Praise for *PC Annoyances*

"Annoyed with your PC? Fight back with this smart, funny, indispensable survival guide."

—*Ed Bott, author,* Microsoft Windows XP Inside Out *and*
Special Edition Using Office 2003

"*PC Annoyances* is packed with amazingly useful tips and tricks. Every flip through the book brings me to something useful that I'm glad to know and didn't before."

—*Steve Gibson, security expert and*
author, ShieldsUP! and SpinRite

"Bass is the smartest and most entertaining technology writer covering personal computers today. This book is a guaranteed cure for whatever ails your PC, from the big errors that can bring a computer to its knees to the glitches that are more trivial but no less maddening."

—*Kevin McKean, CEO and Editorial Director,*
InfoWorld *magazine*

"One of my current favorites...Bass delivers on the book's title by zeroing in on a handful of the most common and most aggravating problem areas in personal computing. Using clear language and everyday examples, Bass systematically tackles such knotty subjects as email, Windows, wfseb surfing, Windows Explorer, digital music and video, and more."

—*John Moran,* The Hartford Courant

Praise for *PC Annoyances*

"By concentrating on the annoyances—and the fixes—Steve Bass cleverly exposes the underlying richness of Windows and your everyday applications. Beyond boosting your own productivity and reducing your blood pressure, you'll be a hero to everyone around you!"

—*Bill Machrone, Columnist and Contributing Editor*, PC Magazine

"Steve Bass's book...is nothing less than a goldmine. It's a lighthearted, easy read that is also jam-packed with serious tips and tricks...*PC Annoyances* won't be gathering any dust on my living room bookshelf; it already has a handy home—right next to my PC!"

—*Linda Webb, Greater Cleveland PC Users Group*

"Jammed into 200 pages are tips, tricks, and tirades that cover everything from codecs to crashes, Acrobat Reader to ZoneAlarm, with humor and the kind of advice that will keep you running to the keyboard to try out each new pointer."

—*James Coates*, Chicago Tribune

"One of the best darned all-around PC books I've seen in a long time."

—*Linda Gonse, reader review*

PC
ANNOYANCES™

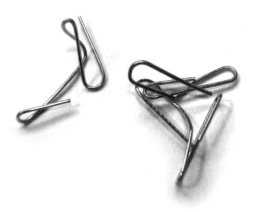

PC ANNOYANCES™

Second Edition

How to Fix the Most ANNOYING Things
About Your Personal Computer,
Windows, and more

Steve Bass

Beijing • Cambridge • Farnham • Köln • Paris • Sebastopol • Taipei • Tokyo

PC Annoyances,™ Second Edition

How to Fix the Most Annoying Things About Your Personal Computer, Windows, and more

by Steve Bass

Illustrations © 2004 and 2005 Hal Mayforth c/o theispot.com.

Published by O'Reilly Media, Inc., 1005 Gravenstein Highway North, Sebastopol, CA 95472.

O'Reilly books may be purchased for educational, business, or sales promotional use. Online editions are also available for most titles (*safari.oreilly.com*). For more information, contact our corporate/institutional sales department: 800-998-9938 or *corporate@oreilly.com*.

Print History:		**Editor:**	Robert Luhn
October 2003:	First Edition.	**Production Editor:**	Genevieve d'Entremont
March 2005:	Second Edition.	**Art Director:**	Michele Wetherbee
		Cover Design:	Ellie Volckhausen
		Interior Designer:	Patti Capaldi

RepKover.™ This book uses RepKover™, a durable and flexible lay-flat binding.

0-596-00882-1
[C]

May the fleas of a thousand camels infest the crotch of the RealPlayer developer who decided to stick icons in my System Tray, Startup menu, and desktop, and may his arms be too short to scratch.

—Snarfed from Internet, author unknown

● ● ●

I want to thank Bill Gates, his Microsofties, and the entire Redmond Empire. Without them, this book wouldn't be possible (or even necessary).

● ● ●

Kvetch: Verb. Pronounced KVETCH, to rhyme with "fetch"; To fret, complain, grunt, sigh. Kvetcher: Noun. Pronounced KVETCHER, to rhyme with "stretcher"; One who complains, often Steve Bass, and always about computers.

—From *The Joys of Yiddish*, Leo Rosten (1968)

Contents

129 Excel Annoyances

137 PowerPoint Annoyances

140 Outlook and Outlook Express Annoyances

5 WINDOWS EXPLORER ANNOYANCES

6   MUSIC, VIDEO, AND CD ANNOYANCES

7 HARDWARE ANNOYANCES

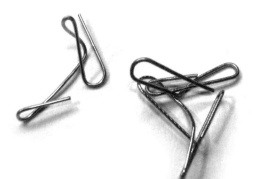

Introduction

Early in October 2002, I got a prank call. "This is Tim O'Reilly. You want to write a book for me?"

"Sure," I reply, thinking it's my buddy Rod, who often calls pretending to be Bill Gates, "but only if you include a free trip to Hawaii and a brand new Volvo."

"No, it's really Tim," he tried again, "and I'm a fan of your 'PC Annoyances' articles." It took me a second to regain my composure (untangling my headset while getting up off the floor isn't easy).

It turns out that Mark Brokering, O'Reilly's VP of Marketing and Sales, was on a flight, picked up a copy of *PC World* and read my latest annual article-cum-kvetchfest. He told me he was able to fix half a dozen of his notebook's annoyances before the plane landed. (Oddly enough, he still hasn't subscribed to the magazine.)

WHY WRITE PC ANNOYANCES?

I've spent nearly 20 years in front of a computer, and I constantly fume at some of the really dumb things programs do to us—and our PCs. I mean, I'm floored that some companies—RealOne and AOL, for instance—actually think it's okay to plaster icons willy-nilly in the Start menu, on the desktop, and in the System Tray. (Windows' system tray, that little box in the lower-right portion of your desktop, doesn't need—no, shouldn't have—two dozen icons in it. See "Protect Your System From Dumb Installations" in Chapter 2 for a tip on how to empty it.)

From the email I receive from *PC World* readers, I know I'm not alone in feeling ticked off, annoyed, and aggravated (not to mention aggrieved). I want people to know that it's not their fault, and, most important, that there are solutions and fixes.

WHY THE BOOK'S ESPECIALLY IMPORTANT RIGHT NOW

Lots of people have purchased computers in the last two years. Many are realizing they've been putting up with dumb things, such as Word's confusing numbering feature, Netscape's incessant ads, or those irritating pop-up ads. (Heck, I'm ticked off just writing about it.)

People have also learned about spyware, adware, and other insidious programs that collect and share information about them behind their backs, or, worse, hijack their home pages or install backdoor worms or viruses.

IS PC ANNOYANCES RIGHT FOR YOU?

If you've ever felt even a drop of animosity toward your PC, this book is for you.

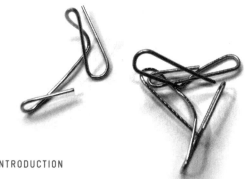

HAVE AN ANNOYANCE?

I'll bet you do, and I'd love to hear about it. Send me an email briefly describing the annoyance, and I'll do my best to cook up a fix. While I can't guarantee an individual response, I will post some of the best on O'Reilly's site for this book, *http://www.oreilly.com/pcannoyances*. Write me at *annoyances@oreilly.com*.

HOW TO USE THIS BOOK

The book is organized into big categories—email, Windows, Office, hardware, file management, Internet, and a spot for CD, music, video, and audio annoyances. As you browse around, you'll see that some chapters are divided into specific applications. For instance, the email chapter starts with irritations common to all programs, followed by sections on the applications most people use—Outlook and Outlook Express, Eudora, AOL, Hotmail, and others.

The best bet is to browse through the book and mark the pages that interest you (I use those little yellow Post-Its) so you can get back to them.

CONVENTIONS USED IN THIS BOOK

The following typographic conventions are used in this book:

Italic is used for filenames, URLs, email addresses, and for emphasis.

`Constant width` is used for commands and items that should be typed verbatim.

`Constant width italic` is used for text that should be replaced with user-supplied values.

THE NONEXISTENT CD (OR "SWING BY THE WEB SITE!")

Did you notice we didn't include a CD? There's a good reason, or actually two: it drives up the price of the book, and it becomes outdated in about 20 minutes. Instead, we decided to create a special web site with more than 150 free tools and utilities aimed at ridding your PC of irritations and annoyances. For these and other treats, head to *http://www.oreilly.com/pcannoyances/*.

HAVE A COUPLE OF LAUGHS

I have a quirky sense of humor and want to share it. So I added lots of links to web sites that poke fun at some of the annoying things PCs (and Macs) do. For instance, spend a minute watching Shotgun Studio's "Bob Gets a New Monitor," a video starring Bob and his twelve-gauge showing a creative way to get rid of your old monitor. It's at *http://snipurl.com/shotgun*. (I feel an annoyance coming on: if the video won't play and you're starting to feel irritated, zip over to Chapter 6 and read "Why Doesn't My Video Play?")

USING THE SNIPURL LINKS

It's the small things that drive me crazy—like having to type the long web links I see in books or magazine articles. So in this book, I use SnipURLs, a free service that shortens the URL into a link that's no more than 14 characters long. (For more details, see "Sending Shorter URLs" in Chapter 1.)

ABOUT THE AUTHOR

Steve Bass first learned about computers in 1982 with an IBM PC he bought from Computerland. When he asked them for support, they said, "Don't use it in the shower." The following day, he founded the Pasadena IBM Users Group. After 24 years, he finally closed the organization, releasing the over 2,400 former members onto the streets (*http://www.pibmug.com*). Be careful out there. In the late 1980s, Steve co-founded the Association of Personal Computer User Groups (*http://www.apcug.org*), a nationwide organization serving user groups.

Steve is a Contributing Editor to *PC World*, writing the "Home Office" column since 1990, the *Home Office Online Newsletter*, and dozens of articles including "Net Phones: Dialing Without Dollars," "The Ultimate PC Troubleshooting Guide," and "Great Windows Shareware for Under $50." His annual "How to Fix the Biggest PC Annoyances" article has won PRSA's prestigious Excellence in Technology Journalism award.

Steve has also written for *Forbes*, *Family Circle*, and *Computer Currents*, and once had a syndicated newspaper column that was way more work than it was worth. But wait, there's more: Steve has a regular spot on KPCC's "Airtalk," an NPR-affiliate radio show, and Pacifica's KPFK's "Digital Village." He's currently producing a new computer show, "Phrenology: The New Topology." It's been a bumpy road.

In a previous life, Steve was a licensed family therapist (so watch what you say); owned PCG Seminars, a training company for mental-health professionals; and met his wife while doing magic at Hollywood's Magic Castle.

ABOUT THE CONTRIBUTORS

Harry McCracken has been swatting PC irritations (or trying to) since 1978, when he learned that the Radio Shack TRS-80's keyboard had a tendency to repeaat chharacterss at ranndom. After discovering that other computers—such as the Atari 400, Apple Macintosh Plus, and Commodore Amiga—were equally aggravating in other ways, he eventually turned to Microsoft Windows—the Mother of All Annoying PC Platforms—and found work in the computer-magazine industry, where they actually pay you to complain about PCs. Currently the editor in chief of *PC World*, the largest monthly computer magazine, Harry has written for *InfoWorld*, *Family Circle*, *USA Today*, and other publications, and has been a guest on "Dateline NBC," NPR's "Marketplace," and many other television and radio programs. He lives in San Francisco's up-and-coming Mervyn Heights neighborhood and wears fashionable eyeglasses.

Dan Tynan is an award-winning journalist, TV commentator, and high-tech guru and has been described as "witty," "smart," and "not as big a geek as you might think" (primarily by his wife). In 16 years of journalism, Dan has won more than 20 national awards and has been published in 13 languages.

Dan began his editorial career in 1986, as a lowly copyeditor at *InfoWorld* magazine. The next year he jumped to *PC World*, where he began a meteoric rise up the editorial food chain. This culminated in 1995 with his appointment as Editor in Chief at *CD-ROM Today* magazine; he later served as Executive Editor for Features at *PC World* for nearly four years. By the time you read this, Dan's first book, *Computer Privacy Annoyances* (O'Reilly), should be heading to the printer.

Most recently, Dan's CNET column, "Inside @ccess," has won two Maggie Awards (in 2002 and 2003) for Best Online Column (each time beating out Steve Bass, who amazingly agreed to let him contribute to this book anyway).

David Jung has co-authored an array of books and articles on programming and debugging Visual Basic, Microsoft Outlook, Java, and other Internet solutions. He is a frequent speaker at seminars and user groups, discussing how technology can be integrated into business solutions. In his spare time (usually after 2:00 a.m.), he writes terrifically useful Windows utility programs that help track down and eliminate system crashes, as well as prevent script-based viruses from spreading on Windows-based computers. Two of his programs, DLL Checker and VBS Defender, received *PC World*'s Editor's Choice award and continue to be sold to users all over the world. (David's web site can be found at *http://vb2java.com*.)

Carl Siechert has been trying (with mixed success) to make sense of personal computers for over 20 years. During that time his firm, Siechert & Wood Professional Documentation, has written manuals, online help, and other documentation for numerous hardware and software products (only the good manuals—not the ones you swear at). In addition, Carl has written a dozen books about Windows and MS-DOS. One recent book, *Microsoft Windows Security Inside Out for Windows XP and Windows 2000*, won an award of merit from the Society for Technical Communication.

When the computing annoyances become too great, Carl goes hiking, returning whenever possible to the Pacific Crest Trail. He recently made a small concession to his no-electronics-in-the-wilderness vow by carrying a small LED flashlight.

Preston Gralla has been annoyed by the PC—and especially digital media (see his contributions to Chapter 6)—since he was knee high to a disk drive. The proud owner of seven computers, Preston is the author of more than 30 books about computing, including *Internet Annoyances*, *Windows XP Hacks*, and *Windows XP Power Hound* (all from O'Reilly). His lengthy experience in computer journalism includes stints at *PC Week*, *PC/Computing* (which he founded and where he was editorial director), and working as an executive editor at both ZDNet and CNET. Preston has won a number of awards, including Best Feature in a Computer Publication from the Computer Press Association.

ABOUT THE TECHNICAL TEAM

Karl Koessel is a *PC World* Senior Editor and the best technical editor ever. Karl scrutinized all the annoyance fixes, duplicated them in his lab, and made sure they worked. He also suffered through a dozen installations of Yahoo's Instant Messenger, Netscape's browser, and, heaven help him, Real's player. Karl doesn't let *anything* slip by and was essential to the book's accuracy.

Dennis O'Reilly is a *PC World* Senior Associate Editor and is the absolute master of headings (and no, he's not related to Tim).

Laura Blackwell is a *PC World* Assistant Editor who fiddled with many of the chapters, doing a marvelous job of making me sound more like me.

ACKNOWLEDGMENTS

Oh, sure, I know, you're here out of courtesy. You'll probably skim the first few lines, maybe look for someone you know, then skip to the first chapter. No one, except those involved in a book, ever reads the acknowledgments. So go ahead, jump ahead while I indulge myself and thank lots of people.

It's the spouse who usually gets short-changed and stuck in the last line of the acknowledgments. But I can't wait.

That's because the book would never have been finished (or started, for that matter) without Judy's incredible patience, support, and unflagging willingness (uh, except that one time in July) to put up with my interminable kvetching and crankiness throughout this ordeal. Sweetie, I couldn't have done it without ya.

My parents, Bernie and Hilda, who, like all good parents, provided nourishment, encouragement, and lots of pastrami sandwiches, and who let me annoy them often.

There are plenty of others.

PC World's black belt schnorrer, Michael Lasky, gave me the original Annoyances article assignment, thus making this book possible. My gratitude to Dennis O'Reilly who tweaked, poked, and massaged my words in the first and second Annoyance articles.

Thanks also to Harry McCracken, who gave the green light to the project, and generously nurtured the relationship between *PC World* and O'Reilly; thanks also to Downloads maven Max Green for smoothing the wheels for the file downloads on PCW's web site.

On the user group front, computing guru Rod Ream filled in dozens of technical holes and came through with bright ideas. A glass of Anchor Steam to Tom Lenzo, David Jung, George Siegal, Mike Lanzarotta, Carl Siechert for their smart (and smart-ass) advice, much of which I used in the book.

A big tip of the hat goes to the members of the Pasadena IBM Users Group. You folks supplied tons of material and remained on my side through thick and thin (and missed newsletters). Ditto for the stevebass list subscribers—your challenging and provocative replies to my seemingly endless requests for more annoyances made the book a more annoying place.

Mark Brokering, O'Reilly's Associate Publisher, Consumer Books, is ultimately responsible for the Annoyances book. He found the *PC World* Annoyance article, ran with the idea, and kept his hand on the tiller, with suggestions, witty repartee, and occasional handholding while we switched editors. Thanks for sticking through it all, Mark.

My editor for the first edition, Linda Mui, the only person I know who reads mail with Unix, took over mid-project and was a godsend. If anyone knows how to work the system (and work a writer), it's LM.

I've also gotta love Uncle Bob, a.k.a. Executive Editor Robert Luhn, who asked me pesky questions when he was my editor at *Computer Currents* and somehow followed me to O'Reilly with, I swear, the same set of pesky questions. Robert, you're a crackerjack and talented guy—you found the goblins that haunted the manuscript. Thanks—I'm glad you're at O'Reilly.

O'REILLY WOULD LIKE TO HEAR FROM YOU

Please address comments and questions concerning this book to the publisher:

O'Reilly Media, Inc.
1005 Gravenstein Highway North
Sebastopol, CA 95472
(800) 998-9938 (in the United States or Canada)
(707) 829-0515 (international or local)
(707) 829-0104 (fax)

There is a web page for this book, where you can download the utilities mentioned, in addition to select articles from *PC World*. You'll also find errata and additional information. You can access this page at:

http://www.oreilly.com/catalog/pcannoy2/

To comment or ask technical questions about this book, send email to:

bookquestions@oreilly.com

For more information about books, conferences, Resource Centers, and the O'Reilly Network, go to:

http://www.oreilly.com

Email
ANNOYANCES

If you're like me, you live in email. That means you also live with all the dumb things your email program does—like hide your attachments or turn them into gobbledygook, or delete messages without permission. It also means that you have to deal with all the joke lists, chain letters, and productivity-gobbling spam filling your mailbox at all hours of the day.

First, I'll show you how to solve general email problems that drive me up the wall. Then I'll guide you through the annoyances in most of the popular email programs—Outlook and its kid sister Outlook Express, Eudora, AOL, Hotmail, Netscape, and Gmail.

Since few people use all of these email programs—unless, of course, they have too much time on their hands—you'll probably find yourself skipping over the parts of this chapter that don't apply to your mailer. Then again, if you're the kind of person who likes to gloat, study them so you can later lord it over your unfortunate friends. But remember: people in glass houses shouldn't throw stones, and people who use Hotmail should be careful when making fun of AOL.

GENERAL EMAIL ANNOYANCES

HIDE THE RECIPIENTS LIST

The Annoyance: It rankles when I get an email and the list of email addresses is longer than the message.

The Fix: When you're sending an email to more than one person, just hide the recipient list using your email application's Blind Copy (Bcc) feature. You can either address the message to yourself or leave the "To" field blank (if your mailer will let you). Then Bcc everyone else.

- To display the Bcc field in Outlook Express, select View and select All Headers.
- In Outlook, choose View and select Bcc Field.
- In Netscape, click the "To" field and scroll to Bcc.
- Eudora's the easiest—just fill in the Bcc field.

DISPLAY EMAIL HEADERS

The Annoyance: My email program works overtime to protect me from headers, and most of the time, that's just fine. Usually, all I want to know is who wrote the email, who received it, and when it was sent. But every now and then I have to dig up email headers to report a problem to tech support or find out why something is bouncing back. How do you find headers in an email?

The Fix: Each email application has a different way of showing headers. To display the header info, follow the steps for your mail program:

Outlook Express 5 and 6
Open the email message, select File → Properties, and click the Details tab.

Outlook 2000 and 2002
Open the email message, click View, and select Options. The data you want is in the Internet Headers dialog box.

Netscape Mail
In Versions 6 and 7 of Netscape, open the email message, click View, and select Message Source. For Netscape's web-based email, open the message and click the little yellow triangle at the bottom right of the message's Subject/Date/From/To pane.

Eudora 5
Open the email and click the Blah Blah Blah (no, I'm not kidding) button on the message window's toolbar. The header information will appear at the top of the message.

AOL
Just above the email message, locate the "sent from the Internet (Details)" line and click "(Details)". The header information appears in the Internet Information dialog box.

Hotmail
Head for Options, choose Mail Display Settings, choose Full, and click OK. Open the email again and repeat the process, choosing None or Basic once you've looked at the headers.

STOP YOUR MAILBOX FROM FILLING UP

The Annoyance: I got a call from a friend that his emails to me are bouncing back. "It says your email box is full," my buddy says with a smirk. But it isn't. What gives?

The Fix: This used to happen to me when friends insisted on sending messages with humongous files attached. When someone sends you an email message, it goes to your Internet Service Provider (ISP), which holds it on an email server so that your email program can, at your leisure, fetch it. Problem is, most ISPs limit you to between 5 and 10 MB of server space for your messages—and once your accumulating email fills that space, your ISP's email server rejects (bounces) any new incoming mail until you make room for the new messages.

My ISP, EarthLink, sends me a warning email when my email box is nearly full. But even if your ISP does you that courtesy, you have to fetch your email regularly. You also need to make sure your POP3 account is set up to delete your mail from the server after you've fetched it, as follows:

- In Outlook Express and Outlook 2000 and 2002, click Tools → Accounts, select the proper account, and click Properties → Advanced. If you have "Leave a copy of message on server" checked, be sure "Remove from server after 5 days" (the default) is checked, but change the 5 to 2.

- In Eudora, select Tools → Options → Incoming Mail. If you have "Leave mail on server" checked, be sure "Delete from server after 0 days" is checked, but change the default 0 to 2.

- In Netscape Mail, select Edit → Mail/News Account Settings, then select Server (Server Settings in Version 7) under the appropriate account name. Make certain that "Delete messages on server when they are deleted locally" is checked. Then select Copies & Folders (under Server or Server Settings) and set the drop-down lists to appropriate local folders.

ENDLESS LOOP VACATIONS

The Annoyance: I came home from vacation and my inbox was filled with hundreds of emails, mostly complaints and flames, from people who are signed up to the same email lists I'm on. Why are they mad at me?

The Fix: If you're subscribed to one of my email lists and go on vacation, do me a favor: don't enable your email program's "out of office" auto-response feature. If you do, every time a message from the list lands in your inbox, your autoresponder will reply to the list. You (and everyone else) will receive the "out of office" message, causing an endless loop when your autoresponder sends yet another "out of office" to the list. The list members are then inundated with your messages until the moderator hunts you down—or throws you off the list.

If you're not subscribed to many lists, the easiest solution is to set each of your lists' preferences to "no mail" while you're on vacation. Not sure how to do it? Write to the list's moderator, often known as the "list mom," for instructions.

THINK OF A CARD

If you don't believe in mind reading, here's a site that will change your mind: *http://mstay.com/free*.

SPAM ZAPPERS EXTRAORDINAIRE

The Annoyance: It's getting so bad that on some days, I get as much spam as legitimate email.

The Fix: Don't spend your time battling spam. In fact, it shouldn't even be on your radar. There are dozens of tools to reduce spam, but I recommend the following three because each is able to capture and mulch between 90 and 98 percent of the spam aimed at me:

MailWasher

This spam attacker has all the characteristics I like in a spam blocker. It works like a charm, is truly easy to set up and use, and nails spam at the door by filtering, bouncing, blacklisting, and removing it. And while there's a MailWasher Pro version, the free one is adequate for most people.

MailWasher works on your incoming missives (POP3 email programs and AOL only) before you open your email program. It goes to the mail server, just as your email program does, but it retrieves only the header information and the first few lines of each message. From there, I take action: I mark messages I recognize as spam, or I agree with MailWasher's suspicion that they're spam. One click and MailWasher spits the message back to the sender, camouflaging it with "address not found." Yep, it really looks like bounced mail.

After a few days, you'll find MailWasher a no-brainer to use. It's easy to add email buddies to a friends list and the junk to MailWasher's spam list. After you've used MailWasher for a while, it collects enough info—through heuristic checking and filtering—that most spam is automatically blocked without any intervention. Grab a copy at *http://www.oreilly.com/pcannoyances*.

iHateSpam

What's neat about iHateSpam is that, unlike MailWasher, it works within your email program, so there's no need to load and use a separate program. iHateSpam adds a toolbar to both Outlook and Outlook Express that lets you bounce email, mark messages as spam (or not spam), and add senders to an enemies or friends list.

What won me over to iHateSpam is that it really, truly blasts spam to smithereens. My wife and I used iHateSpam for more than a month. Her daily use filtered about 98 percent of the spam she received; dummy accounts I set up on Hotmail and CompuServe gave me an even better hit rate. I don't know what sort of algorithmic magic the program uses, but it seems to grow smarter the more I use it. You can grab a trial copy of the $20 utility from *http://www.oreilly.com/pcannoyances*.

Spamnix

There's no doubt that Eudora users need Spamnix, a $30 no-frills plug-in from Spamnix Software. Spamnix examines each message's header and contents. If Spamnix thinks the email isn't spam—but it is—click the Reject This Sender button and Spamnix bans the sender's subsequent messages. Click the Accept button and the program grants immunity to future mail from the sender. Spamnix optionally accepts all email from anyone in Eudora's address book. You can get a copy of the 30-day trial version at *http://www.oreilly.com/pcannoyances*.

If you're using a web-based email service—which typically has built-in spam filters—you may need to dig into the options and turn on or configure filtering:

Hotmail

From Options, choose Junk Mail Filter and choose a filter level. Then click Safe List and add addresses you want to get through the filter, such as friends or business associates. Finally, click Mailing Lists and add any lists you subscribe to so they won't be filtered as junk.

Yahoo!

There's no way to set spam filtering levels. Yahoo! uses SpamGuard, a tool that automatically filters spam.

HIDE YOUR RETURN ADDRESS

If you read mail on newsgroups, keep prying eyes—namely, bots that scoop up email addresses for spammers—from getting a usable email address. You can either insert characters that legitimate users can remove, or you can physically break up your address so a bot can't read it. For instance, in your email program's "Reply to" field under Tools or Options, change your email to something like *bassREMOVETHISgroups@lycos.com*. If your emails have a signature line, break it up like this:

```
_____
bass_    | not
groups   | extractable
@Lycos.  | by
com      | automated means
```

ALTERNATIVE MEDICINE FOR PC VIRUSES

The Annoyance: Help! I think my PC's infected, and I haven't updated my antivirus software in ages.

The Fix: Head for HouseCall, Trend Micro's free, up-to-date online virus scanner, at *http://snipurl.com/housecall*. After a small utility downloads onto your PC, HouseCall scans your computer's hard drive, finding and removing viruses.

Play it safe and do another scan using McAfee's Stinger. It's not a substitute for antivirus software, but a virus removal tool for the virus du jour. As I wrote this book, Stinger looked for and removed such common pests as Fizzer, Lovgate, BackDoor-AQJ, SQLSlammer, Lirva, Yaha, Bugbear, Elkern, Funlove, Nimda, Sircam, and the ever-popular Klez. McAfee updates Stinger depending on how frequently the virus strikes. You can find Stinger at *http://www.oreilly.com/pcannoyances*.

RETURN TO SENDER

What to do if you don't update your antivirus program and inadvertently send your annoyed boss a worm? See *http://snipurl.com/ouch*.

CLEAN UP FORWARDED EMAIL

The Annoyance: My friends complain that my forwarded messages are overloaded with excess baggage—distracting > symbols, extra spaces, carriage returns, and bizarre word wrapping (see Figure 1-1). I have to admit, when I get such emails, I just delete them. How can I (and my friends) clean this digital clutter out?

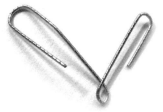

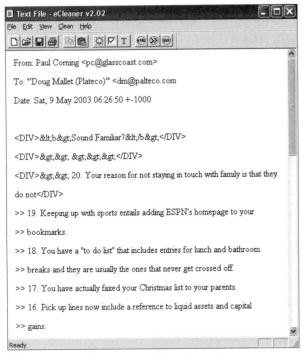

Figure 1-1. This email might be funny if it didn't have all those annoying brackets.

The Fix: There's a very easy fix, and it won't cost you a cent. All it takes is a quick cut and paste into eCleaner, a nifty free utility, to scour the email of junk before you forward it on. Besides removing irritating > symbols, the tool gets rid of HTML code and email headers, and straightens out the word wrap. To clean an email, copy and paste the desired mail into eCleaner and press F1. Select the cleaned text and paste it into a spanking new email. (See Figure 1-2.)

FIX PC ANNOYANCES WITH A MAC

Almost everyone jokes that the number one way to fix any PC annoyance is to switch to a Mac. Before you do, check out this new i-application: *http://snipurl.com/ i_toilet.* **It may change your mind.**

I keep eCleaner on my Windows Quick Launch toolbar for easy one-click access. To add it to the toolbar, open the eCleaner folder, right-click eCleaner, and drag and drop it to the Quick Launch toolbar. Release the mouse button and choose Create Shortcuts Here. You can grab a copy of eCleaner at *http:// snipurl.com/ecleaner.*

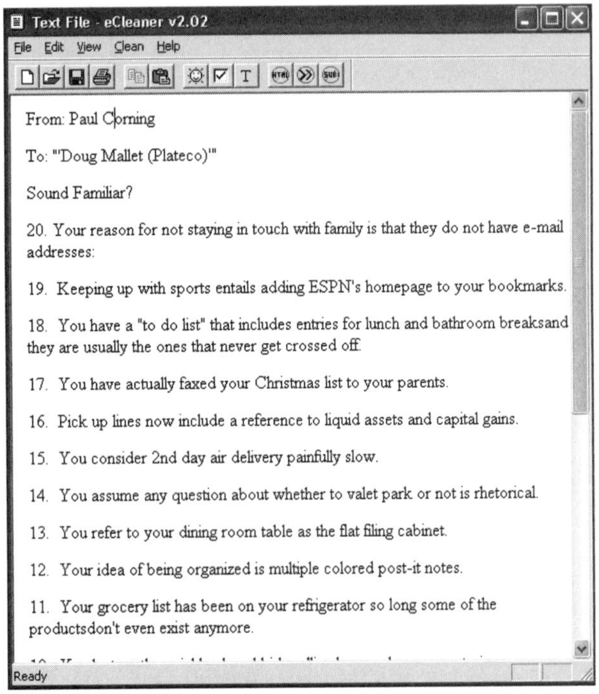

Figure 1-2. With a two-second run through eCleaner, the message is spic and span. Unfortunately, it's still not funny.

If you'd rather roll up your sleeves and banish these pesky brackets manually from your specific email program, follow these steps:

- In Outlook Express 5 and 6, click Tools → Options, and then click the Send tab. In the "Mail Sending Format" section, select the Plain Text radio button, click the Plain Text Settings button, and uncheck the "Indent the original text" box. Click OK, then OK again.

- In Outlook XP and 2003, click Tools → Options, click the Preferences tab, and then click the E-mail Options button. In the "On replies and forwards" section, change both drop-down lists to anything except "Prefix each line of the original message." Click OK, then OK again.

- In Eudora 5 or 6, you'll need to reset the *ReplyPrefix* setting in the *Eudora.ini* file. Eudora makes it easy—just go to the tech support site at *http://snipurl.com/e_settings*, scroll down, and click the *<ReplyPrefix>* item. Flip back to Eudora and you'll see it's been forced to automatically open the Change Option dialog box in a new message. Make sure that the "New value" field is blank, and then click OK. Repeat the process for *<QuotePrefix>*.

SHARE BIG FILES WITHOUT THE ATTACHMENTS

The Annoyance: I have a terrific video to share with a buddy. Unfortunately, it's 30 MB and if I try to attach it to an email message, the ISP police will come knocking at my door.

The Fix: Forget email. If you frequently send and receive large files, use znail (*http://www.znail.com*), an almost-free web site for file storing and sharing. You simply upload a file to znail using your browser, then send your friend an email with a link for file retrieval. There's no cost for up to 5 MB of storage. If you want to be a big spender (and big file-transferrer), a dollar a year gets you 20 MB of storage; 50 MB runs $10 a year.

znail has some download restrictions, but nothing I'd call onerous. If you have 20MB of znail storage, you can download a maximum of 40 MB per day and 100 MB per week. (To share data, you have to share the same username and password with friends or coworkers.) If you're on a dialup line, these uploads and downloads can take forever. So if that's your situation, burn the file on a CD and hand-deliver it to your buddy.

RETURN TO SENDER, ADDRESS UNKNOWN

The Annoyance: There's one guy who sends me the most inane, awful, dumb jokes. I've asked him to remove me from his alleged joke list, to no avail.

EUDORA'S MAGIC INI FILE

Now that you've read "Clean Up Forwarded Mail," you've learned about the slick way to change Eudora's INI settings. Here are three cool tricks:

- Use *<QuoteStart>* to add a custom line at the top of any message you forward, such as "This message was forwarded by Steve Bass." Just click *<QuoteStart>* and type your message in the "New value" box.

- If a sender requests a return receipt, Eudora will ask if you want to notify the sender now, later, or never. I don't want Eudora to ever respond. If you have the same attitude, click *<ReadReceiptNo>* and change the number in the "New value" box from 0 to 1. After you do this, Eudora will automatically deny a request for receipts without bothering you to make a decision. (For another way to do this, see "Turn Off Return Receipt" in this chapter.)

- Want to reply to a message and start the first line with "On Sunday 12/26/2004 at 01:13 PM, [*sendername*] wrote:"? Click *<ReplyAllAttribution>* and add `At %1, %2 you wrote` to the "New value" box.

Don't click options on this INI page willy nilly, *especially* if you don't recognize the command and aren't sure what it does. And before you make any changes to Eudora's INI file, back it up. (Search for *eudora.ini* to find its location on your PC).

The Fix: Here's the sneaky way to get off any joke list. Use the Bounce Spam Mail utility to deliver a fake bounce message. It looks absolutely authentic (see Figure 1-3), and the poor shlub will think your email address is invalid. You'll find Bounce Spam Mail at *http://www.oreilly.com/pcannoyances*.

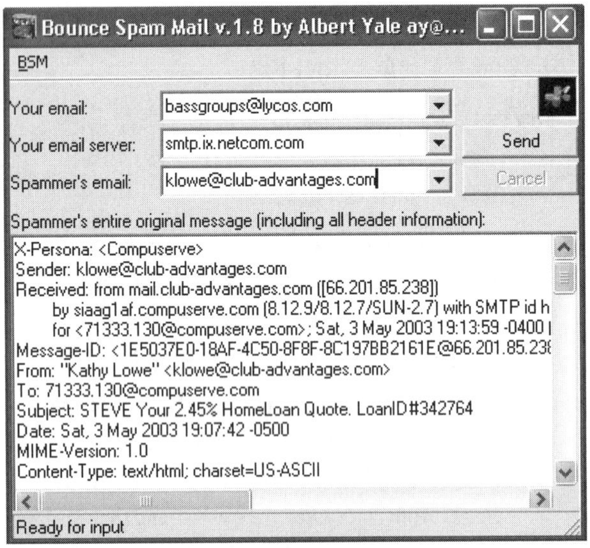

Figure 1-3. Bounce Spam Mail delivers authentic-looking fake bounce messages.

UNDECIPHERABLE ATTACHMENTS

The Annoyance: Occasionally I receive email with a file attachment that's undecipherable. My virus program scans it and gives it a clean bill of health; it's just unreadable.

The Fix: The attachment has probably been encoded with Uuencode, MIME, or BinHex, rendering it seemingly impossible to read with any program in the PC world (see Figure 1-4). You need a copy of Novatix's ExplorerPlus, a $30 Windows Explorer replacement, which has a built-in decoder (and, if you ever need it, an encoder) for UU, XX, MIME base64, and BinHex files (see Figure 1-5). To decode the message, first save it from your email program as a text file. Then in ExplorerPlus, highlight the file, choose Archive, and select Decode files. (By the way, ExplorerPlus is also a terrific file manager. Check the "Dump Windows Explorer" sidebar in Chapter 5 for more details.) You can grab a trial of ExplorerPlus at *http://snipurl.com/explus_trial*.

KEEP IT SHORT AND SIMPLE

Unless you're vacationing on a desert island, your time is tight. If you send me a long message and I don't know you, I probably won't read it, especially if it has an attachment. I read lengthy messages from friends when I have more time. (Messages from my O'Reilly editor, of course, are eloquent and hold my attention to the very end.)

If you want your messages read—whether they're for business or pleasure—follow these handy rules:

Think short. Limit the message to three paragraphs, tops, each with no more than four sentences. If you must write more, provide a single line with a short preview—for instance, "Deadline? Did I miss it?"

Use paragraphs. This sounds like the previous tip, right? Nope, because some people send single paragraphs the length of this page. Break up long paragraphs into three or four smaller ones. Make sure you hit the Enter key between paragraphs; some email programs, most notably AOL, seem to strip out paragraph returns, melding your paragraphs into one.

Avoid fancy formatting, gaudy colors, and flowery backgrounds. Two reasons: first, what's cool on your monitor looks like hell on mine; and second, that extra coding increases the download time when my notebook's using a slow 56 Kbps dialup account.

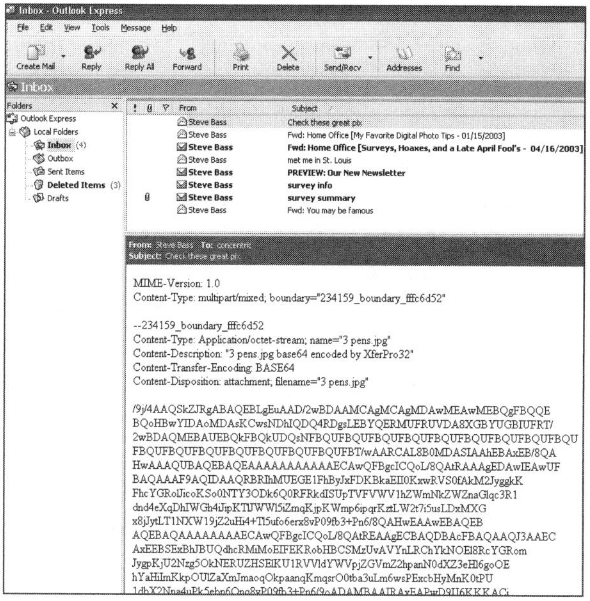

Figure 1-4. Try viewing the image in an Outlook Express message. No way, right?

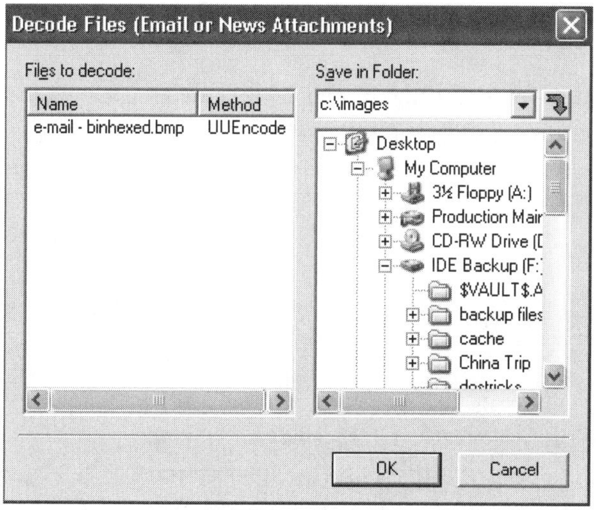

Figure 1-5. The only way you can read a MIMEed message is to decipher it with ExplorerPlus, which converts UU, SS, MIME base64, and BinHex files.

TURN OFF RETURN RECEIPT

The Annoyance: Some people slip a return receipt request into email they send me. Do they think I won't read it otherwise?

The Fix: I give them the benefit of the doubt and assume they don't realize return receipts are a breach of email etiquette. I reject the request and tell the writer how to turn the feature off:

- In Eudora, just don't click the Return Receipt button on the toolbar.

- In Outlook, click Tools → Options, choose the Preferences tab, select Email Options, and click Tracking Options. Make sure "Request a read receipt for all messages I send" is unchecked. If you use Outlook Express 6, click Tools → Options, choose the Receipts tab, and make sure "Request a return receipt for all sent messages" is unchecked. If you want to keep your email reading habits to yourself, check "Never send a response" in Outlook, or "Never send a read receipt" in Outlook Express.

And listen, if their messages are really critical, tell them to use that newfangled thing called a telephone.

IMHO YOU'LL BE ROTFLOL

The Annoyance: I do okay deciphering most email messages, but I'm stymied when it comes to those wacky messaging acronyms. I never knew whether to LOL, sport a VBG, or be MAHANTIA.

The Fix: FWIW (for what it's worth) and IMHO (in my humble opinion), these abbreviations can be TFAOCTKS (tough for an old codger to keep straight). IIRC (if I recall correctly), there's a handy online spot for sorting them out: the Acronym Finder at *http://snipurl.com/acro_finder*. Search for an abbreviation, and you too can be ROTFLOL (rolling on the floor laughing out loud). SGTM (sounds good to me). For a more focused take on online acronyms and abbreviations, try Webopedia (*http://snipurl.com/webopedia*), MacMillan's abbreviations (*http://snipurl.com/macmillandictionary*), or the Free Online Dictionary of Computing (*http://snipurl.com/foldoc*).

CHECK YAHOO! MAIL FROM YOUR EMAIL PROGRAM

The Annoyance: I have a Yahoo! email account for all my joke lists. My only gripe? I hate Yahoo!'s annoying login rigmarole and ads. How can I avoid them?

The Fix: The solution is YPOPs!, a free tool that emulates a POP3 server and lets you check your Yahoo! mail using third-party email clients. YPOPs! works with over a dozen popular email programs, including Outlook, Netscape, Eudora, and Mozilla. Download the tool at *http://snipurl.com/Yahoopops*, and check out the detailed instructions for how to make it work with your email program at *http://snipurl.com/ypops_email*. By the way, it's not just for Windows: the utility also works on Linux, Solaris, and even Mac computers.

EMBED IMAGES IN EMAIL

The Annoyance: Some of the emails I get have images right inside the message, which is very convenient because I don't have to click any icons and hope the image opens in the right viewing program. But putting images in email must be the biggest secret in computing because I can't figure out how to do it.

The Fix: I love revealing secrets. Creating embedded images—sometimes called inline images—isn't all that difficult. Of course, if the recipient's email program doesn't accept messages with HTML code, you're out of luck and will have to send images the old-fashioned way, by attaching them. And if you're corresponding with Luddites who prefer plain-text messages, they may find your embedded images annoying. Otherwise, go ahead and embed images into your email, but don't go overboard. Here's how:

- In Outlook 2000 and 2002, create a new email and insert the picture by using Insert → Picture. Browse to the image you want to insert and click OK.

- In Outlook Express, format the message to be sent as HTML by selecting Format → HTML. Then select Insert → Picture, browse to the image you want to insert, and click OK.

- In Eudora, create a new message, and with your cursor in the text portion of the email, click the Insert Object button on the Formatting toolbar (it's the last one on the right) and choose Picture. An alternative is to choose Edit → Insert → Picture. If Insert → Picture is grayed out, you probably have Eudora set to send plain text only. Change it by selecting Tools → Options → Styled Text and clicking "Send both plain and styled." While you're there, check "Show formatting toolbar" so you'll be able to access the Insert Object button.

- In Netscape, create a new message and choose Insert → Image.

- In AOL, click the little camera icon above the email message, browse to the picture you want, select it, click Open, and choose the sizing option.

FIX THOSE BROKEN LINKS

The Annoyance: My buddy sent me an email with a link to a cool web site. But when I clicked it, my browser popped open and I got an error message. But I know the site exists!

"FYI" Means "Don't Reply"

Some people feel obligated to reply to every email, even if it's just a link they might be interested in or an FYI. Here's a bit of Bass netiquette: end your email with "This is just an FYI. So don't feel obligated to reply." It takes people off the hook when they think they ought to reply with something lame, like "thanks" or "I agree." This is especially helpful when you reply to someone on a mailing list.

The Fix: Broken web links in email messages—where spaces and junk characters get inserted into a URL—drive me batty. One cool, unobtrusive utility that has become part of my personal arsenal is UrlRun, a freebie.

Just download and unzip URLRun and stick it in Windows' Quick Launch toolbar. In any email program, just highlight a URL and copy it. Click URLRun, and the utility strips out spaces and other debris and sticks the better-than-new URL into Internet Explorer's Address field. If your browser isn't running, URLRun opens the browser and takes you right to the page. Outlook users have it even easier, since there's a free plug-in version for Outlook. The tool is at *http://www.oreilly.com/pcannoyances.*

STOP INCLUDING MESSAGES IN REPLIES

The Annoyance: When I reply to emails, I'm apparently including all the text of the original message. How can I stop this?

The Fix: It's easy to avoid this faux pas. By default, most email clients include the original in replies, but you can change the default by following the instructions for your email program:

- To change this setting in Outlook 2000 and 2002, click Tools → Options and, under the Preferences tab, select E-mail Options. Click the drop-down list box under "When replying to a message" and choose "Do not include original message."

- In Outlook Express, choose Tools → Options, select the Send tab, and uncheck "Include message in reply."

- Using Netscape? Click Edit → Preferences, double-click Mail and Newsgroups, select Message Composition from the list, uncheck "Automatically quote the original message when replying," and click OK.

- Eudora has a more elegant solution: simply highlight the text you'd like to include and click the Reply

button. The highlighted text, but no more, is inserted in your reply automatically. (If you don't select any text, the entire original message is included.)

Even if you prefer to keep the original text in your reply by default, you can remove it on a case-by-case basis with two keystrokes. In virtually any email program, press Ctrl-A to select all of the original text, then start typing your reply. The text will magically disappear, replaced by your response.

PRE-ADDRESS YOUR EMAIL

The Annoyance: I send a lot of email to one person—my mother. Yet none of the email programs I've used lets me address an email to a specific person and open the program in one fell swoop.

The Fix: Head for the Windows desktop and create a shortcut. Right-click any unencumbered spot on the desktop and select New Shortcut. In the "Command Line" (98 and Me) or "location" (2000 and XP) field, type `mailto: bassgroups@lycos.com` (substituting Mom's email address after the `mailto:`, of course). Click Next and give your shortcut a name like `Email Mom`. Double-click the shortcut to address an email on the spot. For added convenience, slide the shortcut into Windows' Quick Launch toolbar.

SETTING UP A SIGNATURE

It's easy to have your email program stick a signature line at the bottom of your email. Signatures are valuable because they let the recipient know who's sending the message and how to contact the sender by phone or (gasp) snailmail. A courteous signature is short and to the point—no more than four or five lines—and contains the sender's email address, phone number, and location. As witty as your favorite poetry/movie/inspirational quotation is, leave it out—it just adds to bandwidth bloat.

KEEP A COPY

The Annoyance: I try to keep a copy of any email I send that's really important—missives to the President, complaints I've lodged against the IRS., and so on. The problem is that I don't always remember to do it, so I'm sometimes up the creek when I need to see what I said.

The Fix: I set my email program to store a copy of all my outgoing mail in a separate mailbox. Every week or so, I browse through and purge the mailbox to keep my hard drive free of clutter. Here's how to do this in various email programs:

- In Eudora, select Tools → Options → Sending Mail and check the "Keep copies" box.
- In Outlook Express, select Tools → Options, select the Send tab, and check "Save copy of sent messages in the 'Sent Items' folder."
- In Outlook, select Tools → Options → Preferences, click E-mail Options, and check "Save copy of messages in Sent Items folder."
- In Netscape Mail, go to the email account's Copies & Folders area of Edit → Mail & Newsgroups Account Settings (Mail/News Account Settings in Version 6), check "Place a copy in," and set its drop-down list box to a local folder.

ONE-CLICK EMAIL TO GO—ON STEROIDS

Thanks to "Pre-Address Your Email," you now know how to send a new email message to the same buddy by double-clicking an icon on the desktop. The only problem is that this shortcut can't pop some boilerplate text into the email's subject line or message body. To add a subject and/or message to your email shortcut, right-click it, select Properties, and type the following in the shortcut's command line:

```
mailto:yourbuddy@hisISP.com?subject=Cooltip
inside&body=(Put your message text here).
```

If you have multiple recipients, insert a comma between their names. Now isn't that better?

SENDING SHORTER URLS

The Annoyance: Some URLs I want to forward to friends or coworkers are really long. How can I avoid sending them URLs a mile long?

The Fix: Great guy that I am, I make an effort to be considerate—at least when sending email—by using *SnipURL.com*, a free site that trims long URLs to 13 characters. Add the snipped URL to your email, and when the recipient clicks it, the site invisibly sends them to the lengthy link.

Using SnipURL is a snap. I attached the SnipURL icon to my Internet Explorer toolbar (go to the site and drag and drop the "Snip This" link to IE, Netscape, or Opera). When I'm at a web site with a long URL, one click on the SnipURL icon opens a browser box, pops the shorter URL into the Clipboard, and automatically closes the box. Then I can just paste the shortened URL into my email. Check out SnipURL at *http://www.snipurl.com*.

OUTLOOK AND OUTLOOK EXPRESS 5 AND 6

DISABLE THE PREVIEW PANE

The Annoyance: Outlook Express's preview pane is not only useless, it's dangerous. By default it marks any message as read if it spends more than five seconds in my preview pane, which means I sometimes miss important messages (because OE thinks I've already read them) simply by leaving the preview pane open. Worse, some email—particularly nasty spam—contains scripts that are activated when a message is "read." How can I stop this?

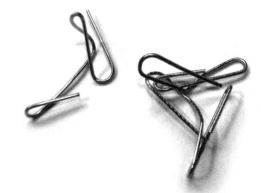

The Fix: First, close the preview pane. Launch Outlook Express and select View → Layout. In the Windows Layout Properties dialog box, uncheck the "Show preview pane" box. Click OK to close the dialog box. In Outlook, choose View → Preview Pane to toggle the pane on and off.

Now tell Outlook Express to stop marking messages as read just because your cursor happens to land on them. Select Tools → Options and click the Read tab. Uncheck the "Mark messages as read after displaying for 5 second(s)" box, click OK, and you're done. In Outlook, select Tools → Options, click the Other tab, click the Preview Pane button, and uncheck the "Mark messages as read in preview window" box. In Outlook 2003, follow the steps above, but in the Other tab, click the Reading Pane button instead.

GIVE OUTLOOK EXPRESS A MAKEOVER

The Annoyance: One of my big complaints about Outlook Express is that its default layout makes no sense. For example, the contact window that OE opens by default when you first use it is pointless. And those huge toolbar icons are wasted real estate. And why doesn't OE open the inbox by default? Stupid, stupid, stupid.

The Fix: Start by selecting View → Layout. To nuke the contacts window, click the box next to the Contacts bar, then click Apply. Now squeeze the icons down to size. With the Windows Layout Properties box still open, click the Customize Toolbar button. Another dialog box opens with two scrollable lists and a bunch of toolbar icons in each one. Under the left list, click the Text Options drop-down menu and choose either "Selective text on right" or "No text labels," depending on how familiar you are with OE's icons. In Icon Options below that, select Small Icons.

Here's where you can also add useful icons like Print or Reply to OE's meager set of default tools. In the window on the left, highlight the icon you want to add, click the place where you want it inserted in the window on the

right, and click the Add button. When you're done, click Close to exit the Customize Toolbar dialog box, then click OK to close the Layout window.

As a final step, force OE to get to work at startup. Select Tools → Options and click the General tab. Click the box next to "When starting, go directly to my inbox folder" and click OK. Now Outlook is ready for action, unhindered by (some of) Microsoft's bad design decisions.

CHOOSE YOUR MESSAGE VIEW

The Annoyance: I like to keep all my messages in Outlook Express, but I don't want to look at them all the time. At other times I'd like to see conversations grouped by topic. Is this possible?

The Fix: Just select View → Current View, and you'll get a drop-down list of different ways to display your messages. Select "Hide Read Messages" to see only those that are new. Pick "Group Messages by Conversation" to see messages displayed along with replies, the way it's done in some online forums and newsgroups. And if you want to get really fancy, you can select "Customize Current View" and add your own rules to show or hide messages.

EXPONENTIALLY GOOD FUN

From the Milky Way Galaxy to your backyard. You'll find the "Powers of Ten" an absorbing view of existence from the very large (galaxies) to the very small (quarks).

[Warning: if you're on a dialup connection, it may take a few minutes to load and run.]

See *http://snipurl.com/power*.

OUTLOOK EXPRESS FIXER-UPPER

Pawing through Outlook Express messages that are filled with replies and quotes is a drag. Thankfully, there's a solution: OE-QuoteFix for Outlook Express. It automatically changes the appearance of your email reply, aligning paragraphs, moving your signature to the bottom of the message, and more. (The following figure shows all the ways you can modify your email reply.) Get a free copy at *http://snipurl.com/OEquoteifx.*

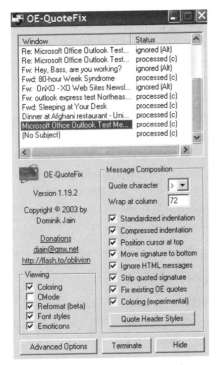

Stop worrying about how your replies look in Outlook Express: just choose the desired options and let OE-QuoteFix do the rest.

By the way, if you've upgraded to Windows XP Service Pack 2 (SP2), some OE-QuoteFix features might not work. The fix is easy. In Outlook Express, select Tools → Options, click the Security tab and uncheck the "Block images and other external content in HTML email," and then click OK.

USE FOLDERS

The Annoyance: The more mail in my inbox, the more slowly Outlook Express loads. The obvious answer is to delete my messages, which will make OE's *inbox.dbx* file much smaller and load more quickly. But what if these are important messages I need to refer to later?

The Fix: Use folders to stash mail that's too important to toss but not important enough to keep in front of you all the time. Creating a folder is child's play: select File → New → Folder. In the Create New Folder window, choose a location for the new folder (most likely, Local Folders), type a name for it, and click OK. Now you can drag mail into that folder and save it for a rainy day.

Even better, use OE's rules to funnel mail directly into a folder without ever sullying your inbox. Select Tools → Message Rules → Mail. If you already have rules set up, you'll see the Message Rules dialog box. Click the Mail tab, then click New. If this is your first rule, OE will automatically display the New Mail Rule dialog.

Here's where you specify the Conditions (when to implement the rule) and Actions (what you want the rule to do). Select a condition—say, "Where the From line contains people"—and an action, such as "Move it to the specified folder." In the Rule Description field you'll see the words "contains people" highlighted. Click that link and select the email addresses of people whose mail should be routed to the folder. (You can type them in or click the Address Book button to select from a list.) Click Add and then OK to return to the New Mail Rule box.

Now click the word "specified" in the Rule Description field; OE will display a list of folders. Pick the folder where you want the mail to go. You can also create a new folder on the fly here by clicking the New Folder button. Click OK.

There's one thing left to do: type in a name for the rule in the last field. When you're done, click OK twice. Now, mail from the specified person will fly directly into its own folder, leaving your inbox untouched.

DRAGGING MAIL INTO SUBFOLDERS

I created folders to unclutter my inbox. Now my folders are bulging with messages, and I still can't find anything. So I created subfolders within each folder. But Outlook Express always starts with the folder views collapsed, so when you want to drag a message from your inbox to a subfolder, you have to expand the view by clicking the little plus sign next to the main folder. Inevitably, I realize this after I've selected the message I want to move.

I've discovered a neat little trick. If I drag the message over the main folder and hold it there for about three seconds, the folder will automatically expand, showing me all the subfolders. Then I just drop the message into the right folder and go on my merry way. Just this once, Microsoft did something right. (The same trick works with folders in Windows Explorer.)

MULTIPLE EMAIL ACCOUNTS ON ONE COMPUTER

The Annoyance: Want a recipe for breaking up a relationship? Share a copy of Outlook Express with your significant other. Sure, you can each set up your own identities, but your long downward spiral into discord will soon follow. Who gets to be the default account? How do you avoid accidentally downloading your partner's mail because he or she has set the thing to automatically download mail at startup?

The Fix: First, if you haven't done so already, set up a separate identity so all your mail doesn't crowd into the same inbox. Select File → Identities → Add New Identity.

Type in your username, and Outlook Express will ask whether you want to switch to the new identity (you do, so click Yes) and, if you're already logged onto the Net, whether you want to stay logged on (sure, why not?). Then you'll need to answer some personal questions posed by the Internet Connection Wizard, such as whether you're adding a new account or an existing one, the names of your email servers, your username and password, and whether you want to import your old contacts.

OK, you've finished creating a new identity. Now what? Go back to File → Identities, but this time, pick Manage Identities. Check the "Use this identity when starting a program" box, click the drop-down menu just below to open the list of identities (there should be at least two in there, yours and your partner's), and pick the one you want to be the default. Click Close.

Wait, you're not done yet. You want to make sure that your partner doesn't accidentally download your email (or vice versa) at startup. Go into Tools → Options, and on the General tab, uncheck the "Send and receive messages at startup" box. Now, wasn't that easier than getting relationship counseling?

THE OTHER IDENTITY CAN BE YOU!

Here's another tip for cleaning out your inbox: create a new identity for yourself, and keep the old mail with your old identity. Select File → Identities → Add New Identity, using a clever name for the new identity (like `Steve's New Email`**), since you can't use the same one twice. Then follow the steps in "Multiple Email Accounts on One Computer" to make your new identity the default. When you want to rifle through your old mail, just switch to that identity (File → Switch Identity) and pick your old one from the list. It's a funky solution, but hey, it works.**

ONE EMAIL ACCOUNT ON MULTIPLE COMPUTERS

The Annoyance: I have a computer at home and at work, and want to read email on both. Problem is, once I download the email at home, I can't read it at work, so I have to forward important messages to myself. Is there a better way?

The Fix: Let's assume you've already created accounts on both computers where you want to check mail. One of them is probably more vital than the other—most likely the one at your office. We'll call that the primary computer, and your home or laptop your secondary computer.

Open Outlook Express on your secondary computer, select Tools → Accounts, and go to the Mail tab. Select the email account that you want to check both at home and in the office, and click the Properties button. Click the Advanced tab and check the "Leave a copy of messages on server" box. Click OK.

Now you'll be able to download the same messages to both your primary and secondary computers. (Note: make sure you *don't* modify your primary machine with these steps, or you'll have endless duplicate messages on both systems.)

But wait, you're not done yet. You probably also want to keep copies of messages you send from your secondary computer. For that, follow the steps in "Keep a Copy," earlier in this chapter.

THE MINOTAUR LABYRINTH

You use a PC, so you're used to crazy challenges. Here's one that will send you 'round the bend. Like your relationship with Microsoft, every step you take toward the exit, you're followed by the Minotaur who's taking two steps. See *http://snipurl.com/minotaur*.

SAVE KEYSTROKES VIA SIGNATURES

The Annoyance: I can't count how many times I've written in an email "Sure, why don't you FedEx that to me" and then had to type in my shipping address...again. Even after placing that information in a text file and inserting it into my messages with Insert → Text From File, it's still annoying. Isn't there a better way?

The Fix: OE's Signatures tool can automatically insert a text file into your email message with just a couple of clicks. Select Tools → Options and click the Signatures tab. Click the New button and enter the text you want in the text box. (You can also tell OE to grab the text from a file, if you want.) Click Rename. Type in a new name for the information (like my home address) and click OK. It doesn't have to be an address; you can insert your favorite quotation, a long diatribe on any topic of your choosing—any text that you don't want to retype endlessly for the rest of your life.

The next time you need to insert this text in a message, just click Insert → Signature and pick the one you want from the submenu (assuming you have more than one sig, of course—but you're too smart to attach your home address and FedEx account number to every email you send, so you have at least two). To have Outlook Express automatically insert the signature line, select Tools → Options → Signatures and check the "Add signatures to all outgoing messages" box. In Outlook, select Tools → Options, click the Mail Format tab, and select the desired signature you've created from the pull-down "Use this Signature by default" menu.

BACK UP EMAIL

The Annoyance: My email messages and address book are some of the most important stuff on my computer. But does Microsoft give you any way to automatically back up your inbox, folders, or contacts? Noooooo. What's the trick?

The Fix: Here's how to copy your email messages and address book manually. Locate where Outlook Express has squirreled away your mail messages on your hard drive. The easiest way to do this is to select Tools → Options and click the Maintenance tab, then the Store Folder button. In the Store Location window you'll see the beginning of an inscrutable series of letters and numbers (like *C:\WINDOWS\ Application Data\Identities\{86291360-DB6F-11D6-8F3A-444553540000}\Microsoft\Outlook Express*). Believe it or not, this is the name of the folder where OE keeps your mail. Highlight the entire folder name by dragging the mouse pointer from the first letter all the way to the end of the name, and press Ctrl-C to copy it. Now click Cancel twice in a row to get the heck out of there before you screw something up.

Next, go to Start → Run, press Ctrl-V to paste that ridiculous folder name into the field, and click OK. Windows Explorer will appear and open the folder, which should show a series of *.dbx* files. These files hold all the email in your inbox and any folders you've created, one file per folder.

Simply select the files and copy them to your backup destination of choice. If you're like me, there will be many megabytes of files, so use the largest capacity disc you can lay your hands on—a 100 MB (or better yet, 250 MB)

BACK UP EMAIL EASILY

Manually backing up OE is fairly annoying in its own right. The good news is that there's an easier way. The bad news is that it'll cost you.

The solution is a backup utility that does the dirty work automatically: Genie-Soft's Outlook Express Backup 6.0 (*http://snipurl.com/oebackup*). This $30 utility (a 15-day free trial is at *http://www.oreilly.com/pcannoyances*) is truly easy to use—just click along with the wizard to back up mail files, address book, and browser favorites. It can save each of your OE identities separately, split huge backups across multiple discs, and let you schedule regular automated backups. It's fast, too—Outlook Express Backup copied and verified 280 MB of my data in less than five minutes.

Zip disc, or a CD-R or CD-RW if the file tonnage exceeds 250 MB. A quick way to tell: the bottom of the Outlook Express folder should display the number of objects (files) and total megabytes.

BACK UP YOUR ADDRESS BOOK

The Annoyance: But wait, there's more! I also want to back up my address book in case my PC goes kaput. But there doesn't seem to be any way to do this. Thank you, Microsoft!

The Fix: You have two options: find your Windows Address Book (WAB) files hidden on your hard drive, or export your contacts to a text file, which you can reimport later. (On Windows 9x and Me systems, the files are stored in the *\Windows\Application Data\Identities* folder; on Windows 2000 and XP systems, it's in *\Documents and Settings\userprofile\Application Data\Microsoft\Address Book*.) The latter option is the easier of the two, so that's what I'll focus on here.

In OE, Select File → Export → Address Book. Click "Text file (comma separated values)" to highlight it and click Export. In the next window, type the name of the backup file (address book backup, perhaps), click Browse, and pick the folder where you want to store the backup. (Store it on the same disk where you're backing up your email files.) Click Next, then pick the fields (name, address, phone) you want to export. If you're unsure which to pick, check all of them. Click Finish, and when the file stops copying, click Close to close the Export Tool Box.

WHERE DID THAT ATTACHMENT GO?

The Annoyance: Outlook uses the kookiest places for storing email attachments! When I open an attachment, Outlook saves the file in an obscure temporary directory. (On one of my computers, each time I opened an attached file, Outlook saved it in *C:\Documents and Settings\Steve\ Local Settings\Temporary Internet Files\OLK3F.*) I often make changes to an attached file I've opened, save it (without thinking about where it's being saved), and then close it. When I need it later, I don't have a clue where to search.

The Fix: The simplest solution: don't open attachments within a message. Instead, save the attachment to a folder you pick, and open it from there. But that's a cop-out; the real solution is to change the default folder where Outlook saves attachments. To do that, you'll have to wade into the Windows Registry, as follows:

1. Select Start → Run, type `regedit`, and click OK to open the Registry Editor.

2. In the Registry Editor, navigate to the key that's appropriate for the version of Outlook you're using:

   Office XP (Outlook 2002)
   ```
   HKEY_CURRENT_USER\Software\Microsoft\
   Office\10.0\Outlook\Security
   ```

   Office 2000
   ```
   HKEY_CURRENT_USER\Software\Microsoft\
   Office\9.0\Outlook\Security
   ```

3. Double-click the OutlookSecureTempFolder value.

4. In the Value Data box, type the complete path of the folder where you want Outlook to store attached files that you open. Be sure you put a slash at the end of the path, like this:

   ```
   C:\Documents and Settings\Steve\My Documents\
   Attachments\
   ```

Making this change has a minor security benefit as well. Certain hackers expect to find Outlook's attachment folder in a known, standard location. You can thwart such attacks by specifying your own, not-so-well-known folder.

CREATE FILE ATTACHMENTS

The Annoyance: When I choose Insert → File to attach a file to a message, Outlook Express (and Outlook) looks in My Documents. The same thing happens when I choose File → Save Attachments to save an attachment. But I want to insert and save files from and to my *DOC* folder!

The Fix: I've finally succumbed to the Microsoft Way and use My Documents as the source folder for all my personal documents. But if you're one of those stalwarts who must use a different folder, the fix is obvious enough: just change Outlook's default folder.

Changing the default folder is not at all obvious, however. You can use a Registry tweak, but there's a better way. Visit the Simpler-Webb site at *http://snipurl.com/OutlookDefPath*

MANAGING OUTLOOK ATTACHMENTS

Email programs like Eudora neatly save attachments in their own, easy-to-find folder. But Outlook cleverly(?) stores all attachments with the messages in a mysterious database file. If you're using Exchange Server, the attachments and all your messages are stored in an Exchange mailbox on the server; otherwise, all your attachments and messages are jumbled together in a Personal Folders (*.pst*) file. Outlook is the only way Microsoft lets you get at these contents.

As is often the case, outsiders have come to the rescue. You'll find an extensive list of third-party tools for managing attachments within Outlook files at *http://www.snipurl.com/addins/*. While you're there, check out the rest of Diane Poremsky's excellent Slipstick Systems Outlook & Exchange Solutions Center at *http://www.snipurl.com/slap.*

---

and pick up a copy of OutlookDefPath, a free add-in for Outlook. This little program adds an OLDefPath command to the Tools menu, which lets you change the default folder.

AUTOMATIC ZIP ATTACHMENTS IN OUTLOOK

The Annoyance: Many of my computing buddies are still on dialup. (I can't decide whether they're cheapskates or just in no hurry.) I don't want to risk losing their friendship, so I always compress any big files I send them, but doing this manually is a pain.

The Fix: Save your fingers. bxAutoZip is a free Outlook add-in that compresses email attachments with one click. If the recipient doesn't have an unzipping program, tell your pal to use bxAutoZip's self-extracting archive option. The program works with Windows 95 through XP and is compatible with Outlook 98 to 2003. There's also a version for Outlook Express 5 and 6. Browse to *http://snipurl.com/bxAutoZip* to download either program.

AOL ANNOYANCES

MUZZLE AOL

The Annoyance: Call me a grump, but whenever I hear AOL's chirpy "You've got mail," I feel a migraine coming on. If I want to check my mail, I can do it without AOL's prompting, thank you very much.

The Fix: Good thing there's an easy way to tell it to pipe down. Log onto AOL, and on the AOL toolbar, select Settings → Preferences and click Toolbar & Sound. At the bottom of the dialog box, uncheck the line "Enable AOL sounds such as the Welcome greeting and Instant Message chimes" box. Click Save, and the next time you check your mail, you can do so in blessed silence.

GIVING AOL'S COMPANION THE BOOT

The Annoyance: I installed AOL 9 and found I'd gotten myself a new sidekick—and not one I particularly wanted. The AOL Companion pops up onscreen whenever I have a Net connection—and keeps hanging around until I forcibly remove it.

The Fix: Giving the Companion the permanent boot is pretty simple. Click the little X (the Close icon) in the upper-right corner to close the AOL Companion. AOL will ask whether you really, truly want to do this. You do, but first deselect "Autolaunch AOL Companion" and check the "Do Not Show This Message Again" box. That should banish the little bugger—at least until AOL gets corrupted and you have to reinstall it.

TURN OFF POP-UP ADS

While you're in AOL's Preferences window, you might as well fix a few other AOL irritants. Hate pop-up ads? In Version 9, type Keyword: Popup controls and select "Block all web pop-ups" and on the Pop-Ups from AOL tab, select "Block pop-ups from AOL". In Version 8, click the Pop-Ups link, then check the "Suppress AOL member-only special offers" and "Suppress pop-ups from Web sites I visit using AOL software"boxes. Click Save and OK. For Version 7, click the Marketing link, click the Pop-Up button, and click the radio button labeled "No, I do not want to receive special AOL members-only pop-up offers." Click OK twice, but leave the Marketing Preferences window open. Here's where you can also tell AOL and its advertising partners to stop sending you special offers via email, snail mail, and over the phone. (In Version 8, click Marketing Options → Marketing Options; in Version 9, type Keyword: Marketing Preferences.)

If you use more than one AOL screen name, you'll have to set your preferences for each one.

HOLD ON TO YOUR AOL MAIL

The Annoyance: I like to hang on to my email for a long time. Unfortunately, AOL tosses read messages out with the garbage after about a week.

The Fix: There's a way to hang on to the messages you really want. Select Settings → Preferences, click Filing Cabinet, and check the "Retain all mail I read in my Personal Filing Cabinet" and "Retain all mail I send in my Personal Filing Cabinet" boxes. Your mail will then stay in your inbox as long as you want.

AOL'S HIDDEN TOLL-FREE SUPPORT

The Annoyance: AOL is one of the last bastions of toll-free, 24/7 phone support, but they do their best to keep it a secret. They're trying to keep their costs down by forcing people to use web-based support, like live chat and email.

The Fix: Well, too bad. Email's slow, and chat's messy. Don't bother searching AOL, typing keyword Help, or clicking one of the "Get Live Help" links on the AOL Help window (that just takes you to a live chat session).

If you type keyword Call AOL, you'll get a list of toll-free numbers to call. But I'll save you the trouble: Windows users can get support at 888-346-3704; Mac users (assuming there are any reading this) can try 888-265-8007.

DUMP AOL'S EMAIL

The Annoyance: I hate AOL's brain-dead email client. What's the alternative?

The Fix: For starters, use AOL's very own AOL Communicator program (Keyword: AOL Communicator). This application is amazingly—dare I say—robust. You get email, instant messaging, antispam tools (including pretty sophisticated filtering), and mail management in one place. Better yet, you don't need to load AOL proper to do it. (For more, see *http://www.pcworld.com/news/article/0,aid,111887,00.asp*).

Really, really hate AOL? Use Netscape 7.0's built-in mail program, which knows how to pick up AOL and Netscape mail. Just download and install Netscape; then, to configure mail, select Window → Mail & Newsgroups. From the New Account Setup screen, click "AOL Account," and in the subsequent screens, supply your name, screen name, and password, and that's it. Netscape checks your AOL box on the spot. Another plus: Netscape works with multiple accounts, and it can check your AOL mail via a non-AOL broadband connection.

LEAVING AOL—AND TAKING YOUR FAVORITES

The Annoyance: It's great news that I can use another email program to check AOL's email. But I'm ready to switch to another service and leave AOL for good. Exporting all my goodies—address book and favorites—is nearly impossible unless I fork over $25 for a utility. Is there a freebie?

The Fix: There sure is, and it's a great web service with a funny name—linkaGoGo. Head for *http://snipurl.com/AOLconvert*, and you'll see how you can easily convert favorites/bookmarks to and from a number of browsers, including AOL, Netscape, IE, MSN, and Opera. However, first you have to export your Favorite Places from AOL so that linkaGoGo can do its stuff. Here's how:

- In AOL 8.0, go to Keyword: **Favorites**, choose Favorite Places, click the Manage button, choose "Save My Favorite Places as a Favorites File on my Computer," and click OK.

- In AOL 9.0, go to Keyword: **Favorites**, click the Save/Replace button, choose "Save My Favorite Places as a Favorites File on my Computer," and click OK.

The file that's exported will have a *.pfc* file extension and can be imported to another browser with linkaGoGo.

What about your AOL 8.0 or 9.0 address book? Hie thee to AOL Keyword: **Sync** and click the Download Now button. Follow the prompts to install the Intellisync for AOL program (see Figure 1-6). Pick the screen name whose Favorite Places you want to export, then find the "Desktop

Application/Handheld Device" drop-down list and select either Outlook or Outlook Express. (The options for Palm or Pocket PC will work only if you have the appropriate device installed on your system.) If you export to Outlook Express, Intellisync will output your address book; exporting to Outlook and Intellisync will output your address book *and* calendar. You don't have to import anything—Intellisync plugs the information into Outlook and Outlook Express for you.

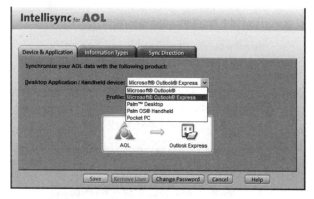

Figure 1-6. Want to kiss AOL goodbye? With its sync tool, you can export your AOL address book to Outlook or Outlook Express with just a few clicks.

But wait—you say you're not interested in switching to Outlook Express and don't even have a Palm? Ah, but now that your AOL information is in Outlook Express or Outlook, you can simply export it from these programs in a format that other email programs can read.

To export your Outlook Express and Outlook address books, take these steps:

- In Outlook Express, go to File → Export → Address Book and choose Text File (Comma Separated Values).
- In Outlook, go to File → Import and Export → "Export to a file" and click Next. Your best bet is to choose Comma Separated Values (Windows) because most email programs can accept this format. Click Next, choose Contacts, and save the file to a folder you'll be able to easily find.

KEEP IMAGES SHARP IN AOL

The Annoyance: Hmmmm—all the images I view in AOL look a tad blurry. Should I call my ophthalmologist for a special prescription just for AOL use?

The Fix: Put down the phone. Blurry images are a byproduct of compressing graphics aggressively so they'll load quickly over slow phone lines. When AOL decompresses them, some of the detail is lost.

If you connect over dialup, you might consider this a fair tradeoff. But if you've got a cable or DSL line with plenty of zip, or if you would just prefer crisper, albeit slower-loading, pictures, tell AOL not to put the squeeze on pictures. Select Settings → Preferences, then click "Internet Properties (WWW)." In the dialog box, click the Web Graphics tab, select Never Compress Graphics, and click OK.

A SQUEAKY-CLEAN AOL SCREEN

I hate AOL's screen clutter. Its interface is a blinking mess of overlapping windows and pop-up ads, not to mention garish menus and useless lists. To hell with it, I say. And you can, too, by making the following tweaks.

First, unless you're a die-hard Instant Messenger fan, lose the Buddy List that crowds the right side of the screen. Select Settings → Preferences, click Privacy, choose the General Buddy tab, uncheck the "Show me my Buddy List at sign on" box, and click Save.

Now reduce the size of the toolbar across the top of the screen by going into the Toolbar & Sound Preferences screen (see "Muzzle AOL" earlier). Under Toolbar Preferences, find "Display the following in my Toolbar," click "Text only," and save.

Finally, minimize the Welcome Window so that it doesn't crowd your screen at logon. Shrink the window by clicking the minimize button in the upper right corner, select Window → Remember Window Size and Position, and then quit AOL entirely. Next time you launch AOL and sign on, your screen will be nice and clean.

EUDORA ANNOYANCES

MANAGING EUDORA'S ALPHABETICAL MAILBOXES

The Annoyance: I switched from Outlook to Eudora and I have to know—are folders mailboxes or are mailboxes folders?

The Fix: Eudora's designers went to great lengths to make their mailboxes and folders annoying *and* confusing. Mailboxes, which are designated by tiny inbox icons, store messages. Folders, on the other hand, aren't meant to hold messages, only mailboxes. I know, it's bass-ackwards. One smart cookie at Eudora decided mailboxes ought to be alphabetical, which is fine, except that unlike Outlook, you can't drag and drop them out of order. So if you want to place your mailboxes in some other order, like with "Really Really Important Stuff" up top, it takes a workaround, such as renaming them to something that'll push them to the top of the alphabetical list. For instance, I access my *PC World* mailbox often, so I renamed it "1 PC World." Same thing for "1 VIP," a mailbox for my wife and others in my family. Less important stuff goes at the bottom of the stack, tagged by the letter "z," as in "z pesky editors."

By the way, you can transfer a message from one Eudora mailbox to another by highlighting or opening the message, right-clicking, selecting Transfer, and scrolling to the new mailbox. (A neat alternative: copy the message by holding the Shift key while transferring it.)

DUCT TAPE WALL HANGINGS

You thought duct tape was just for fixing leaky radiator hoses? It's also good for decorative wall hangings. See *http://snipurl.com/walltapings*.

KEYBOARD SHORTCUTS FOR MAIL MANAGEMENT

Busy typing messages and need to attach a file or run a quick spellcheck? There's nothing more distracting than having to reach for the mouse.

Hey, I'm with you. Eudora has some of the weirdest keyboard shortcuts since the ancient word processor WordStar, but here are the finger-flicking shortcuts I use:

- Use Ctrl-N to create a new message.

- Attach a document with Ctrl-H, and run a system tray with Ctrl-6.

- If you're reading new mail and want to add the recipient to your address book, press Ctrl-K. To quickly pop open the address book, use Ctrl-L.

- Want to send a message right away (or queue it if you're offline)? Use Shift-Ctrl-E.

- Using the four arrow keys to navigate through multiple listings in the address book is much faster than double-clicking the mouse.

SLIMMING DOWN EUDORA'S HEADERS

The Annoyance: The header information in a message shouldn't be longer than its content. Eudora is famous for its tweakability, and I'll bet there's a way to futz with the headers, but there's nothing in Help that tells me how.

The Fix: You can indeed keep the header size to a minimum but still include the essential info, such as "From," "To," "Date," "CC," "Subject," and "Reply-to." First, close Eudora (that's *essential*). Next, find *eudora.ini*, the file that contains all of Eudora's settings; you can have Windows search for it, or you might look for a folder named something like *C:\Program Files\Qualcomm\Eudora* or *C:\ Documents and Settings\username\Application Data\ Qualcomm\Eudora* or just *C:\Eudora*. Once found, double-click *eudora.ini*. Your text editor (Notepad by default) should open. (If it doesn't, you'll be asked to give Windows some guidance; choose Notepad from a list.) In the [Settings] section, find the line that begins with TabooHeaders and replace it with the following (or insert the following if you don't already have a TabooHeaders line):

```
TabooHeaders="a,b,co,dis,e,g,h,i,j,k,l,m,n,o,p,
rec,ref,res,ret,q,s,u,v,w,x,y,z"
```

Save the file and run Eudora. Remember, if you want to see the entire header in a message, just click Eudora's Blah Blah Blah button.

FIND MAIL FASTER WITH FILTERS

The Annoyance: Wouldn't it be neat if Eudora made it easy for you to see whether incoming email had attachments? Sure, but Eudora doesn't work that way unless you force it to.

The Fix: Think filters. Eudora's filters are smart, and you can create one in a flash (as you'll see in the next few tips). I have Eudora flag messages with attachments by slapping them with a bright color. Select Tools → Filters and click the New button. In the pane to the right, check the Incoming and Manual boxes. In the Header drop-down menu, choose <Body>. The next field should already say "contains"; type `attachment converted` into the field directly to the right. Skip down to the Action area, click the first drop-down menu, choose Make Label, click inside the field that appears, and choose a color. Save the filter with Ctrl-S and close the Filters window. Now every email with an attachment will stand out from the other messages. (See Figure 1-7.)

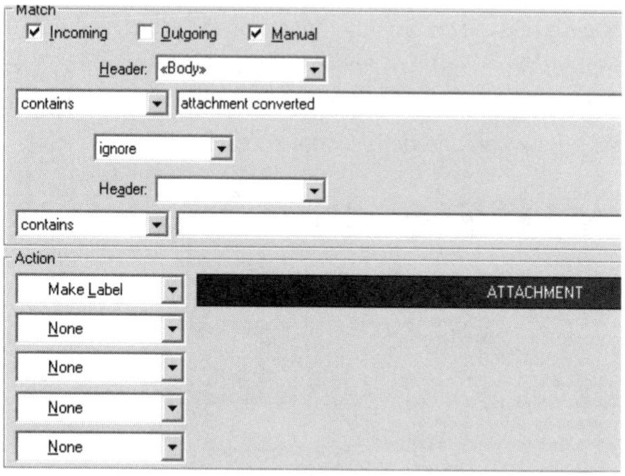

Figure 1-7. Use this Eudora filter to automatically mark each message that has an attachment with a label.

> **BUG ALERT**
>
> **I'm a hardcore Eudora user and I love the product. I also hate it with a passion. On the one hand, it has tremendously powerful features and allows almost unlimited customizations via the *eudora.ini* file. What's annoying about Eudora is that it still has bugs. I've badgered the developers, the PR flacks—even the author—to no avail. The somewhat good news is that the bugs are obscure and I've provided workarounds for a few of the more annoying ones. Better news—Eudora's Version 6 should have even fewer gnarly bugs. (Check for the latest version at *http://www.eudora.com*.).**

> **tip**
>
> **Like the preview pane in Eudora but want to turn it off temporarily? Press F7. To make it reappear, press F7 again.**

FILTER OUT VIRUSES AND WORMS

The Annoyance: Every time another new virus or worm makes the rounds, one of my not-so-bright computing buddies passes it my way. I'm protected by my antivirus program, but that's not the problem. When the Klez worm hit, I often got a dozen or more of these unwanted messages clogging up my inbox in a single day. How about some help from Eudora?

The Fix: Now that you know how to create a filter, you can craft one for messages generated by Klez—or most other viruses of its ilk. My antivirus program, Grisoft's free AVG, gleefully adds a sentence to the disinfected email giving me the name of the virus or worm it caught; I use the name in a filter to send the message directly to the trash. (If your antivirus program doesn't provide a name, consider switching to AVG.) Figure 1-8 shows how to create a filter that works for both the Klez and the I-Worm/Palyh.A worms. When a new worm or virus appears on the scene, just create another filter. You can grab a copy of AVG Anti-Virus Free Edition (for use in home and non-commercial settings) at *http://www.oreilly.com/pcannoyances.*

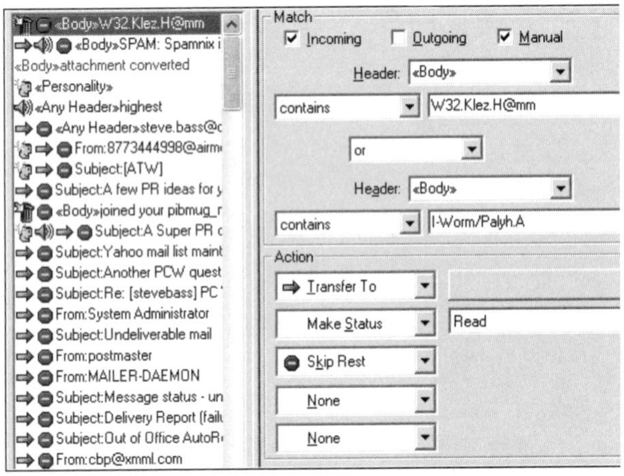

Figure 1-8. Create this filter in Eudora, and those endless messages with Klez will be dumped right into the trash.

SMART SORTING

The Annoyance: It seems I can sort mail in Eudora by only one field, such as Date. Am I missing something?

The Fix: Sorting is one of Eudora's many strong points. You can sort by clicking any field header, such as Who, Date, or Subject. Complex sorting is, of course, more complex: hold down the Ctrl key and click one column (such as Date), then click another column (such as Subject), and the columns will be sorted in just that order: the messages will sort chronologically, and then alphabetically by subject. To sort in the opposite order, hold down the Shift key while clicking. You can sort on as many as eight fields. To cancel the new arrangement, click the column with the number "1" in the triangle.

FILTERING SPAM

The Annoyance: Spam. Need I say more?

The Fix: You can complain about spam forever—or you can get rid of lots of it, with about 10 minutes of work. I have two nifty Eudora filters that will send every email that's not addressed to you into your spam folder.

Select Tools → Address Book, click the New button, and create a nickname called Me. Enter all the email addresses from which you receive mail, each address separated by a comma. Now select Tools → Filters and click the New button. In the Header drop-down menu, choose <Any Recipient>, click the field just below and to the left and choose "intersects nickname," and type Me into the field to the right. Under Action, click inside the first drop-down menu and choose Skip Rest; leave the other fields blank. (Don't be discouraged, folks; this is worth it.)

EUDORA PLUG-INS

If you're using Eudora, you have access to several nifty plug-ins for a variety of message-massaging tricks. For instance, if there are tons of brackets or a few lines of text in all capitals, highlight the offending text, click the right mouse button, select Plug-ins, and choose the best one for the job.

To install a plug-in, close Eudora, and download and unzip the plug-in (usually a *.dll*) into *\Program Files\ Eudora\Plugins*. When you launch Eudora, the plug-ins will be ready to go.

For all the plug-ins I use (removing brackets and word-wrap, changing word case, and sorting text), head to *http://snipurl.com/eudora_plugin.*

Following the same steps, create a second filter, choosing <Any Header> for the Header field, replace "contains" with "appears", and leave the field to its right blank. Under Action, set the first field to Transfer To, click the In button that appears, and choose your spam mailbox. Save the changes when prompted. Finally, move these two filters to the bottom of your filter list so that they'll be the last to execute.

IMPROVE PERFORMANCE WITH NEW MAILBOXES

It's easy to get ticked off when Eudora's performance becomes sluggish, which happens because Eudora's In, Out, and Trash mailboxes can never be filled to the brim. The reason could be that you took my advice in "Managing Eudora's Alphabetical Mailboxes." You'll take a big performance hit, since Eudora gobbles memory faster than a teenager downloading music from a file-sharing server. Cut the clutter by transferring messages to other mailboxes, and open only the mailboxes you need at the time. The more mailboxes you have open, the more memory Eudora needs.

Start by selecting Tools → Filters, and click New. In the pane on the right, check the Outgoing box. Click the Header drop-down menu and choose From. The next field should already say "contains"; type your email address into the field directly to its right. Skip down to Action, click the first field, and choose Transfer To from the list. To the right, a button with "in" will appear—click it, click New, and type Sent into the field (and no, don't make it a folder). In the next Action field, choose Skip Rest (at the bottom of the list) and save the filter with Ctrl-S. Every time you send an email using that email address, the message will be transferred to the Sent mailbox

---

EUDORA'S TOOLBAR: DUMB AS DIRT

The Annoyance: Eudora's toolbars look great, but sometimes half the toolbar buttons go missing, nowhere to be found.

The Fix: This is my very favorite Eudora annoyance, and there's no real cure. But I have a personal Bass Kludge™, a virtual whack to the side of the toolbar that you're welcome to use:

1. Arrange your toolbar so it's just right. Double-check all your other Eudora settings in Tools → Options and make sure you're happy with them all. That's because you're going to preserve Eudora's *.ini* file, *the* master file that holds all the precious details about how you want Eudora to behave.

IS IT NEW MAIL OR JUST NOT READ YET?

Outlook Express is smart—it displays new messages in bold. But in Eudora, it's just not obvious whether email is "new" or just "unread." Once you know the secret to Eudora's silly Status symbols (the Status column is the one on the far left), it becomes clear:

- A blue ball indicates the message has *not* been read.

- No icon in that spot means the message has been read.

- If you see a left arrow, it means you've replied.

- A right arrow means you've forwarded the message.

You can change a message's status by right-clicking the message and selecting Change Status. Finally, if you have the Preview setting on, viewing the message—by simply highlighting it and seeing it in the Preview Pane—changes the message's setting to read (past tense). Don't want to do that? Go to Tools → Options → Viewing Mail and uncheck "Mark messages as unread after _ seconds." Another trick: turn the Preview settings off. Select Tools → Options → Viewing Mail and uncheck the "Show message preview pane" box.

2. Close Eudora and use Windows Explorer to navigate to Eudora's folder (it's usually at *\Program Files\Eudora* or *\Documentsand Settings\username\Application Data\Qualcomm\Eudora*). Copy *eudora.ini* and stash it away; I copied mine to my desktop so it would be easy to get to.

3. Next time you launch Eudora and you discover the toolbar's been hosed, close Eudora and copy the pristine *eudora.ini* file into the appropriate folder (perhaps *\Program Files\Eudora* or *\Documents and Settings\username\Application Data\Qualcomm\Eudora*), overwriting the old one.

> Did you know that Eudora collects embedded images in the *\Program Files\Eudora\embedded* folder? (In XP, they're usually in *Documents and Settings\username\Application Data\Qualcomm\Eudora*.) Clean them out every so often and reclaim some hard drive space.

SHARPER TOOLBAR BUTTONS

The Annoyance: I've customized the toolbar, and every so often when I load Eudora, many of the toolbar buttons look blurry and strange—almost like TV sets full of static. I don't know why it happens, and I don't really care. But I'm tired of it.

The Fix: Among Eudora's endearing qualities is the undependable, unstable toolbar. There are a few ways to make Eudora's toolbar behave, and all take just a few minutes:

EUDORA'S PASSWORD RECOVERY TOOL

Can't remember your mail account password? *No problemo, señors y señoras.* Download EudoraPass, click its Decode button, and your password's revealed. Grab a copy at *http://snipurl.com/eudorapass.*

NERDY TOOLS FOR EUDORA

If you use Eudora, you have a nerd gene in your DNA. That's okay—I do, too. That's why I love the Eudora plug-ins and obscure, but valuable, tools found on the Bujenovic site. For instance, there's the Search & Replace Plugin that lets you find and replace text in messages, something missing in Eudora. Or the Delete Duplicates Plugin, which compares and gets rid of duplicate messages. To install any of these plug-ins, download the file to your drive, unzip it, and drag the contents into Eudora's plug-in folder. Fair warning: you've got be a nerd to enjoy and use these tools. Get them at *http://snipurl.com/Bujenovic.*

---

1. Resize the buttons. Select Tools → Options, scroll the Category icon list to find Display, click it, and uncheck the "Show large buttons" box. Close and launch Eudora. No luck? Keep reading.

2. Type `<x-eudora-option:ToolbarDisplayFix=1>` right into the message area of a new Eudora message, making sure to include the brackets. Don't send the message to anyone (especially not to me). The text should be blue (if not, press Enter). Press the Alt key while you click the link. You'll see a window asking to confirm the change; click OK, exit, and relaunch Eudora.

3. If that doesn't work, repeat the process in Step 2 using the line `<x-eudora-option:ToolbarDisplayFix=2>` instead.

4. If the toolbars still look awful, you might have to fiddle with Windows settings and lower the graphics acceleration level, or try changing the color depth of your display. From the control panel, open Display, select the Settings tab, click the Advanced button, and click the Performance (98 and Me) or Troubleshooting (2000 and XP) tab. Lower the "Hardware acceleration" level a tad and click OK. Take Eudora's temperature by closing, relaunching, and looking at the toolbar. Futzing with your graphics adapter's color depth is next. Follow the

Eudora's Extreme Resetting

If Eudora crashes a lot, strip all but the essential parts out of *eudora.ini*. (The settings for sending and receiving mail will survive cleansing.) When you have Eudora strip the *.ini* file, it first makes a copy of the current *eudora.ini* (probably named *eudini.sav*), but my advice is to first save a copy of the file yourself (see "Eudora's Toolbar: Dumb as Dirt"). Then hold down the Control and Shift keys while you select Tools → Options.

EUDORA TOOLS ON THE WEB

There's a wealth of cool Eudora tools and support from Eudora users on the Internet:

- Sign up for the very best Eudora for Windows mailing list, where you'll find experts who can answer your pithy questions, at *http://snipurl.com/ eudora_win*.

- Cecil Williams, a Washington State University professor and Eudora tinkerer, put together a wonderful site that explains how to use Eudora filters. He's got it down to a science with filters that, according to him, will catch 99 percent of spam. You can find his filters at *http://snipurl.com/filters*.

- Daniel Jacobson's Bookmarks page has a Eudora E-mail Application section with comprehensive, up-to-date links to many of the best Eudora spots; see *http://snipurl.com/1f3p*.

previous steps, and at the Settings tab, click inside the Colors ("Color quality" in XP) drop-down menu. Switch to 16 bit if it's set to 32 bit, or vice versa.

5. If, after all these workarounds, your toolbar still looks lousy, here's the final stop: switch to Outlook Express.

HOTMAIL ANNOYANCES

BOOKMARK YOUR HOTMAIL INBOX

The Annoyance: I check my Hotmail inbox more often than I check my wristwatch. But what a hassle! I go to *http://www.hotmail.com*, and instead of landing in my mailbox, I get a page of news briefs, ads for other MSN gewgaws, newsletter solicitations, and various other items I never asked for.

The Fix: Take a minute and set things up so you can zip right to your mail. First, go to *http://www.hotmail.com* and type your email address and password into the appropriate fields. Check the "Sign me in automatically" box and click the Sign In button. (Heads up: this allows anyone who gets access to your browser to get into your Hotmail account without supplying the password, so don't try this if you have snoopy coworkers or nosy relatives.)

Click the Inbox tab and bookmark *this* page in your browser. From now on, use the bookmark and you'll land smack dab in your inbox, no additional clicks required.

A COOL ILLUSION

Dizzy from reading all these annoyances? Here's a neat optical illusion that'll calm you: *http://snipurl.com/ illusion*.

USE OUTLOOK EXPRESS TO EXCISE HOTMAIL SPAM

The Annoyance: I sometimes think that the only reason Hotmail exists is to attract spam. (Wait—isn't that AOL's job?) If I wait a few days before checking my inbox, I'll sometimes rack up 150 pieces of junk mail. And getting rid of them takes way too many clicks, since you have to select them one at a time. There's got to be a better way.

The Fix: How about using Outlook Express to do some heavy-duty spam weeding?

Launch Outlook Express and select Tools → Accounts, click the Add button, and choose Mail. A wizard will pop up; enter your name, then your Hotmail address. (Outlook Express will fill in the "E-mail Server Names" screen automatically). You're then asked for your password. Enter it, click Finish, and then click Close to leave Accounts. Outlook will ask if you want to download folders from the mail server—click Yes, and supply your password again.

Now OE will download copies of all your Hotmail messages. Your Hotmail account now lives inside Outlook Express, along with any other email accounts you've set up there in the past.

MANAGING TONS OF EMAIL

1. **Get and stay organized. Create additional mailboxes and use filters to automatically move messages to specific mailboxes. Filters let you take control of your email so you aren't overwhelmed with 100 email messages in your solitary inbox. Instead, you can see immediately that 10 messages arrived from your brother-in-law who's asking for money again.**

2. **Use mailboxes to set priorities. Create three mailboxes for messages with high, medium, and low importance. For instance, items needing a response today go into the *high* mailbox, and you must force yourself to resolve those as soon as possible. If necessary, create another mailbox for items held in abeyance. Get the idea?**

3. **In Eudora, use Spamnix to get rid of spam; Outlook and Outlook Express users can use iHateSpam. (See the earlier topic, "Spam Zappers Extraordinaire," for more about these two products.)**

4. **Encourage people not to respond to you unless necessary. This will save you the hassle of opening a bunch of messages with a one-word reply—"Thanks!" To discourage replies, I might say something like this:**

   ```
   This is just an FYI. So don't feel obligated
   to reply.
   —Steve
   ```

5. **Realize that some people blind copy their messages to a dozen people—not just to you—so it's okay not to respond.**

6. **If you use Eudora, switch to the preview mode (go to Tools → Options, click Viewing Mail, and check the** "Show message preview pane" box). This allows you to quickly glance at a message and know whether it can be immediately deleted. Unfortunately, it's another story in Outlook and Outlook Express; I don't recommend using preview mode in these programs because the risk of catching a virus or worm by just previewing a message is too great. Disable the preview pane in Outlook by going to your inbox and selecting View → Preview Pane. In Outlook Express, also from your inbox, select View → Layout and uncheck the "Show preview pane" box.

7. **If you receive email that bogs down your business day, create a fictitious project and send a boilerplate response, such as:**

   ```
   Ordinarily I'd respond with a quick verifi-
   cation that I got your email, and I'd say
   something bright or witty. But I'm afraid I
   can't do that today.

   While I'll continue reading your email, I
   won't have time to respond. That's because I'm
   writing a book and plan to be working on it
   for the next five years or so. I have a short
   attention span and I'm easily distracted, es-
   pecially by email.

   Important: Don't hesitate if you need to send
   me a business email; don't worry, I'll read it
   and you'll get a response.

   Thanks
   —Steve
   ```

From now on, you can do some or all of your Hotmailing inside OE if it strikes your fancy. At the very least, it's a much better tool for deleting messages en masse. For instance, click the Hotmail Inbox in the Folders pane, click a message, hold down the Shift key, use the down arrow key to highlight a range of messages you want to purge, and press the Delete key. They'll be erased in OE—and next time you check Hotmail with your browser, you'll see they're gone there, too.

HIDE HOTMAIL'S SPAM

The Annoyance: The previous Fix helps me delete spam only after it's already infested my inbox and driven me bonkers. What I really want to do is stop spam from the get-go, but Hotmail's so-called spam filter isn't worth a hoot.

The Fix: Here's a two-click trick that hides all spam instantly: click the "Show me mail from" drop-down menu above Hotmail's inbox and choose "People I Know." Bam— all the junk will vanish. It's still there, lurking in the background, but Hotmail is showing only mail that came from folks in your Contacts address book.

Know somebody who isn't in your Contacts? Open a message from that person and click the Save Address(es) button, and the address will be added to the address book.

MANAGING TONS OF EMAIL (*continued*)

8. **Use more boilerplates! A prewritten response lets you quickly reply with the same response to similar messages. For example, many people write and ask me if the "A Card for You" is a hoax. Here's my boilerplate:**

   ```
   Yep, the "A Card for You" is a hoax. Here's
   how the message starts:

   It's the WORST VIRUS EVER!!!...CNN ANNOUNCED
   PLEASE SEND THIS TO EVERYONE YOU KNOW!!! A new
   virus has just been discovered that has been
   classified by Microsoft as the most destructive
   ever!!!!

   For hoax details, look at these two Web sites:
   http://snipurl.com/card_hoax
   http://www.vmyths.com

   (BTW, about the only thing MS has sent out
   that's been destructive is Win Me, but that's
   another story.)
   ```

9. **All email programs let you create boilerplate, but Eudora has some of the most powerful tools around. For instance, you can take any reply and, with one click, turn the message into a boilerplate: type the text and save the message when prompted. To send this text, choose the email you're replying to, select Message → Reply With, and pick the appropriate stationery.**

   In Outlook Express 6, click Tools → Options → Signatures and click the New button. Enter your text in the Text box, then click the Rename button and give the text a name. Click OK, and when you're ready to enter the text in an email, just click Insert → Signature. If you've created only one "signature," it will appear automatically. If you've made more than one, choose the desired text from the Signature submenu.

   If you use Outlook 2002, choose Tools → Options, click the Mail Format tab, check the "Use Microsoft Word to edit email messages" box, and click OK. Type your boilerplate text into a new message, select it, and choose Insert → AutoText → New. Enter an abbreviation and click OK. When you're ready to use the boilerplate in a reply, choose Insert → AutoText → AutoText and find your boilerplate in the list of entries.

10. **Remember Bass's golden rule of email: you're under no legal or moral obligation to respond to every email you receive.**

Do this with mass mailings you want to see, too—say, newsletters you actually enjoy receiving—so they don't disappear along with the spam.

Normally, this spam-free view stays in effect only for your current Hotmail session; log in later, and you're back to seeing your entire inbox, junk and all. Aggravating as this is, it's fixable. Just follow the "Bookmark Your Hotmail Inbox" tip above—but before you bookmark the page, select the "People I Know" inbox view. When you return to Hotmail via the bookmark, you'll go right to your de-spammified inbox.

MAKE HOTMAIL YOUR DEFAULT EMAIL PROGRAM

The Annoyance: Ninety-nine percent of email programs on the planet tick you off by incessantly asking whether you want to make them your default email program. Here's a switch: Hotmail irritates you by not only *not* asking whether you'd like it to be the default, but also by not allowing you to set it as the default. Which means that if you click an email address in your browser, it'll probably launch some other mail program you don't use.

The Fix: Stay calm. You can make Hotmail your preferred email program—you just can't do it in Hotmail. Open your Internet Options settings (which is both an item in Internet Explorer's Tools menu and an icon in the Windows control panel) and click the Programs tab. Click the E-mail drop-down menu, choose Hotmail, and click OK. Now when you click an email address in your browser, Hotmail will appear and address a message for you. Feel better?

IMPORT YOUR ADDRESS BOOK VIA OUTLOOK EXPRESS

The Annoyance: Let's be realistic: Hotmail works a lot better as a backup mail service. But if you've got another account, you've got another address book that you might want to use in Hotmail. Hunt around Hotmail, and you'll see no way to import it.

The Fix: Don't retype anything! And don't pay anybody to put a hex on Microsoft, either. With typical Redmondian logic, the company hid Hotmail's address-book importing feature in Outlook Express, where it's called Synchronize Now and doesn't mention Hotmail. Very clever, guys.

The good news: if OE is your main email program, the Synchronize Now feature makes it easy to get contacts into Hotmail. And even if you're a Netscape fiend or Eudora maven, you can use OE as an intermediary. Start by following the instructions in "Use Outlook Express to Excise Hotmail Spam" (earlier in this section) to set up your Hotmail account in OE.

In OE, click the Addresses button, and in the Address Book window, select Tools → Synchronize Now. Not only will your OE address book be exported into Hotmail, but any contacts you entered in Hotmail will make the journey back into OE, so all your buddies show up in both email applications. Pretty slick, I must admit.

If you use an email program other than OE, you must import your contacts into OE first. In OE, choose File → Import → Other Address Book to see a list of the formats OE understands. It may take some tinkering to figure out which one you need—for instance, even though OE's Eudora Pro filter specifies that it's for Version 3.0, it works fine for Eudora 5.2. But don't try the stale old Netscape filters if you use Netscape Mail 6 or 7—instead, use Tools → Export in Netscape Mail to save a copy of the address book in LDIF (a file format supported by OE).

If all else fails—say, if you use an oddball email program that OE doesn't know from Adam—see if you can export your address book as a comma-separated value (CSV) file. It's a bare-bones format, but any email client worth its salt should handle it.

Still with me? Once your contacts are in OE by hook, crook, or CSV, you can use Synchronize Now to squirt them over to Hotmail. Mission accomplished.

GMAIL ANNOYANCES

GET GMAIL

The Annoyance: Everyone's talking about Gmail and you may already have an account. That's swell for you—but I don't have one. And I haven't a clue where to get one.

The Fix: It's a bummer. At press time, Gmail was still in testing (known cryptically as "beta"), and most of us can't get a Gmail account until it's publicly released. The trick is to find someone with an account, because they can send you an invitation. Beg, plead, and, if necessary, grovel until they send you the invite. One way to get an account is at the Gmail Forums page (go to *http://snipurl.com/swapgmail*, scroll down a bit, and click "Accounts and Invitations"). Traders desperate for an invite have offered such goods as a "one slightly used husband," "6 months of homemade cookies," and "a pound of 100% pure kona coffee." Another approach: do a Google search for "gmail invites" or "gmail invitations" and find a web site that may let you trade your first born for an account.

THE GMAIL STORY

Google's new web-based email service—named Gmail—is getting lots of buzz. And well it should: it's a hot product, and I like it for lots of reasons. Why is Gmail so insanely popular even before its official release? First, it offers one gigabyte of storage, which competing services have yet to match. (At press time, Yahoo! Mail was offering 250 MB.) Second, Gmail doesn't bludgeon you with ads. Gmail reads your incoming email (no humans read it; it's scanned by a computer), determines the content, and posts a text ad on the page. The ads are unobtrusive, just like the ones you see on a Google search results page. This beats MSN Hotmail and Yahoo! Mail, which clutter the screen with banner ads.

IMPORT ADDRESS BOOKS

The Annoyance: I like Gmail well enough to give up my Hotmail account. But how do I import my 500 names and email addresses into Gmail?

The Fix: Importing your email program's contact or address book into Gmail can be done in short order. Export your existing email program's contact list or address book as a comma-separated values (CSV) file. Most email programs can do that, including Outlook, Hotmail, and Yahoo! Mail. If you're having trouble exporting the address book, check Gmail's Help page. Once you've logged in, click Help (it's in the upper-right corner of the Gmail screen) and insert "export address book" in the search field. Look for an entry titled "How do I export CSV files?" Here's how to import the address book into Gmail:

1. Log into Gmail, click Contacts, and you'll see a new browser window.

2. Click the Import Contacts link, choose Browse..., and locate the CSV file you generated.

3. Select the file, click Import Contacts, and the file will be uploaded and imported into Gmail. The dialog will show you which entries were added to Gmail's Contacts list.

GMAIL SAYS: "YOU'VE GOT MAIL"

The Annoyance: I love Gmail, but I hate having to log in to see if there's any new mail. There has to be an easier way.

The Fix: Turn to the handy Gmail Notifier. You can find it by clicking on Gmail's Settings link. Once installed, you'll see an icon in Windows' System Tray that shows all your

unread Gmail messages, including the subject, sender, and a morsel of the message (see Figure 1-9). Just click an item to load the browser and go directly to your Gmail inbox.

Figure 1-9. Got mail? Find out by checking the Windows System Tray.

GMAIL NIXES EXES AND ZIPS

The Annoyance: Google's Gmail won't let me send or receive an email with a program attached. I guess that's a good thing, security-wise. But Gmail's restrictions are ridiculous—I can't send a zipped file as an attachment, either.

The Fix: Annoying yes, but Google's trying to protect you from viruses, which is a very good idea. If you're an experienced user and know what you're doing, there's a workaround: just rename files ending in *EXE* to *EX_*. You can use the same technique with zipped files. (BTW, this trick also works when I send mail to my wife at work, where the overzealous IT guys even block JPEGs.)

Fair warning: once the Google kids get wind of this, they'll probably figure out a way to block these attachments, too. But by then I'll have a new Annoyances book with another workaround.

BREAKING THE 10 MB LIMIT

The Annoyance: My ISP says I can send file attachments up to 10 MB in size. I've tried and I can't send a 10 MB, 9 MB, or even 8 MB file. All I've been able to get through is a 7.3 MB file. What's the deal? And can Gmail do any better?

Drop the Dot in Gmail

Many users took Gmail's recommendation and created email addresses using their first and last names separated with a period. Did you know that you can ignore the period in Gmail addresses? For instance, *bill.gates@gmail* and *billgates@gmail.com* will both arrive in Bill's inbox. If Bill had a Gmail account, that is….

The Fix: You're a victim of the attachment conundrum (and no, that isn't a virus). When you attach a file to a message, the file is converted into encoded text and shoved inside the message. Your recipient's email program then removes the encoded text from the body of the message and turns it back into a separate file.

The problem: the encoded text is typically 10 to 20% larger than the source file. So a 10 MB file may actually take up 12 MB or more.

That's another advantage of Gmail. No matter how bloated a 10 MB file attachment might be, Gmail is okay with this because it ignores the size of encoded text and simply looks at the attached source file.

If you don't use Gmail and must send 10 MB or larger file attachments, use a splitting program. That way you can send the file in two, three, or more separate emails. (The recipient, of course, must have the same program in order to reassemble all the parts.) My recommendation: grab a copy of Marc Bjorklund's File Splitter, a freebie available at *http://snipurl.com/file_split*.

Addicted to Gmail?

If you love Gmail and hunger for still more tips, paddle over to the delicious GmailGems at *http://snipurl.com/gmailgems*. Not enough? Try the Gmail Forum (*http://www.gmailforums.com*), the Gmail-Users group (*http://snipurl.com/Gmail_Users*), and Mark Lyon's Gmail page (*http://snipurl.com/Gmail_hacks*) for all sorts of cool Gmail utilities.

USE GMAIL TO STORE BIG FILES

Need to store your files online? Gmail's 1GB allotment per account might be the perfect parking spot. You can even call on a parking attendant: Viksoe's GMail Drive, which makes Gmail an extension of your PC. Log in and GMail Drive creates a virtual filesystem on top of your Gmail account, treating it like a disk drive. To move files from your PC, just drag and drop from Windows Explorer to your virtual Gmail folder.

Behind the scenes, the GMail Drive adds the file to Gmail's inbox (see the figure below). If you want to use the file, reverse the procedure—drag the file from the Gmail Drive folder back to your PC. Delete a file from the Gmail Drive folder and it's removed from your Gmail inbox. The one downside is that you're limited to files 10MB or smaller. Grab a copy at *http://snipurl.com/GmailDrive*.

				Create a filter
Compose Mail	Archive	Report Spam	More Actions ... ▾ Refresh	1 - 10 of 10
Inbox (8)	Select: All, Read, Unread, Starred, Unstarred, None			
Starred ☆	☐ ☆ me	» GMAILFS: /CPS.jpg [30159;a;1] -		🖉 1:00pm
Sent Mail	☐ ☆ me	» GMAILFS: /parachute.swf [111926;a;1] -		🖉 1:00pm
Drafts (1)	›☐ ☆ me	» GMAILFS: /15488_300.jpg [55216;a;1] -		🖉 12:58pm
All Mail	☐ ☆ PC World	» Home Office [IM Is More Than Chatting - 12/01/...		11:03am
Spam (4)	☐ ☆ PC World	» Announcing PC World's Online Guide to Di...		10:32am
Trash				

Windows
ANNOYANCES

Annoyances and *Windows*—the two words are inseparable. Windows is your portal to every application on your PC and is therefore your first source of irritation each and every day.

In this chapter, I'll arm you with simple workarounds, subtle tricks, and nifty configuration tweaks to circumvent the multitude of Windows annoyances. Some of the tips involve fiddling with the Registry, but don't worry—I'll make it as safe and painless for you as I possibly can.

GENERAL WINDOWS ANNOYANCES

WINDOWS XP IS THE CURE FOR ME (AND 98, AND 95)

The Annoyance: I'm using Windows 98 and I hate it when—

The Fix: Hold it right there. After years of frustration, I've found a solution to lots of Windows annoyances: dump what you're using and upgrade to XP. I'm not kidding. If you're using Windows 98 (or Windows Me or, worse, Windows 95), you should seriously consider upgrading to Windows XP. I don't like to shill for Microsoft, but Windows XP is the finest operating system to come out of Redmond since Bill Gates made his first billion. It offers better stability (no more daily reboots or frequent blue screen crashes), memory management (you won't run out of resources, even when you open dozens of windows simultaneously), and security (you can't bypass the password prompt merely by pressing Esc!). In short, Windows XP has far fewer annoyances.

Before you throw your current Windows out the window, however, be sure that Windows XP is compatible with your hardware and software. You can perform a quick compatibility check with PC Pitstop's XP Readiness Test (*http://snipurl.com/pcpitstop_full*), which tells you how your system stacks up against XP's minimum and recommended hardware specs. (See Figure 2-1.)

Windows XP Upgrade Advisor, a far more comprehensive compatibility checker, is a Microsoft tool that takes stock of your current setup and warns you about programs or devices that won't work with Windows XP. If a new, compatible version or driver is available, Upgrade Advisor tells you about it. If you can get your hands on a Windows XP CD, you've got Upgrade Advisor. Insert the CD, and on the main menu that appears, click Check System Compatibility. If you don't have access to a Windows XP CD, you can

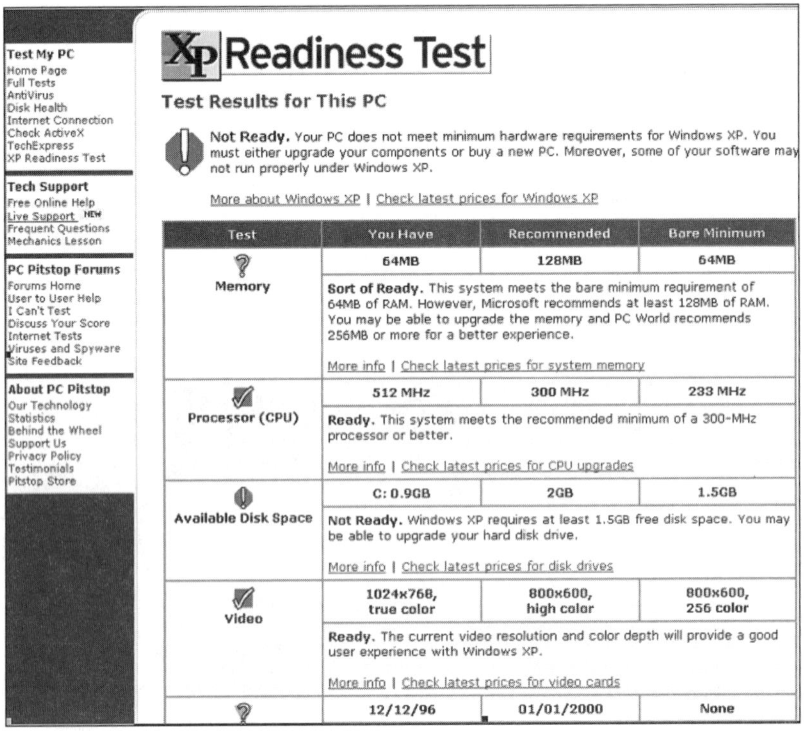

Figure 2-1. PC Pitstop's XP Readiness Test runs a slew of diagnostic tests to determine how ready your PC is for a Windows XP upgrade. While you're on the site, you might as well let PC Pitstop examine your PC and give you some pointers for tuning it up. See *http://snipurl.com/pcpitstop_full*.

download Upgrade Advisor from *http://snipurl.com/ upgrade_advisor*. Be forewarned, however: at about 32 MB, it's a huge download.

Whether you have the CD or a downloaded copy, make sure you're connected to the Internet when you run Upgrade Advisor. Upgrade Advisor will snag the most current hardware and software compatibility report for your system.

HELP THAT'S ACTUALLY HELPFUL

The Annoyance: I hate it when I'm using Windows XP and—

The Fix: Sorry to keep interrupting, but I have to tell you about one of the niftiest features in Windows XP: the help system. Yep, believe it or not, online help in Windows XP (which uses a completely different help engine than previous versions of Windows) often leads to *useful* information about actual problems. Don't believe me? Check out the incredibly comprehensive Network Diagnostics window in Figure 2-2.

When you encounter a problem in Windows, your first step ought to be choosing Start → Help and Support. The opening window lets you browse through various topics, but typing a few words in the Search box usually gets quicker results. The help system returns matching results in three categories: suggested topics (articles that are most likely to answer your question), full-text search matches (all topics that contain the words you typed), and relevant articles from the Microsoft Knowledge Base web site.

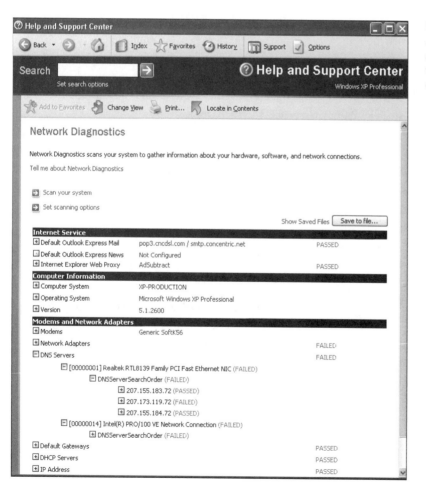

Figure 2-2. XP's Handy Network Diagnostics and Annoyance Basher told me I needed to contact my ISP and obtain correct DNS IP addresses. Just try getting this sort of detailed analysis from Windows Me, 98, or (ha!) 95.

A MOST ANNOYING ANNOYANCE: WINDOWS PRODUCT ACTIVATION

The Annoyance: I was on an airplane without Internet access or a phone, working on a memo in Word, when Windows XP froze me out because I hadn't activated the software I'd paid for. I was hosed.

The Fix: Understanding what Windows Product Activation does can help you to avoid inopportune freeze-outs and embarrassing situations—like when you're making a presentation to members of your church and Windows acts like it's a stolen copy.

At each startup, Windows examines 10 components of your computer, including the volume serial number of the hard drive's system partition, the processor type, the processor serial number, the amount of installed RAM, and so on. Windows creates a one-way hash value (see the sidebar on this page for more on hash values) from these components and compares it to the hash value stored in \Windows\System32\Wpa.dbl, a file created on your computer when you activate Windows.

Bottom line: invasion of privacy is not an issue with Windows Product Activation. Potentially getting locked out of your PC is the real problem if you don't activate.

Note that Windows does not contact the Mother Ship (a.k.a. Microsoft); it looks only to the *Wpa.dbl* file stored on your computer. If either of the following conditions exist, Windows requires you to activate before you can log on:

- The *Wpa.dbl* file does not exist or is corrupt.
- During a 120-day period, you change more than 4 of the 10 components.

In either case, you must activate XP by contacting Microsoft via Internet or phone. With the original version of Windows XP, you had to activate right away in such situations. With Service Pack 1 installed, Windows squawks but gives you another three days to solve the problem or reactivate before it locks you out altogether.

Every 120 days, *Wpa.dbl* is updated to match your current array of components.

To avoid activation hassles:

- Install Service Pack 1 for Windows XP. Go to Start → All Programs and choose Windows Update at the top of the menu. Once the analysis is done, click "Scan for updates," then "Review and Install Updates," and select the service pack.
- When you upgrade hardware components, restart Windows and make sure it's working before you get to that remote island without Internet access.

If you do get caught with your activation down, you can run XP in safe mode. Press F8 while your computer boots, and choose a safe mode from the menu that appears.

SPEED UP MENUS BY SKIPPING TRANSITIONS

The Annoyance: I'm primed for a fast PC experience: I have a speedy 3.0 GHz processor with 768MB of RAM on my XP system. But here I am, tapping my fingers, waiting for menus to fade into view.

The Fix: You want sharp, snappy menus? In Windows 98, Me, and 2000, right-click the desktop, choose Properties, and select the Effects tab. With one click of the mouse, uncheck that confounded "Animate windows, menus and lists" (98) or "Use transition effects for menus and tooltips" (Me and 2000) box. In Windows XP, right-click the desktop, choose Properties, click the Appearance tab, and click the Effects button (see Figure 2-3). Now uncheck the "Use the following transition effect for menus and tooltips" box. Faster now?

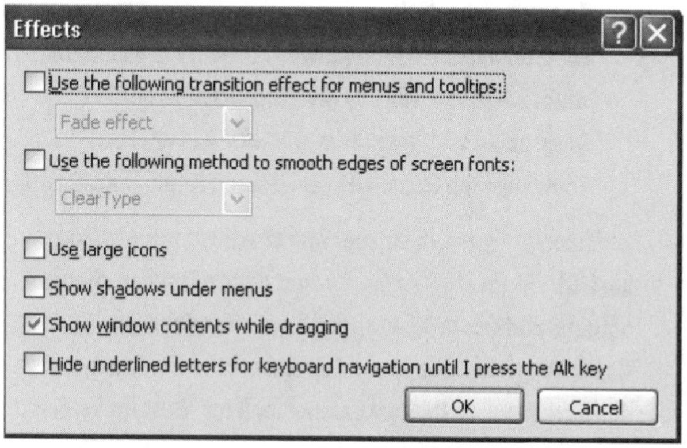

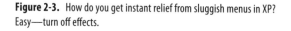

Figure 2-3. How do you get instant relief from sluggish menus in XP? Easy—turn off effects.

SCREEN RESOLUTION: I CAN SEE CLEARLY NOW

The Annoyance: XP's user-accounts feature is a nifty way to create personalized workspaces, but why can't I set a different display resolution for each user? My mother, who's no spring chicken, needs a magnifying glass to see an elephant, so I'd like to use a low resolution (say, 800 × 600) for her. My eyesight's better, so I'd like a nice 1280 × 1024 resolution.

The Fix: Unfortunately, whatever display resolution you choose (the one you set by right-clicking the desktop, choosing Properties, clicking the Settings tab, and adjusting the "Screen resolution" slider) applies to everyone who uses your computer.

However, there are a few Mom-oriented settings to increase the size of icons, text, and other Windows objects that make high-resolution screens easier to use. On the Settings tab, click the Advanced button. On the General tab of the dialog box that appears, select a larger DPI setting for your mom. Click OK until you return to Display Properties, then click the Appearance tab. Click the "Windows and buttons" drop-down menu and select "Windows Classic style." Then select a color scheme and font size that your mom can read. On the Settings tab, set the resolution at the highest level anyone using your computer wants.

An alternative is to set the resolution for your sharper eyes and let Mom use the zoom feature (often in the View menu) found in many applications.

MONITOR ANNOYANCES

If you're using an LCD monitor or notebook, jump to "Clear and Sharp LCD Fonts" in Chapter 7 and see how ClearType can make a world of difference on your XP system.

A NEAT ZOOM TRICK

If your mouse has a wheel button, hold down the Ctrl key and roll the wheel. In many programs, that action zooms the image in or out, depending on the direction you turn the wheel.

OLD DOS GAMES MAKE IT TO THE BIG SCREEN

The Annoyance: Many older games run at 640 × 480 resolution and leave a blank border around the screen when Windows is configured at a higher resolution. (Windows XP doesn't even offer 640 × 480 resolution, although the driver on your graphics card may).

The Fix: Here's how to make those games fill the screen:

- For a DOS-based game, right-click the game's icon and choose Properties. On the Screen tab, select Full-screen. (You can test full-screen mode without making this change permanent. After you start the program, press Alt-Enter, which toggles between full-screen and windowed modes.)

- For a Windows-based game, right-click the game's icon and choose Properties. On the Compatibility tab, select "Run in 640 by 480 screen resolution." Some games may run more smoothly if you select "Run this program in compatibility mode for" and specify the Windows version the program was designed for.

TAKE CHARGE OF YOUR START MENU AND SYSTEM TRAY

The Annoyance: First Windows XP hides infrequently used icons in the System Tray, then it adds program shortcuts to my Start menu's left pane. Enough!

The Fix: Take charge of your System Tray icons: right-click the Start button and choose Properties to open your system's Taskbar and Start Menu Properties dialog box. Select the Taskbar tab and uncheck the "Hide inactive icons" box.

You can decide for yourself which System Tray icons you want to see and which you want out of the way. Leave "Hide inactive icons" checked, click the Customize button,

and then choose each icon one at a time and set its Behavior to "Always show," "Always hide," or "Hide when inactive."

If you don't want XP to add items to the list of frequently used programs in the Start menu, reopen the Taskbar and Start Menu Properties dialog box, choose the Start Menu tab, click the Customize button, and set "Number of programs on Start menu" to a figure of your choosing. Note: this tip doesn't work with the Classic Start menu.

CLEAR YOUR DESKTOP ONCE AND FOR ALL

If you really like to be tidy, make your desktop an icon-free zone:

- In Windows 98, right-click the desktop and choose Active Desktop→View As Web Page. Then right-click the desktop, click Properties, select the Effects tab, and check the "Hide icons when the desktop is viewed as a Web page" box.

- For later versions of Windows, right-click the desktop, choose Arrange Icons By (in Windows XP) or Active Desktop (in Windows Me and 2000), and uncheck Show Desktop Icons. All your desktop items vanish.

Don't worry—you can still get fast access to your desktop shortcuts. Right-click an empty spot on the Taskbar, choose Toolbars, and select Desktop if it's not already checked. The desktop icons disappear. To access those shortcuts, slide back down to the Taskbar and look for "Desktop >>". Click the >> and the desktop icons reappear in a pop-up menu. Another cool trick: double-click the vertical bar to the left of any Taskbar group and the icons will collapse or expand to fill the space.

KEEP OUT

Finally, a System Tray utility everyone can agree on (*http://snipurl.com/keepout*).

PROGRAM FILENAMES THAT MAKE SENSE

The Annoyance: When I download a program or an upgrade, the last thing I want the file named is *setup.exe* or *install*. Because I don't always install the program right away, I may lose track of it. Worse, other downloads invariably have the same name, making it even harder to figure out which is which.

The Fix: There's no earthly reason why installation files can't be named something sensible. I simply rename the file in the Save As dialog box before I download it, using something more descriptive, such as the program's name and version.

KEEP YOUR FOLDER NAMES SHORT AND SWEET

The Annoyance: I get really annoyed—no, steamed!—with the long folder names some companies create in my Program Files folder. I'm surprised they haven't figured out a way to make folder names flash in neon.

The Fix: There's an easy way around it: when the installation asks where you'd like to install the program, make a change. I do it all the time with no ill effects. See Figures 2-4 and 2-5.

LOADED SYSTEM TRAY

Want to see a system that's been collecting icons since 1983? Check out *http://snipurl.com/systray1*.

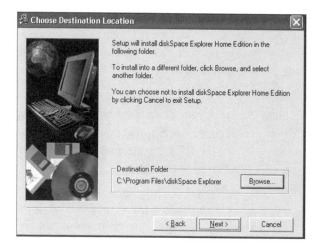

Figure 2-4. When the installation routine asks if you're happy with the folder name, click Browse...

Figure 2-5. ... and change it to something you're happy with.

ONE-CLICK XP SHUTOWNS

The Annoyance: No matter how I want to do it—Turn Off, Restart, Stand By, or Hibernate—shutting down requires too many mouse clicks or keystrokes. Select Start, Shut Down, and then Shut Down again. There's got to be a faster way!

The Fix: Windows XP includes a command-line utility called *Shutdown.exe*, but it doesn't support some key features, such as hibernation. Some better alternatives offer more control, work with all versions of Windows, and are free:

- Show Stopper, from Karen Kenworthy (*http://www. oreilly.com/pcannoyances*), makes it easy to shut down, reboot, log off, hibernate, or stand by with just a click or a command line.

- Wizmo, from Steve Gibson (*http://www.oreilly.com/ pcannoyances*), provides a simple way to shut down, and it also offers command-line control of screen savers, speakers, and CD drives.

- CloseWin creates shortcuts on the desktop that close Windows with a double click. Another time-saver is Presstart, which adds a Start button to the desktop. To put these tools on the Quick Launch toolbar for one-click operations, just drag the icons from the desktop to the toolbar. Both tools are free, and you can download them from *http://snipurl.com/cooltools*.

Launching a program or typing a command line to shut down your computer is no easier than using the standard Windows shutdown procedure, of course. What makes these programs shine is that you can create a shortcut that performs the exact actions you want. You can put the shortcut on your desktop, on the Quick Launch toolbar, or some other convenient place. You can also run the shortcut as a scheduled task if you want to shut down your computer at a particular time.

Here are two other options to consider:

- You can have Windows stand by or hibernate automatically after a period of inactivity. You don't need any extra tools, batch files, shortcuts, or scheduled tasks—just go to Power Options in the control panel to set up a schedule on the Power Schemes tab.

- You can configure your computer's power button (and the sleep button on your keyboard, if it has one) to perform the shutdown action of your choice. Visit the Advanced tab in the Power Options control panel.

WHAT DO THE FOUR XP SHUTDOWN OPTIONS DO?

Turn Off

(Appears as Shut Down on some systems.) Closes all programs and turns off the power. The next time, you'll have to turn on your PC's power switch and go through the full boot process.

Restart

Closes all programs, shuts down Windows, and then restarts Windows.

Stand By

Quickly switches to a low-power state by shutting down hard drives, monitors, fans, and other power hogs, but it continues to draw enough power to preserve the contents of memory. You can resume from standby very quickly, but this convenience comes with a risk: if you should lose power altogether during standby (your battery dies or there's a power failure), the contents of memory—and with it, any unsaved work—are lost.

Hibernate

Stores the contents of memory to your hard drive and then turns off the power. When you turn the power back on, Windows loads the stored contents back into memory and picks up right where you left off. Hibernation takes longer to initiate and resume than standby does, but there's almost no danger of losing data. The other downside of hibernation is that it requires a big chunk of free disk space, though with today's hard-drive capacities, that requirement is less of an issue.

Note that the XP Pro logoff feature shuts down all your applications and takes you back to XP's Welcome screen, where you can log onto any account established on your system.

ALL HAIL THE WINDOWS KEY!

The Annoyance: I have a keyboard with a Windows key stuck between the Alt and Ctrl keys. What else is this key good for besides bringing up the Start menu?

The Fix: Plenty—if you combine it with other keys. For example, WinKey-E brings up Windows Explorer (My Computer). Some other useful key combos:

WinKey-D
> Minimizes all open windows and takes you to the desktop. Do it again and you're taken back to the last active application.

HIDDEN XP SHUTDOWN OPTIONS

Finally, after years of unfulfilled promises, power management features in Windows XP actually work (most of the time). Now you can put your machine in a no-power hibernation state, and when you awaken your computer from its slumber, Windows reappears in a flash.

The Hibernate option can be hard to find. Here's the trick: when you reach the "Turn off computer" screen, hold down the Shift key. The Stand By button miraculously turns into a Hibernate button, as shown below. Click and snooze!

Don't see the Hibernate option? Hibernation was probably disabled on your system. To enable it, open the Power Options control panel, click the Hibernate tab, and check the "Enable Hibernation" box.

WinKey-E
> Opens Windows Explorer (My Computer).

WinKey-R
> Opens the Run dialog.

WinKey-L
> Brings up the Log On screen.

WinKey-F
> Opens the Search Companion screen.

WinKey-M
> Minimizes all windows.

WinKey-Shift-M
> Use this key combo to undo the "minimize all" command (WinKey-M).

WinKey-Pause/Break
> Opens System Properties.

WinKey-F1
> Brings up Windows Help.

For a complete list of WinKey combinations—plus shortcut keys for Word, Excel, and Windows in general—go to the Computer Hope site at *http://snipurl.com/ch_shortcut*.

AN EVEN BETTER WINDOWS KEY

The Windows key *is* great, but we're just scratching the surface here. If you like these shortcuts, you'll *love* WinKey, a small, free utility that expands the Windows key with over 200 configurable key assignments.

For instance, I have Word, Eudora (my email program), and half a dozen utilities assigned to my keyboard's Windows key using WinKey. I no longer have to hunt around in the Start menu for these tools; I just tap a WinKey combination. Grab a copy at *http://snipurl.com/winkey*.

OPEN CLOSED STARTUP PROGRAMS WITHOUT RESTARTING

The Annoyance: I was using a program that resides in the System Tray and accidentally closed it. I can't find the program anywhere in my Start menu. Do I have to reboot to reload this program?

The Fix: This happens to me all the time, especially with programs that you can unload too easily. My quick fix is to head for the Start menu and select Programs → Startup. Chances are good that a shortcut to your program is right there. Just click it, and you're on your way.

If it's not there, don't fret: select Start → Programs → Accessories → System Tools → System Information. In the left pane of the System Information dialog box, expand the Software Environment item, then select the subcategory Startup Programs. In the right pane are all the programs that run at startup.

You should find what you're looking for in this list. Select it, press Ctrl-C to copy the line (System Information won't let you copy just the command you need), open the Run dialog box (Start → Run), and press Ctrl-V to paste the line into the Open field. (If you use Windows 2000, right-click the line; select Save As Text File; name, save, and open the text file; and copy the command from there.) Delete everything except the command and its path, press Enter, and your System Tray icon should reappear.

LAPTOP NETWORK SWITCHES MADE EASY

The Annoyance: I take my notebook when traveling, and it's a pain to change my network settings to connect to the hotel LAN or my client's network. I have to carry around a piece of paper with my network settings, and every time I make the changes, Windows forces me to reboot.

The Fix: You're suffering from Multiple Network Disorder, an affliction I'd still be suffering from if I hadn't found NetSwitcher. With NetSwitcher, I can save a set of network settings for each situation. When I'm at a new location, such as a client's office, I change and save the new network settings. Once I'm home, I restore my previous network settings with a few clicks. NetSwitcher is a $14 shareware gem (see Figure 2-6), and it's cheap insurance—and a lifesaver—when I have to fiddle with my PC's network settings.

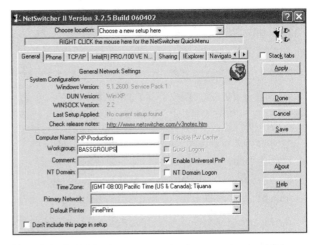

Figure 2-6. NetSwitcher lets you save and restore your network and dialup settings. Think of it as a $14 insurance policy that guarantees you never lose your network settings again.

Unlike Windows, NetSwitcher requires a reboot *only* if you modify a parameter that needs a reboot to take effect. A 30-day trial of NetSwitcher is available at *http://www.oreilly.com/pcannoyances*.

SET THE WINDOWS CLOCK

The Annoyance: A cheap wristwatch seems to keep better time than my $2,500 PC.

The Fix: By default, Windows XP (but not earlier versions of Windows) periodically synchronizes the computer's clock with an accurate timeserver on the Internet. (If your Windows XP computer is joined to a domain, it synchronizes with the domain controller.) Initially, Windows XP checks with the timeserver once a week, but if it needs to make too much of an adjustment, it checks more frequently to maintain two-second accuracy.

You can see when the last successful synchronization occurred and when the next one is scheduled by viewing the Internet Time tab in the Date and Time Properties dialog box. (You can get there through the control panel, but the quickest way is to double-click the clock in the Windows systray.)

You can force Windows to synchronize immediately by clicking the Update Now button or by entering the command `w32tm /resync` in the Start → Run dialog box's Open field, a command prompt window, or a program shortcut.

Sometimes the Windows Time service gets mightily confused, and the clock in your Windows XP computer gets pretty far off. If that happens, give the service a swift kick. Open a command prompt window (choose Start → Run, type `cmd`, and click OK) and type the following commands at the prompt, pressing Enter at the end of each line:

```
net stop w32time
w32tm.exe /unregister
w32tm.exe /unregister
w32tm.exe /register
net start w32time
exit
```

If you're not using XP, you'll need a third-party program to synchronize your computer's clock to an Internet timeserver. One I've used with success is AtomTime98 (*http://www.oreilly.com/pcannoyances*).

You can set each computer on your network to synchronize to an Internet server, but you might find it easier to synchronize only one and then let the other computers on the network synchronize to that master. To synchronize your computer's clock with another computer on your network, type `net time \\computer /set /y` (where *computer* is the name of the computer whose time you want to adopt) in a command prompt window. Since this is a one-time synchronization, save the command in a program shortcut or batch file that runs each time you start Windows.

Virtual Time Check

Does anyone know what time it is? I didn't think so. (And don't furrow your brow—this isn't a trick question.) The industrious web site has the straight skinny on time, with a unique and amusing way of showing the year, month, day, hour minutes, and all the seconds in between: *http://snipurl.com/v_time*.

AN INADVERTENT TRIP TO THE FUTURE

It was an ordinary morning—the sun was shining, and, as usual, I was late on a deadline. The big difference? I booted my system and received a dozen alerts—my uninterruptible power supply warned me its battery needing replacing, four shareware programs insisted I'd gone beyond the 30-day trial period, Outlook popped up 100 reminders, and every program in my System Tray wanted to check for updated versions. Yep, you've got it. I had intentionally set my system's clock to 2015 (don't ask why; it's too embarrassing) and forgot to set it back. Lesson? If you futz with the clock, remember to reset it when you're done.

A CURE FOR COCK-EYED CALENDARS

The Annoyance: Sometimes, my computer's system date suddenly changes to the wrong date, but the time remains correct.

The Fix: This one had me scratching my head when I noticed that all the files I had recently saved in a particular folder were dated several weeks in the future. I checked the system date (hover the mouse pointer over the time in the lower-right corner of the systray until the date pops up), and sure enough, it was wrong.

After a bit of sleuthing, I discovered that someone (who shall remain nameless, but she lives with me and occasionally uses my PC) needed to see a calendar to schedule a vacation. So she went to the built-in calendar in Windows by double-clicking the time in the Taskbar, skipped ahead a few months, and when she was all done, clicked OK to close the dialog box. That set the computer's system date to the date she had selected. This faux pas could have been avoided in a number of ways:

- If you use the Date and Time Properties dialog box as a quick way to view a calendar, be sure to use Cancel to exit the dialog box instead of clicking OK.

- If other users of your computer won't heed the above, and you use Windows 2000 or XP, change their account privileges so they're not allowed to change the system time. In Windows 2000, select Start → Settings → Control Panel and open the Users and Passwords control panel. If you haven't yet given the user an account, select Add and follow the directions, selecting "Restricted user" when asked to choose an access level. If the user has an account, double-click the account name, select the Group Membership tab, and select "Restricted user." In Windows XP, open the User Accounts control panel, select "Create a new account" or pick the account to change, and set or change the account type from "Computer administrator" to "Limited."

- Use a different calendar! You probably have a better one in another program (do you have Microsoft Outlook?). If not, try Calendar Magic—it's freeware, and you can create reminders for events, set audible warnings for imminent events, and calculate equinoxes, solstices, and moon phases through the year 3000 (see Figure 2-7). Grab a copy at *http://www.oreilly.com/pcannoyances*. There are also plenty of freeware and inexpensive shareware tools at *http://snipurl.com/pcw_calendars*.

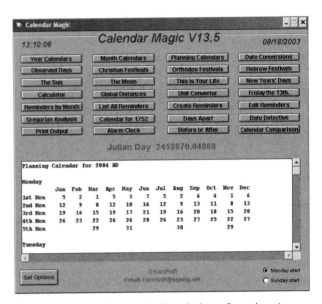

Figure 2-7. Instead of using the calendar in the System Tray and messing up your PC's time and date, use the free Calendar Magic.

A QUICK FIX FOR MISSING QUICK LAUNCH TOOLBARS

The Annoyance: During a lengthy session with Windows Explorer, I somehow deleted the Quick Launch toolbar and can't figure out how to get it back.

The Fix: The disappearance of the Quick Launch toolbar is inexplicable, but it's a no-brainer to bring it back. Right-click a free space on the Taskbar (you may have to close some programs to do so), and choose Toolbars → Quick Launch.

RESTORE MIA QUICK LAUNCH SHORTCUTS

The Annoyance: The other day I accidentally deleted the Show Desktop icon in the Quick Launch toolbar—the icon that minimizes all open windows and shows the desktop. Worse, in trying to get the shortcut back, I inadvertently erased the clock from the System Tray!

The Fix: Sometimes the tendency to tinker gets one in trouble, but fortunately these two *faux pas* are easy to reverse. To restore the clock, right-click a blank area in the Taskbar and select Properties. In Windows XP, check the "Show the clock" box and click OK. In Windows 98, Me, and 2000, select the General tab (Taskbar Options in 98), check "Show clock", and click OK.

To retrieve the Show Desktop icon, turn to a great free utility written by Doug Knox, aptly named "Restore Missing Show Desktop Icon to Quick Launch" (*http://snipurl.com/ showdesktop*). After you download, unzip, and install the program, run it to recover your shortcut. Now you can get back to fiddling with your PC's settings without losing track of time.

PREVENT ACCIDENTAL FILE DELETIONS

The Annoyance: My buddy stopped by my home office, and I made the mistake of letting him fiddle with my system. He changed something in the Recycle Bin, and I no longer get a dialog box that asks if I'm sure I want to delete files. The confirmation was annoying, but it was also reassuring. How do I get it back?

The Fix: Right-click the Recycle Bin either on the desktop or in a Windows Explorer or folder window, choose Properties, check the "Display delete confirmation dialog" box, then click OK. And don't let your pal near your PC again, okay?

PLAY WITH PROPERTIES

You can find dozens of ways to modify how your PC works by poking around in Properties. Try it on everything— drives, files, icons, etc. Just right-click the item, choose Properties, and explore.

PHONE REBOOTS

The Annoyance: My Aunt Blossom is happy as a Jersey clam using dialup for Internet access. The only problem is that when her computer is on but not connected to the Internet, the PC restarts whenever her phone rings. By the way, the restarts never happen when she's already dialed into the Internet.

The Fix: It's not a bug—it's a feature! Luckily, Aunt Blossom can turn this "feature" off. Open the Control Panel, and if you're in Windows XP's Category view, click "Performance and Maintenance." If you're not, or you're running Windows 2000 or Me, open the System control panel, click the Hardware tab, and then click the Device Manager button. (In Windows 98, open the System control panel and click the Device Manager tab.) In the tree-like list in Device Manager, open the Modems item. Right-click your modem and select Properties. On the Power Management tab, uncheck the "Allow this device to bring the computer out of standby" box and click OK.

If you don't see a Power Management tab, this setting isn't causing the restarts. Instead, here's the other possible culprit: your system's BIOS may be set to trigger a restart when the phone rings. Exit Windows and restart your PC. Press the key that opens your CMOS Setup screen (typically F1, Del, or F10.) Once you're in your PC's Setup program, look for options labeled "Power" or "Power Management" (the wording varies from system to system). If you see a "Wake Ring-on" option, disable it.

PRINTING FAXES, NO WIZARD REQUIRED

The Annoyance: The fax capability in Windows XP has saved me untold aggravation. I don't need a standalone fax machine or that slippery thermal paper. But it's not entirely a bed of roses. It takes at least five clicks to print a received fax because Windows insists on dragging me through the Photo Printing Wizard.

The Fix: When you receive a fax, the normal procedure is to read it on-screen. Clicking the Print tool invokes the blasted Photo Printing Wizard. One way you can foil the wizard is to close Windows Picture and Fax Viewer (the window in which the fax is displayed), select the fax in Fax Console's Inbox, and choose File → Print.

But this is a kludgy fix. Since a fax file is just a TIF, associate it with a viewer other than Windows Picture and Fax Viewer. Changing the file association also prevents the Photo Printing Wizard from popping up.

- Any program that can view and print TIF files will do. If you have a favorite image editor (and it's not a slow-loading memory hog like Adobe PhotoShop), you can use it. I recommend IrfanView, a fast, small, free viewer for all kinds of graphic and multimedia files. You can download IrfanView from *http://snipurl.com/irfanview*. If you missed the option to associate TIF files with IrfanView during setup, just open IrfanView and choose Options → Set File Associations.

- If you have Office XP, you have a viable alternative in Office Document Imaging, which displays and prints faxes. (It also claims to perform optical character recognition, but don't bother with this anemic feature.) If the Photo Printing Wizard appears when you view a fax, open Control Panel, open Add/Remove Programs, select Microsoft Office XP, and click the Change button. Select "Add or Remove Features," click Next, then expand the Office Tools item, and you'll find Microsoft Office Document Imaging. Click its icon and choose Run From My Computer, and then click the Update button to complete the setup.

If you install Office Document Imaging, IrfanView, or another image viewer, but Windows Picture and Fax Viewer (along with its evil spawn, the Photo Printing Wizard) still appear as your default fax viewer, you need to set the file association manually. In a Windows Explorer window, choose Tools → Folder Options. Click the File Types tab, scroll down to the TIF entry, and select it. Click Change and select your viewer program from the list that appears. Repeat for the TIFF entry.

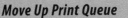

Move Up Print Queue

Sometimes right after you've sent several documents to your printer, you realize you want the last one sent to print first. Double-click the printer icon in your System Tray and drag the last document in the file list to the top of the queue. It will print immediately after the file currently being processed.

FASTER ACCESS TO YOUR CONTROL PANEL

The Annoyance: Often the instructions for adjusting certain settings—including a lot of the instructions in this book—direct me to a Control Panel application. But when I go to Control Panel, the specified application or icon isn't there!

The Fix: Over the years, Control Panel applications have proliferated, making it increasingly difficult to wade through them all and find a particular icon. (A basic installation of Windows 3.1 had only a dozen icons in Control Panel. A typical installation of Windows XP has nearly three times that many.) In Windows XP, the default Control Panel view (called Category View) divides the Control Panel icons into logical groups. Category View gives Control Panel a simpler, prettier face, but it means an extra click (and a little extra thought) to find the icon you want.

To restore the old view—the one with all Control Panel icons in an ordinary Explorer window—click the "Switch to Classic View" link in the task pane on the left side of the window.

If you want really quick access to Control Panel items (and you're not put off by a lengthy menu), try this:

1. In Control Panel, open "Taskbar and Start Menu." (If you're still using that pesky Category View, you'll find it in the Appearance and Themes category.)

2. Click the Start Menu tab, select "Start menu" if it's not already chosen, and click Customize.

3. Click the Advanced tab. In the "Start menu items" list box, under Control Panel, select "Display as a menu." Click OK twice to confirm your choices.

Control Panel items now appear on a cascading menu (complete with submenus) that opens when you choose Start → Control Panel, as shown in Figure 2-8.

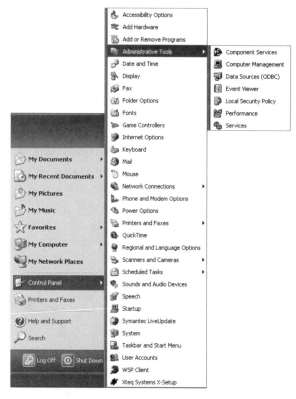

Figure 2-8. If you use Control Panel applications frequently, you might prefer to set up Control Panel as a cascading menu on the Start menu.

THE CASE OF THE MISSING ICONS

The Annoyance: I'm one of those compulsive types who insist that everything be in its place. I spend hours meticulously arranging icons on my Windows desktop. But when my system crashes, my precious arrangement of desktop icons comes up scrambled.

The Fix: Several freeware programs can keep those desktop icons in line. Should your system crash, the graphics mode change, or someone mess with the desktop icons, you simply restore the saved arrangement. Check 'em out:

- Save My Desktop!, from Johnny Tucker (*http://www. oreilly.com/pcannoyances*), is a simple program with the single purpose of saving and restoring the desktop icon arrangement.

- Iconoid, from SillySot Software (*http://www.oreilly. com/pcannoyances*), saves and restores icon arrangements, and offers options for controlling colors and for hiding icons and windows.

> **tip**
>
> Save My Desktop! is also perfect insurance for putting your desktop icons back in order when you have to boot to Safe Mode or if you experiment and change your graphics adapter's resolution.

> **EXPLODING GRAPES**
>
> No matter how busy you are fending off annoyances, there's always time to make some grapes explode. All you need is a plate, a few grapes, a microwave oven and several friends with way too much time on their hands (*http://snipurl.com/grape*).

CRUSH INTRUSIVE DESKTOP WEB ITEMS

The Annoyance: I was traipsing around the Internet and saw an image I thought would look cute on my desktop. So I right-clicked on the image, chose "Set as Desktop Item," and answered a couple of prompts. But in the cold light of day, the image isn't that cute, and I can't figure out how to get rid of it. (See Figure 2-9.)

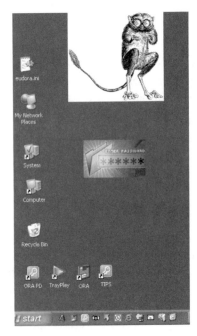

Figure 2-9. That creature's cute, but how in the world did it end up on your desktop?

The Fix: Selecting "Set as Desktop Item" creates a live Active Desktop item (see Figure 2-10), and now you've got a small—or humongous—web page object on your desktop.

> **tip**
>
> Choose "Save Picture As" instead. Then you can deal with the image as a file rather than an Active Desktop item.

Figure 2-10. Top: It's pretty easy to click "Set as Desktop Item" instead of "Save Picture As." Bottom: And even easier to confirm whether that's what you really want!

It's happened to me, too, and it's exasperating trying to delete it. But don't fret; renovation will take less than two minutes:

1. Click the desktop and move your mouse pointer across the object towards its upper left corner. Click the down arrow on the left side of the bar that appears above the object.

2. Click Customize My Desktop on the menu that appears.

3. From the Desktop Items dialog, click the Web tab (see Figure 2-11).

4. Uncheck the item (or items) that begin with *http://*. If you're sure you never want to see the item on your desktop again, click Delete and answer "yes" to the prompt. Click OK and OK again to confirm.

Desktop Items dialog

General | **Web**

To display a Web page on your desktop, select it from the following list. To add a Web page to the list, click New. To update Web page content, click Synchronize.

Web pages:

☑ http://oreilly.com/images/animals/vi_guy.gif
☑ http://www.pcworld.com/home/graphics/hp_(
☐ My Current Home Page

[New...] [Delete] [Properties] [Synchronize]

To prevent moving or resizing of Web items on your desktop, select the following check box.

☐ Lock desktop items

[OK] [Cancel]

Figure 2-11. You can get rid of Active Desktop items temporarily by unchecking the boxes—or permanently by clicking Delete.

PUMP UP YOUR ICONS

The Annoyance: I set my large, 21-inch monitor at a screen resolution of 1152 by 864 pixels to get a bigger view of all my open applications. That was cool, but the microscopic size of the desktop icons and fonts at that resolution was decidedly uncool. How can I puff these up a bit?

The Fix: Changing the size of your desktop icons may also change their positions on screen, which is an annoyance in itself. So before you do anything, download and install the free Save My Desktop! utility (see "The Case of the Missing Icons"). Run the program and save a snapshot of the desktop. Then, to adjust the size of your desktop icons, right-click the desktop, choose Properties, click the Appearance tab, and click the Advanced button. Choose Icon from the Item drop-down menu, and increase the number of pixels under Size. Keep in mind, however, that many of your icons will look blurry when you make them bigger.

DELETING ANNOYING ICONS

The top section of the All Program menu is where developers stick their program icons. If you don't like 'em, what recourse do you have? Delete 'em. Just right-click the icon and select Delete.

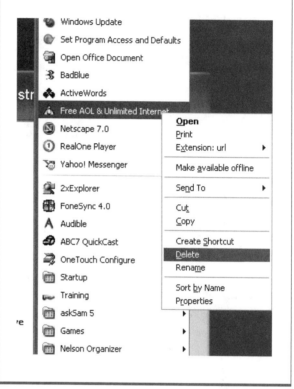

INTERNET EXPLORER HAS SHRUNKEN MENUS

The Annoyance: I was fiddling with some of the tricks you mentioned in "Pump Up Your Icons", and here's a follow-up annoyance: when I rebooted my system, the Minimize, Maximize, and Close buttons in the upper right of the screen in Internet Explorer's menu bar shrunk to half size, which makes them hard to click, but the toolbars are normal size. How do I return the menu bar to its original size?

The Fix: Odd, but fixable. Open the Display control panel, click the Themes tab, choose a theme other than what's currently selected, and click the Apply button. Repeat the process and select the Windows theme of your choice.

BIG ICONS IN THE QUICK LAUNCH

The Annoyance: I don't know how or why, but the icons in the Quick Launch toolbar are enormous. Everything else in the Taskbar locks fine. Weird, you know?

The Fix: If it's not shrunken menus, it's huge icons. I agree that it's strange, but there's an easy fix.

Right-click a blank area in WinXP's Taskbar and make sure that "Lock the Taskbar" is unchecked.

This part's a little tricky: right-click a blank area (i.e., one that doesn't have an icon) in the Quick Launch area of the Taskbar. The best spot is near the double line that's used to adjust the size of the Quick Launch area. (If the first menu item you see when you right-click is Open, you need to try a different spot.)

When you right-click a blank area, the first menu item will be View. Select View → Small Icons to bring the icons in the Quick Launch toolbar back to the right size.

On the other hand, to make your Quick Launch icons bigger, right-click a blank area in the toolbar, make sure that Lock the Taskbar is unchecked, and select View → Large Icons. Neat, eh?

A COOL FEATURE MOST PEOPLE DON'T KNOW ABOUT

If you right-click the Taskbar button that represents a group of buttons, several handy commands are available. You can arrange all the windows in the group (by choosing Cascade, Tile Horizontally, or Tile Vertically) without affecting other open windows, and you can minimize or close all the windows in a group. Or, if you have a large monitor, you can give up a little bit of screen for a double-tall Taskbar.

BUTTON UP YOUR OVERCROWDED TASKBAR

The Annoyance: When I opened more and more windows in earlier versions of Windows, the Taskbar buttons got tinier and tinier. They wound up with no text at all, so I couldn't tell which button controlled which window. In Windows XP, the Taskbar combines multiple open documents from the same application under a single button. That's a wonderful improvement, but it's erratic. Sometimes buttons combine and sometimes each window maintains its own button. What's going on?

The Fix: Taskbar grouping kicks in when you have so many open documents from a single application that the buttons begin to get too small. The exact number varies depending on your screen resolution, theme settings, how many other windows are open, and other obscure factors. With a minor tweak, you can exert some control over how Taskbar grouping behaves.

Using the Tweak UI PowerToy from Microsoft (see *http://snipurl.com/powertoys*), navigate to Taskbar → Grouping. There you'll find three options:

Group the least-used applications first
By default, when the Taskbar fills up, Windows first groups the buttons for the application you haven't used for the longest time. If the Taskbar is still too full, Windows groups buttons for applications that you have used more recently.

Group the applications with the most windows first
When the Taskbar fills up, Windows groups the buttons for the application with the most open windows.

Group any application with at least *x* windows
Windows groups buttons for any application that has at least x open windows—even if the Taskbar isn't full. (You specify the value for *x*.)

If you don't have Tweak UI, you can create these same settings by editing the Windows Registry:

1. First, back up the Registry. Select Start → Run, type **regedit**, and select File → Export. Enter a filename, check All in the Export section below, then click the Save button.

2. Back in regedit, open *HKEY_CURRENT_USER\Software\Microsoft\Windows\CurrentVersion\Explorer\Advanced.*

3. Scroll down the list on the right and look for an item named TaskbarGroupSize. If it doesn't exist, select Edit → New → DWORD Value, type **TaskbarGroupSize**, and press Enter.

4. Press Enter again to **TaskbarGroupSize** and set its values. In the Value data field, type:
   - 0 to use least-used grouping (the default)
   - 1 to use most-windows grouping
   - Any other number to group the buttons for an application when that number of windows are open

EUDORA DEFAULTS TO TASKBAR

The Annoyance: This is weird. Every time I open Eudora, it immediately minimizes to the Taskbar. If I want to use the program, I have to click its icon in the Taskbar. And no, it doesn't happen with any other program.

The Fix: You won't believe this, but Windows is doing exactly what you asked it to do—open and run minimized. I can't explain how you set Eudora to do that, but it's easy to change. In the Start menu, locate the Eudora icon, right-click it, and select Properties. In the Run drop-down menu, select "Normal window" and click OK.

REARRANGE THE TASKBAR

The Annoyance: When I close Outlook Express and open it again, it's at the tail end of the Taskbar. I like to have my open programs in the same spot on the Taskbar. Can I do this?

The Fix: Well that is a strange request, but hey, who am I to question what annoys you? For the price of a download, grab TaskArrange (*http://snipurl.com/taskarrange*). In short order, it will let you control the order of applications in the Taskbar.

TASKBAR, SYSTEM TRAY, AND QUICK LAUNCH WOES

The Annoyance: I don't get it: every time I reboot my PC, my Quick Launch area is blank. I have to go to Taskbar properties, uncheck Lock the Taskbar, and select Toolbars → Quick Launch. I really need a fix for this irritation.

The Annoyance: Whenever I boot up my PC, a Search Assistant shows up in the Taskbar. Worse, my Quick Launch icons are out of sequence and I have to rearrange them every time I boot. I hate Windows!

The Annoyance: The icons in my System Tray are screwed up. The ones I've marked hidden are in the tray, and others designated as "Hide when inactive" are always hidden, even when they're active.

The Fix: Perhaps the most miraculous tool in this book is the Taskbar Repair Tool Plus! (*http://snipurl.com/Taskbarplus*), written by the miraculous Kelly Theriot. The tool fixes all manner of Quick Launch, Taskbar, and Systray glitches, from missing icons to lost toolbars and many other related shenanigans (see Figure 2-12).

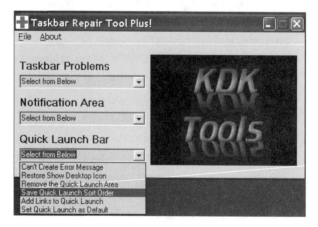

Figure 2-12. If you're having trouble with the Taskbar, System Tray, or Quick Launch toolbar, Taskbar Repair Tool Plus! is a must.

By the way, most of the tool's functions are free; some require you to purchase a license. But get this—the cost is a scant $5. I encourage you to make the payment and support the author.

SAVE DISK SPACE BY DITCHING OLD RESTORE POINTS

The Annoyance: My disk is filling up with old System Restore points, and I can't figure out how to delete them.

The Fix: System Restore points are the files Windows saves (mostly system files and the Registry) so that you can roll your PC back to an earlier state if a change to your PC screws things up. In Windows Me and XP, open My Computer, right-click your *C:* drive, select Properties, and click the Disk Cleanup button. After Disk Cleanup finishes its calculations, click its More Options tab and get rid of old, space-hogging restore points by clicking the "Clean up" button under System Restore (see Figures 2-13 and 2-14). Click OK and then Yes.

WHAT'S THE REGISTRY?

The Registry is a database that holds the configuration information on your system hardware, installed programs, and property settings. Every detail is stored in what looks like an intricate set of file folders, and practically every setting is available for you to change (but please don't). While Windows is running, it's constantly referencing information in the Registry.

The cool part about fiddling with the Registry is that you can make all sorts of remarkable changes to your Windows system. And if you're careful, backing up the Registry before you make any change, the risk of doing damage is decreased. To back up the Registry, select Start→Run; type `regedit`, and press Enter. In Regedit, select File→Export. Select a destination and enter a filename, check "All" in the Export Range section below, then click the Save button.

The Registry editor that comes with Windows is accessed from the Run command (Start→Run; type `regedit`, and press Enter). But if you plan on playing with the Registry, I recommend you use RegEditX, a free utility that adds features to Regedit that make it easier to use. (Go to *http://snipurl.com/regeditx*.) For instance, instead of plowing through the Registry's massive tree to navigate to a specific key, RegEditX lets you enter a long Registry key into the address field and be whisked right to it (see figure).

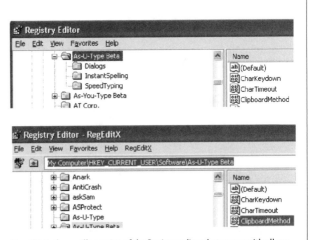

Top: This is the vanilla version of the Registry editor that comes with all current versions of Windows. Bottom: Here's the same editor with the RegEditX add-on—with a handy address bar that lets you cut and paste a long Registry key without having to dig your way down the Registry key tree.

But don't make changes willy-nilly to the Registry just to see what happens. *Nothing* good will come of this and you'll be a very unhappy camper (as will your computer). When you make changes to the Registry based on one of my recommendations, follow the directions carefully. If you're still feeling squeamish about fiddling with the Registry, read "Step-By-Step: Care and Feeding of the Windows Registry," a PC World tutorial you may find useful (*http://snipurl.com/Registry_tweaking*).

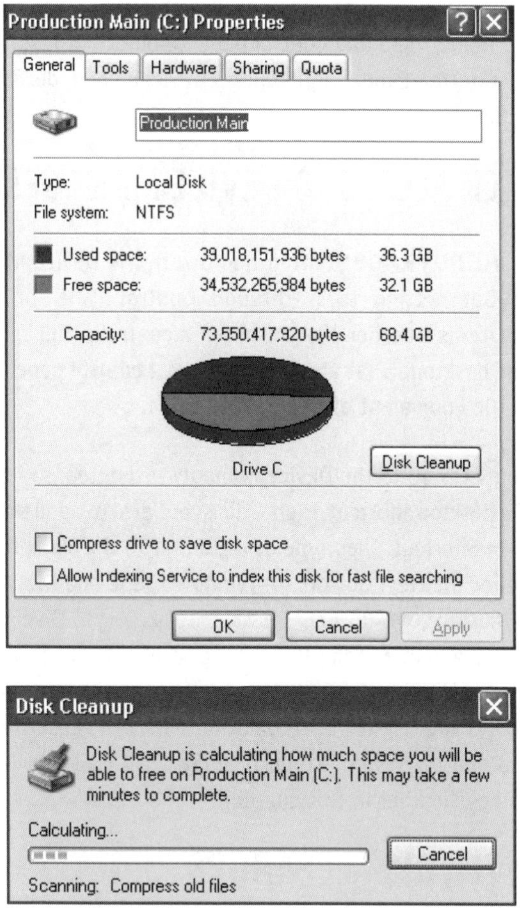

Figure 2-13. Top: The first step in dumping wasteful System Restore points is running Disk Cleanup. Bottom: It may take a few minutes—longer if you don't do it often—for Windows to find the files that can be deleted.

EASY INSURANCE

If you use Windows XP or Me, use System Restore to stick in a restore point every time you install a new program. It's cheap insurance and can save your bacon when the installation program hoses your system.

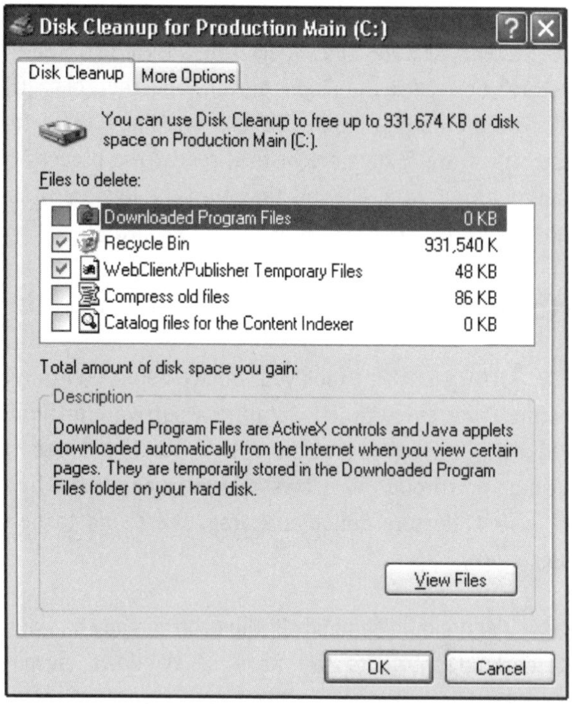

Figure 2-14. While you're here, you might as well clean house, empty your Recycle Bin, and get rid of other old files. Click OK when you're ready to do the housecleaning.

DON'T RESTORE THAT VIRUS!

The Annoyance: I update and run my antivirus program diligently, and it recently removed an annoying virus from my system. That's great, but I later did a scan and it found the exact same virus again—but couldn't remove it!

The Fix: I point my fickle finger of fault at XP's System Restore feature. Although your antivirus (AV) program nipped the virus the first time around, a copy of it was automatically stored in your System Restore folder. The next time you scanned for viruses, your AV program spotted the virus but couldn't get to it. As you might guess, if you restore a virus-laden restore point, you'll re-infect your PC. To squash the bug, start by updating your antivirus program with the latest virus filters (that's critical) and scanning your system to make sure it's squeaky clean and free from viruses. (Don't worry about the one in the System Restore folder.) Next, remove all of your restore points: right-click My Computer, select Properties, click the System Restore tab, check the "Turn off System Restore" box, click the Apply button, and then click OK and exit the dialog. Ignore the dire warnings. Once the System Restore folders are history, repeat the process of running an AV scan, but this time turn the Restore functions back on—and make a fresh restore point.

SYSTEM RESTORE ON YOUR DESKTOP

The Annoyance: I took your advice about creating a Restore Point every time I install new software or fiddle with my PC's settings (see the "Easy Insurance" sidebar). But digging through Windows' menus to get to the buried System Restore dialog is a drag. There's gotta be a quicker way.

The Fix: It would be handy if Microsoft already had prefab desktop shortcuts for many of Windows' system functions, but it doesn't. So make your own. First, go to Start → Programs → Accessories → System Tools, and find the System Restore icon. Right-click it, drag it to the desktop, release the mouse button, and click Copy Here. This places a copy of the System Restore icon on the desktop and leaves the original icon in the System Tools menu.

Instead of "Copy Here", you might see "Create Shortcut(s) Here".

If you can't find the icon, no sweat—you can create it from scratch directly on the desktop. Right-click any empty spot on the desktop and select New → Shortcut. In the blank field, type `%SystemRoot%\System32\restore\rstrui.exe`. Click the Next button, give your shortcut a name (such as "SysRestore"), and click the Finish button. Double-click the shortcut that appears on the desktop, and up pops the System Restore dialog.

As you might imagine, you can use this trick with other menu items, including control panel applets. For instance, open Control Panel, right-click any icon, and do some dragging.

QUICK ACCESS TO DEVICE MANAGER

The Annoyance: I often fiddle with the Device Manager. But getting to it through Control Panel or My Computer is a bother. If you can put a control panel applet on the desktop, what about a tab from a control panel—or even the equivalent of a button from a tab?

The Fix: I go to the Device Manager often, too, so I created a desktop shortcut. Right-click your desktop and select New → Shortcut. Then type `devmgmt.msc` in the blank field, and click the Next button. (In Windows 98SE and Me, type `C:\WINDOWS\CONTROL.EXE sysdm.cpl,system,1`.) Give your shortcut a name—something snappy like "Device Manager"—and click the Finish button. If your keyboard has a Windows key, use it in combination with the Pause/Break key to pop up System Properties. (See "All Hail the Windows Key!" earlier in this chapter.)

FASTER DISK CLEANUPS

The Annoyance: No matter how big my hard disk is, I can always fill it up. Microsoft's Disk Cleanup seems to take forever to calculate how much space I can save by compressing files. I stare at a so-called "progress" bar for a long time, and it takes even longer to actually compress the files. And actually using the files later (and waiting for them to decompress) has me drumming my fingers. Is there some way to speed up any of these processes?

The Fix: In Windows 2000 and Windows XP, files on an NTFS volume can be compressed so they occupy less disk space. Compressed files look and act just like any other file, except that they're a tiny bit slower to use because of the computations required to decompress and recompress them. Using compression with rarely used files is an effective way to regain some disk space.

Therefore, I recommend that you do *not* follow the advice of the experts who suggest deleting a particular Registry value to break Disk Cleanup's link to the compression feature. Instead, take one of the following approaches to avoid the lengthy wait for the compression process:

- By default, Windows looks at all files that haven't been used in more than 50 days and analyzes them to calculate potential space savings. Each time you run this analysis on a system with a lot of old, uncompressed files, it takes a long time. So here's a workaround: tell Disk Cleanup to look only at *really* old files (about a year old). When the Disk Cleanup dialog box finally appears, scroll down in the "Files to delete" list and check the "Compress old files" box, then click the "Compress old files" name itself. Click the Options button that appears and specify a higher number of days. Over time, you can reduce the number of days each time you run Disk Cleanup. You'll soon have all but your most frequently used files compressed—and you won't have to endure lengthy waits to run Disk Cleanup.

- Automate the Disk Cleanup process and run it when you're not using your computer. Start by saving a collection of Disk Cleanup settings. Click Start → Run and type **cleanmgr /sageset:1**. This opens a Disk Cleanup Settings dialog box that looks a lot like the regular Disk Cleanup dialog box. The difference is that once you create your settings (remember—check a box, then click the name to reveal a button to set options) and click OK, nothing appears to happen. In fact, all Windows does is save the settings. To run Disk Cleanup with the saved settings, use the command **cleanmgr /sagerun:1** from the Run dialog box. But a much better way is to create a program shortcut with this command and run it as a scheduled task. To create the shortcut, right-click any blank spot on the desktop and select New → Shortcut. In the "Command Line"

(98 and Me) or "location" (2000 and XP) field, type **cleanmgr /sagerun:1**. Click Next and give your shortcut a name, such as Cleanup. Note that you can use any number (up to 65535) in place of 1 in the commands so that you can save and run different groups of settings.

SQUEEZE YOUR WHOLE DRIVE

Why doesn't Disk Cleanup ever find any old files to compress? This can happen if you back up your disk frequently, because backing up a file is considered a "use." (By the way, congratulations on your backup discipline!) If you're short on disk space, consider compressing your entire drive. Right-click the drive's icon in Windows Explorer and, on the General tab, check the "Compress drive to save disk space" checkbox (see figure below).

If you're running low on disk space and are too frugal to buy a bigger hard drive, check the "Compress drive to save disk space" box.

DEFRAGUS INTERRUPTUS

The Annoyance: Whenever I try to defrag the hard drive on my Windows 98 PC, the Disk Defragmenter tool starts, defrags about 3% of the disk, and then restarts—over and over. This happens even though I've closed all open applications and shut down my antivirus, firewall, and other background programs.

The Fix: Well, some background program is interrupting the defrag. I suspect it's Windows' indexing function, which supposedly makes searches faster, but I've never noticed a speed-up. To turn off indexing in Windows 98 and Me, click Start → Run, type msconfig, and press the Enter key. If you see an entry for FastFind, disable it. In Windows XP, right-click the C: drive in My Computer or Windows Explorer, select Properties, and click the General tab. Uncheck the "Allow Indexing Service to index this disk for fast file searching" box (at the bottom of the window) and click OK (see Figure 2-15). Repeat these steps for all your hard drives, both internal and external.

Figure 2-15. If you want your defragger to run uninterrupted, turn off Indexing.

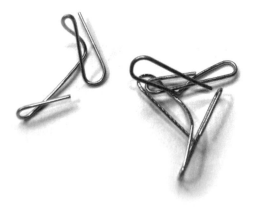

USE NTFS FOR A BOOST

The Annoyance: I upgraded my system from Windows 98 to XP and I already see a speed improvement. But my buddy told me there's a hard-drive trick that will squeeze out even more performance. What is it?

The Fix: My guess is that even though you upgraded your OS, your hard drive is still using the old FAT32 file structure. You can boost your drive's performance and reliability by converting to NTFS (short for NT File System). NTFS also lets you save files larger than FAT32's 4GB limit, and it lets you encrypt folders for added security. Better yet, NTFS uses a smaller cluster size—which means less wasted storage space—so you'll get more drive bang for your buck. Keep in mind, however, that you won't notice a performance boost with NTFS if your hard drive is smaller than 10GB, or if it runs at 5,400 rpm.

To confirm you're using FAT, right-click the hard drive in Windows Explorer, select Properties, click the General tab, and see what the "File system" line says. If it says FAT or FAT32, you can make the move to NTFS.

> **Warning. . .**
> As with any system-level change, back up your PC before you make this conversion.

To convert a FAT32 drive to NTFS, click Start → Run and type `cmd`. In the command prompt window, enter `convert c: /fs:ntfs`, where `c:` is your hard drive's letter. (Don't forget the spaces before and after the driver letter.) One potential gotcha: if you later want to go back to FAT32, you'll need a third-party program, such as Symantec's Partition Magic.

WORK AROUND SCHEDULED TASKS' LIMITATIONS

The Annoyance: When I discovered Scheduled Tasks in Windows, I thought I could just sit back and let the computer take care of itself. I set up scheduled tasks to update virus definitions, clean unneeded files from my hard disk, defragment my drives, cook my lunch.... But guess what: some scheduled tasks don't run. When I go back to the Scheduled Tasks control panel, or choose Start → Programs → Accessories → System Tools → Scheduled Tasks, I discover that the Last Run Time column shows "Never" for each task.

The Fix: If your scheduled tasks are not running, the password for your user account is probably blank. (I won't take this opportunity to chide you for this poor security practice.) A security feature in Windows XP prevents accounts with no password from using the "Run as" feature, which scheduled tasks rely upon. Even if you're logged on when a scheduled task is supposed to fire up, it won't. There are two easy workarounds to put those tasks back on schedule:

- Assign a password to your account, which you can do by opening the User Accounts control panel.
- If entering a password each time you log on is too much to bear, create a separate account for running scheduled tasks and assign a password to that account. To create the account and assign a password, visit the User Accounts control panel. To change the user for existing tasks, open Scheduled Tasks, double-click the task name, and change the username in the "Run as" box on the Task tab. Then click Set Password.

WINDOWS UPDATES YOU CAN SHARE

The Annoyance: I have several computers on my network, and I try to keep them updated with the latest service packs, hotfixes, patches, updates, driver revisions, and whatever else Microsoft calls the bug fix du jour. Windows Update downloads and installs a bug fix on one computer, but it doesn't save the file in a way that I can use with my other computers, so I have to start the process from scratch on each computer.

The Fix: A site called Windows Update Catalog offers all the update files in a form that you can download and reuse whenever you want. You can make these files available on one computer on your network, or you might burn them onto a CD. (Putting them on a CD also saves time if you have to format the hard drive on one of your PCs and reinstall Windows from scratch. But see the next topic for a better solution.) Windows Update Catalog offers downloadable files for Windows 98, Windows Me, Windows 2000, Windows XP, and Windows 2003 Server.

To get to Windows Update Catalog, choose Start → Windows Update, or in Internet Explorer, choose Tools → Windows Update. At the Windows Update site, click Personalize Windows Update (in the left pane), then check the "Display the link to the Windows Update Catalog under See

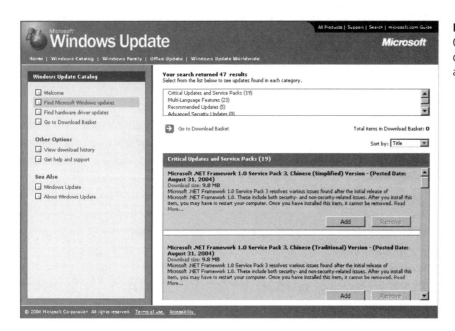

Figure 2-16. Clicking the Windows Update Catalog icon takes you to a page where you can download update files to install at your leisure and reuse on other computers.

Also" box. Click the Save Settings button, and a link to Windows Update Catalog will appear in the left pane each time you go to Windows Update (see Figure 2-16).

If you don't want to go through those shenanigans, use this direct link to Windows Update Catalog: *http://snipurl.com/winupdate.*

ADD SERVICE PACKS TO YOUR WINDOWS CD

The Annoyance: When I reinstall Windows, I have to reinstall all the service packs and other updates. Is there any shortcut?

The Fix: Previous versions of Windows would get so fouled up that it was practically a necessity to periodically scrub the disks and start over with a fresh installation. With Windows XP, accumulated detritus in the Registry and on the hard drive don't have nearly the deleterious effects (such as extreme slowdowns or frequent crashes). And problems caused by things like a buggy driver can usually be fixed without resorting to a complete Windows makeover. But sometimes reinstalling Windows is the only answer.

To save time, you can incorporate the latest service pack into your installation by creating a bootable CD that includes Windows XP or Windows 2000 (but not other versions of Windows) with the service pack files merged in. After you install Windows from such a CD, you need to install only hotfixes that were released after the service pack. Creating a bootable CD is a somewhat tricky process, with many steps that must be followed precisely. Several web sites explain the procedure in great detail, including these three:

- Bart's popular page at *http://snipurl.com/bootcd* provides loads of information about bootable CDs, including step-by-step instructions for creating Windows XP and Windows 2000 CDs with integrated service packs.

- HelpWithWindows.com explains how to create a bootable Windows XP CD with SP2 using IsoBuster and Nero Burning ROM 6 at *http://snipurl.com/Neroburn.*

- TackTech explains how to create a bootable Windows XP CD with SP1 and SP2 using Roxio Easy CD Creator and other tools at *http://snipurl.com/roxiocd.*

SMALLER AND LONGER PRODUCT KEYS

The product keys for Microsoft products—the registration number to activate a program—are getting longer. And the font Microsoft uses on the activation sticker found on the CD case is getting smaller. (Yeah, I could also be getting older and need reading glasses, too.) My trick? I type the activation code into a document with the font set to 18 points, print it out, and tape the enlarged number right onto the CD case.

REMEDIAL ACROBAT READER

The Annoyance: A while back I was trying to read my user group's PDF newsletter from its web site. The Adobe Acrobat Reader appeared, then said "Error reading linearized hint data" and wouldn't open the newsletter.

The Fix: There's an easy workaround for this problem. With Acrobat Reader 5 open, press Ctrl-K, select Options from the lefthand list, and uncheck the "Allow Fast Web View" box. Click OK to save the changes, reopen your browser, and you'll be able to open the PDF. In Adobe Reader 6, press Ctrl-K, choose Internet, and uncheck the "Allow Fast Web View" box.

PROTECT YOUR SYSTEM FROM DUMB INSTALLATIONS

The Annoyance: If one more program installs an icon in my System Tray without permission, I'm going to buy a Mac. I don't want icons and links scattered all over my desktop, Start menu, and System Tray.

The Fix: There are plenty of arrogant companies that toss their icons around—Netscape, AOL, RealOne, and Yahoo!, to name just a few. (Real is probably the worst, and I've banned the program from my PC.)

You can stop this icon madness by following these five tips:

Watch the installation. Stay alert during the installation. If you have the option, *always* opt for the custom installation. You'll probably have a choice of where the program plants its icons. Besides avoiding System Tray litter, you can also stop programs from adding icons to the Start menu and desktop.

Protect your System Tray. WinPatrol is a free early-warning system that stops unsavory programs, such as Trojans, phone dialers, and spyware, from doing damage to your system or reporting your surfing habits to others. WinPatrol watches for anything that adds itself to the Startup group or Windows Registry, flags suspicious items, and offers to remove nasty programs. In order to remove or disinfect the offending program, you'll still need a spyware removal tool, such as Spybot, and an antivirus program. When WinPatrol starts yelling about an unwelcome entry, you can allow the program into your Startup group if it's legit; if you say no, and the program tries again, WinPatrol blocks subsequent attempts. That's especially handy for notoriously insistent programs such as QuickTime, RealPlayer, and MSN Messenger. WinPatrol also lets you see a list of Active Tasks, cookies, and Win XP's running Services, and it works with all versions of Windows. In most cases, you can also gain some insight into the applet's source and purpose (see Figure 2-17). For $19.95, WinPatrol Plus

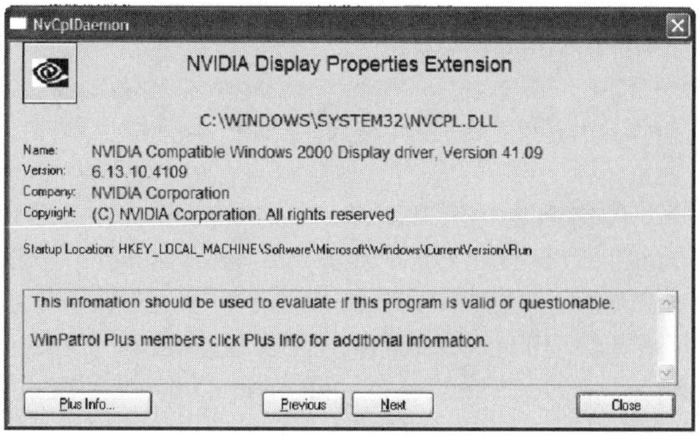

Figure 2-17. WinPatrol's Startup Programs tab helps you determine what program each applet belongs to. Upgrade to the inexpensive $19.95 Plus version, and you're whisked to WinPatrol's online database with more extensive information.

provides an extensive database to further identify what's trying to get into your System Tray. The program is available at *http://www.oreilly.com/pcannoyances*.

Make a clean sweep. Start by hovering the pointer over the icon to identify the application it belongs to—then decide if the icon needs to be in the System Tray. (Most don't. Programs such as RealOne Player, Real-Player Jukebox, ATI's Video Manager, and AOL's Instant Messenger are typical culprits.) Select Start → Programs ("All Programs" in XP) → Startup to see what's in your Startup group, and you'll probably find a few programs you can dump. To dig deeper, use Windows' msconfig (select Start → Run, type `msconfig`, and press Enter) or use Startup Control Panel, a free utility that lets you examine and remove programs that are loaded at startup (get it at *http://www.oreilly.com/pcannoyances*).

Extra ammunition. Many programs have mysterious, abbreviated filenames, so check the Greatis Startup Application Database (see *http://snipurl.com/greatis*) for an extensive list that identifies and explains the function—and potential danger—of the programs in your System Tray and Startup group.

Block that call. If the program insists on phoning home regularly for new ads or for something more sinister, such as your surfing habits, block the outgoing call with your firewall. I use Zone Labs' ZoneAlarm to block the outgoing missive temporarily a few times to see if it incapacitates the program; if it doesn't, I make the block permanent.

CUSTOMIZE WINDOWS UPDATE

The Annoyance: The same old updates—ones I don't want, like the Euro Conversion Tool—keep showing up in Windows Update, even though I've declined to install them many times before. The list of updates gets longer and longer, which makes it harder and harder to pick out the new, potentially useful updates from the dreck.

The Fix: Like so many Windows fixes, this one is easy but not obvious. In Windows Update, click the Personalize Windows Update link in the left pane. In the right pane, uncheck boxes for any updates that you haven't installed and don't want to see every time you view the list. (See Figure 2-18.)

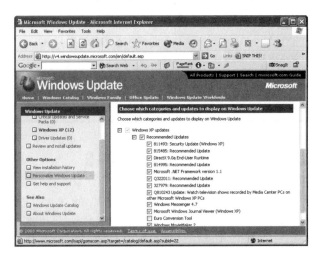

Figure 2-18. Personalize Windows Update by omitting from the list any updates that you never want to install.

SAVE DISK SPACE BY TOSSING OLD UNINSTALL FILES

The Annoyance: My hard drive is filling up with folders that contain the files needed to uninstall service packs and other updates. Because they're hidden folders, they're easy to overlook, but they take up a good chunk of disk space. These folders are usually named something like *$NtUninstallQ328310$*. Since everything is working fine, I'd like to nuke these files.

The Fix: Go ahead, nuke 'em. If you're certain that you don't need to uninstall an update, you can safely delete any of the hidden folders with names that begin with *$NtUninstall* or *$NtServicePackUninstall$*. These hidden folders are located in the *%SystemRoot%* folder (in *C:\ Windows* on most systems). To make them visible, open a Windows Explorer or folder window, choose Tools → Folder Options, click the View tab, and select "Show hidden files and folders."

Deleting the *$NtUninstall* folders doesn't delete their entries in the Control Panel's Add or Remove Programs tool, however. To do that, you'll have to dip into the Registry. Using the Registry Editor, expand the *HKEY_LOCAL_MACHINE\ SOFTWARE\Microsoft\Windows\CurrentVersion\Uninstall* item. Delete the subkey for each of the service packs or updates whose folder you deleted. The subkey (which is below the Uninstall item in the Registry tree) for a service pack has a name like "Windows XP Service Pack"; subkeys for updates are named with the same "Q number" that forms part of the folder name. If you're squeamish about deleting Registry keys, just about any Registry cleaning utility (such as Norton's Win Doctor) will find and delete these orphaned uninstall keys for you.

SERVICEPACKFILES

While poking around in the *%SystemRoot%* folder, you might notice a folder called *ServicePackFiles*. Although it occupies gobs of disk space, don't delete it! It contains files used by Windows File Protection (a feature that automatically repairs Windows files that are corrupted or deleted). You might need them if you add any optional Windows components or device drivers.

I CAN'T INSTALL ANYTHING

The Annoyance: When I click on the actual *SETUP.EXE* file to install a new program, nothing happens. The program doesn't install and the screen just stares blankly at me.

The Fix: Staring back probably won't help. Chances are the installation drivers and hardware drivers already running in memory are duking it out. Two possible fixes: before you install any program, close all other applications. Most installation programs warn you to do this, but most people (hmm, maybe you?) ignore the advice. Better yet, exit Windows and reboot your system, so you can start your installation with a clean slate. If that doesn't help, another

installation program might be running in the background. A conflict between two installation engines will definitely prevent you from installing a program.

To dump the conflicting program, press Ctrl-Alt-Del to summon the Task Manager. (You can also right-click a blank area in the Taskbar and select Task Manager). Click the Processes tab and check for these installation programs:

- *idriver.exe*
- *ikernel.exe*
- *isetup.exe*
- *IsUn16.exe*
- *IsUninst.exe*
- *msiexec.exe*
- *setup.exe*
- *Uninst.exe*
- *Uninst16.exe*

Kill any installation process by selecting it and then clicking the End Process button. Now try installing your new program.

I CAN'T INSTALL ANYTHING, PART 2

The Annoyance: I tried your advice in "I Can't Install Anything" and I'm still having trouble. What else do you have?

The Fix: You'll have to take a more drastic approach and update InstallShield, a program that's used by many software vendors for installing their products. Use Windows Explorer to browse to *C:\Program Files\Common Files\ InstallShield\engine*. Delete the Engine folder, and then install the latest version of the engine (known as the iKernel Engine). It's available at *http://snipurl.com/ikernal_update*.

I CAN'T INSTALL ANYTHING EASILY

The Annoyance: When I try installing a new program, a message appears saying a specific file can't be found. When I click OK, another dialog pops up and if I click Cancel (often as many as three times!), the program finally installs. Why the foot dragging?

The Fix: The problem is due to *other* programs you've installed or improperly uninstalled. The last time you installed a program, you may have stopped the process before it completed. That could have corrupted the files the installer needed to later uninstall the program. When that occurs, subsequent installations go kaflooey because some files are shared by two or more unrelated programs. The other possibility—which I've been guilty of committing—is deleting an application's folder instead of properly uninstalling a program via Windows' Add or Remove Programs control panel. If you likewise made this blunder, you'll probably get this arcane error message: "1706: No valid source could be found for the *application*. The windows installer cannot continue", where *application* is the name of the file that can't be found. My workaround solves this problem most of the time. First, note the application named in the error message and reinstall it. Make sure you install it in the same directory as you did the first time. Then, uninstall the program using the Add or Remove Programs control panel. Success? Now install that new application.

If you *still* can't install that new app, I can offer two recommendations. First, give your PC away and get a Mac. (Kidding!) Second, run Microsoft's Windows Installer Clean-Up Utility (*http://snipurl.com/uninstalltool*) to clear out any miscellaneous installation clutter for the application created by Windows (obscurely abbreviated as MSI files). The utility leaves any data files you created with the application intact.

You might also visit Macrovision's InstallShield Consumer Central, where you'll find solutions to other common installation errors, at *http://snipurl.com/installshield*.

LOCK NUMBERS OUT, ARROW KEYS IN

The Annoyance: I use the keys on the number keypad for navigation, *never* for numbers. I'm tired of clicking NumLock to turn the function off.

The Fix: You can turn it off in your PC's CMOS Setup program, but there are two quicker, easier ways to do it:

- For a permanent fix, edit the Registry (once you've backed it up). From the Start menu, click Run, type **regedit**, press Enter, and navigate your way to *HKEY_CURRENT_USER\Control Panel\Keyboard*. Double-click InitialKeyboardIndicators in the right pane, and change the value to 2. Close RegEdit.

- If you don't want to fiddle with the Registry—or if you want a handy way to toggle NumLock on and off—use the *numlock.vbs* script. You can drag and drop a copy of the file into your Start Menu's Startup Group (hold down the Ctrl key while you drag it) to turn NumLock off when your system boots, and drag a copy to your desktop so you can toggle NumLock back on. Grab a copy from *http://www.oreilly.com/pcannoyances*.

NUMLOCK FOR GEEKS ONLY

If you want to turn NumLock on and off as a program (say, Quicken) loads, stick *numlock.vbs* into a batch file.

BRING BACK YOUR TASK PANE

The Annoyance: I thought Windows XP folder screens were supposed to have a column on the left side filled with terrifically useful information. I used to be able to click the X at the upper right corner of the Search or Folders pane to reveal it, but when I went to the My Network Places folder, there was no extra panel to be found.

The Fix: You probably fiddled with the Folders settings and changed the view back the classic mode. It's easy to fix: in Windows Explorer, go to Tools → Folder Options, and on the General tab, click "Show common tasks in folders." Click OK, and the left pane of the folder window will now reveal those luscious (and valuable) hyperlinks to common folder tasks and other spots on your PC.

EASY SCREEN CAPTURES

If you use Windows, it's inevitable that one day you'll be on the horn with tech-support agents (or worse, the black hole known as your company's IT department), becoming more and more annoyed at how they just don't understand your description of a problem. That's when a picture of your screen is worth a thousand calls.

What you need is a screen capture—a snapshot of your screen. They're easy to create; the most primitive way is to tap your keyboard's Print Screen key. Voilà—an image of your entire screen is in the Clipboard. Press Alt-Print Screen to capture just the active window. But you have to save the file in the clipboard in the *.bmp* format or paste it into another program (such as Windows Paint)—both rather inelegant solutions.

Better to whip out Screen Hunter, a nifty little tool that takes a picture of a portion of a window or of your entire screen. With the press of a hot key, Screen Hunter grabs the image and saves it to a file in *.jpg*, *.bmp*, and *.gif* file formats (see figure below). Then you can email proof positive of what you're seeing. ScreenHunter is free and available at *http://www.oreilly.com/pcannoyances*.

It takes all of five seconds to grab an image from the screen and save it to a file with ScreenHunter, a free utility.

For industrial-strength screen captures with the ability to edit and annotate the images, you need Techsmith's SnagIt (see figure below). It's the program I used to capture the illustrations in this book. You can capture screens in all sorts of ways—from specific areas and windows, multiple pages of screens, or even freehand captures. (Why freehand? So I can carve out and grab a picture of, say, a specific feather from a page full of them for my wife's "How Birds Fly" PowerPoint presentation.)

A SnagIt screen capture of this page early in the editing process.

SnagIt's been around for a long time, and Techsmith knows what users need. Besides hot keys, I've added SnagIt icons to Internet Explorer, Word, and Windows Explorer toolbars for quick captures. Heck, SnagIt's cataloging feature alone has been a terrific help in keeping the screen captures for this book organized. SnagIt is fast, flexible, and for what it does, dirt cheap at $40. (Yes, I'm jazzed about the product—it does everything I need.) Watch a quick promotional video at *http://snipurl.com/snagit_vid* or download the trial version from *http://snipurl.com/snagit_trial*.

DIALOG BOXES THAT WORK YOUR WAY

The Annoyance: Every Microsoft program automatically tries to save every file I create in the My Documents folder. I never use that folder, so it's the last place I look for a file I've misplaced. Also, Microsoft Office applications don't let me add or remove options from the left panel of the Open and Save dialog boxes, so I'm stuck with the History, My Documents, Desktop, Favorites, and My Network Places shortcuts there. Finally, Windows (or the Windows application) often opens a dialog box the size of a postage stamp whenever I open or save a file.

The Fix: There may be no cure for My Documents dumbness, but I stopped grumbling about it when I discovered utilities that make dialog boxes work my way. My favorite is FileBox eXtender, a $20 utility that adds several buttons to file-open and file-save dialog boxes—notably, buttons that show your favorites and recent folders in *any* program, not just Microsoft products (see Figure 2-19).

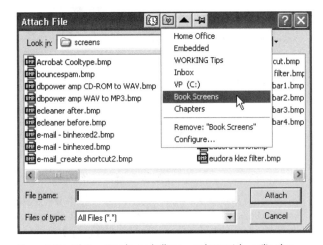

Figure 2-19. FileBox eXtender is a brilliant—and essential—utility that saves you tons of time by supplying a list of your favorite folders. Navigating to folders in dialog boxes has never been so easy.

But wait, there's more! Click the triangle to roll up the dialog box so all you see is the menu bar; the push-pin allows you to keep the box viewable above all other windows and dialog boxes. The program can also enlarge tiny dialog boxes. Configuring FileBox eXtender doesn't take much work—the easiest way is to drag and drop folders onto its menu editor (see Figure 2-20). You can download the demo version from *http://www.oreilly.com/pcannoyances.*

Figure 2-20. If you find yourself using a specific folder often, drag and drop it onto FileBox eXtender's Menu Editor, and give it a name you'll remember.

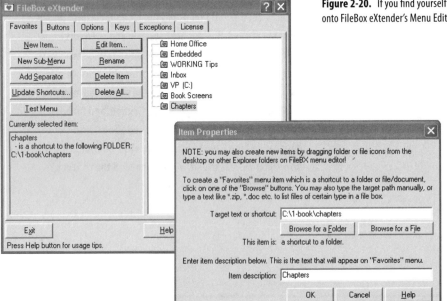

WHERE'S TASK MANAGER'S TOOLBAR?

The Annoyance: There I was, minding my own business, when all of a sudden Task Manager's menu bar and tabs pulled a vanishing act. Without the menu bar—and File → Exit Task Manager—it's almost impossible to close the program.

The Fix: Actually, you can close the Task Manager by either pressing Esc or right-clicking its Taskbar icon and selecting Close. But why did the vanishing act happen in the first place? (See Figures 2-21 and 2-22.) I'll bet you inadvertently clicked one of the lines that bracket a title on one of the tabs (such as "CPU Usage History"). This is easy to do, and for all I know it's a Task Manager feature. To get the menu bar and tabs back, just double-click a blank area on the Task Manager window.

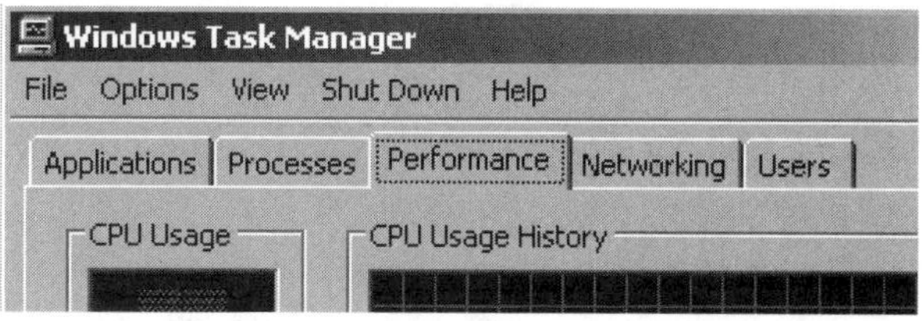

Figure 2-21. If you accidentally click one of the little lines bracketing a title on Task Manager, such as "CPU Usage History"...

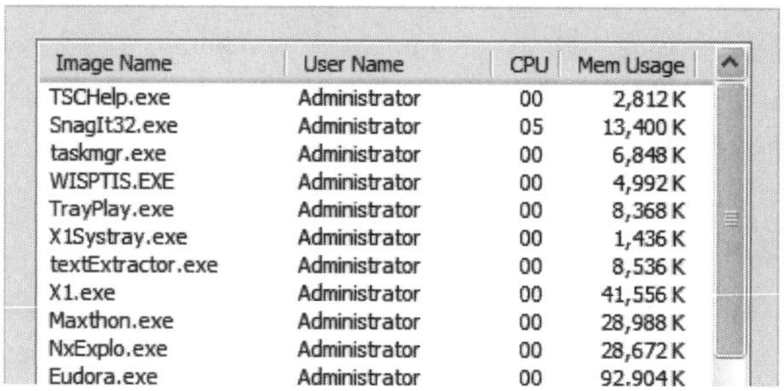

Image Name	User Name	CPU	Mem Usage
TSCHelp.exe	Administrator	00	2,812 K
SnagIt32.exe	Administrator	05	13,400 K
taskmgr.exe	Administrator	00	6,848 K
WISPTIS.EXE	Administrator	00	4,992 K
TrayPlay.exe	Administrator	00	8,368 K
X1Systray.exe	Administrator	00	1,436 K
textExtractor.exe	Administrator	00	8,536 K
X1.exe	Administrator	00	41,556 K
Maxthon.exe	Administrator	00	28,988 K
NxExplo.exe	Administrator	00	28,672 K
Eudora.exe	Administrator	00	92,904 K

Figure 2-22. ...Task Manager's menu bar may disappear!

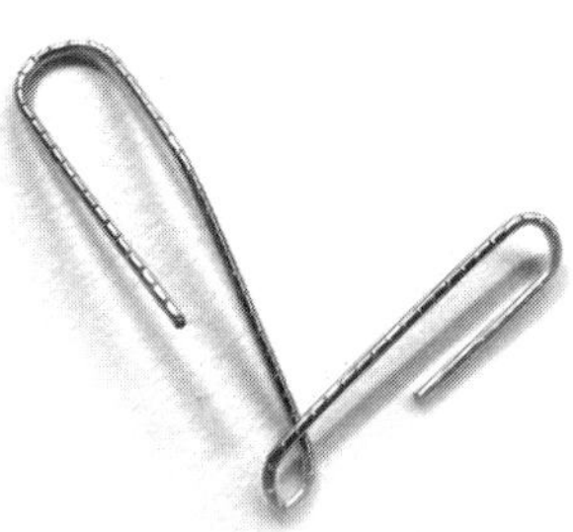

GET TASK MANAGER AFTER A CRASH

You normally beckon the Task Manager using your three-fingered salute: Ctrl-Alt-Del. Aside from letting you shut down misbehaving applications and processes, the Task Manager lets you monitor network performance, CPU usage, and physical and kernel memory. But what happens if your system freezes and your three-finger salute fails? Try your mouse. Right-click a blank area in the Taskbar area and select Task Manager from the pop-up menu. No blank area available? Try the same procedure on a blank spot in the System Tray. For future system meltdowns, put a Task Manager icon on the desktop for quick clickin'. Open Windows Explorer, navigate to the *\Windows\System32* folder, and drag *Taskmgr.exe* to the desktop.

STOP ANNOYING CRASH REPORTS

The Annoyance: I'm getting *really* tired of XP asking me if I want to send an error report to Microsoft every time a program crashes. I think the company should spend its time *reducing* crashes, don't you?

The Fix: I'll bet Microsoft's tired of taking all your reports, too, but that's another story. Stopping these report prompts is easy. Open the System control panel, click the Advanced tab and then the Error Reporting button. If you want absolutely no notification about any errors, check "Disable error reporting" and uncheck the "But notify me when critical errors occur" box. (FYI: I leave this box checked so I can see details of the crash, something that helps me troubleshoot system problems.) Click OK, then OK again.

STOP QUICK LAUNCH POP-UPS

The Annoyance: Whenever my cursor hovers over the Quick Launch toolbar, enormous yellow pop-ups appear with tons of text. They block the other icons, and besides, I already know what the icon represents.

The Fix: The biggest offenders are—surprise, surprise—Microsoft applications. Outlook's descriptive pop-ups are billboard size, and they're definitely annoying (see Figure 2-23).

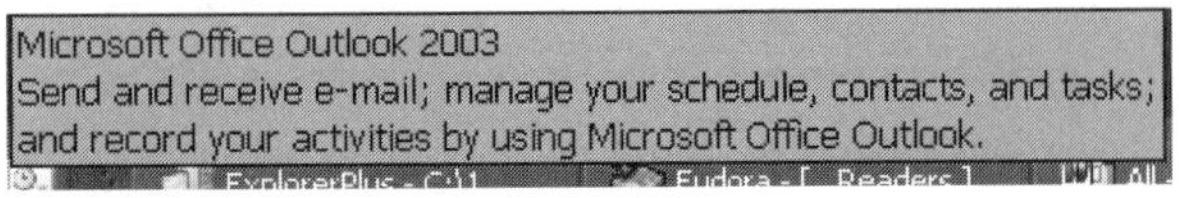

Figure 2-23. Hover your mouse over Outlook's Quick Launch icon, and it insists on providing a lengthy explanation of what it does for a living.

Rather than eliminate the pop-up, shrink it down to size. Right-click the icon in the Quick Launch toolbar, choose Properties, and change—or remove—the text in the Comment field (see Figure 2-24). I changed mine to simply "Outlook." Easy, eh?

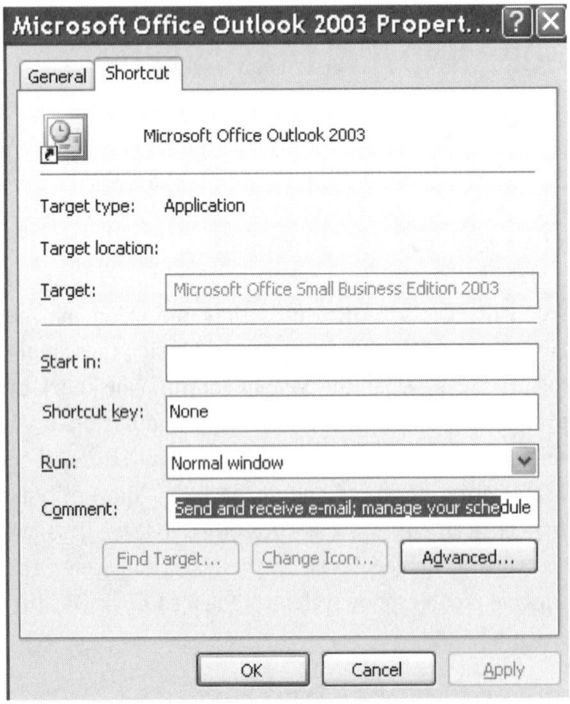

Figure 2-24. Highlight and remove the text in the Comment field, and you'll no longer see Outlook's built-in advertising.

BAN ANNOYING BOOT LOGOS

The Annoyance: I just bought a new PC. When the system boots, I see the manufacturer's irritating logo. How can I banish it?

The Fix: IMHO, watching the logo screen is more than just annoying; it deprives you of valuable troubleshooting and diagnostic information that's served up while the PC's booting. This annoyance is pretty easily dispensed with, provided your system's BIOS allows you to turn off the logo screen.

As your PC boots up, tap the key that summons the CMOS Setup. Browse through the various BIOS options until you find something similar to "disable the Logo Screen," and then disable the feature.

SERVICE PACK 2 ANNOYANCES

THE ANNOYING UPGRADE YOU REALLY NEED

Doing a major operating system upgrade is like cleaning out rain gutters or checking under the bed for the bogeyman—it's gotta be done, but most of us (me included) put it off for as long as possible. If you haven't upgraded to Service Pack 2 (SP2) yet, come out from under the covers. SP2 won't hurt you. In fact, it might already be on your PC and doing it some good.

First, see if your PC hasn't already been upgraded. Open the System control panel. If you see Service Pack 2 on the General tab, you're in like Flynn. Of course, SP2 has been known to introduce some annoyances with Outlook Express and other programs. And some SP features, such as the new Security Center, can drive you crazy with alerts. We'll get to those and other annoyances in a sec. If you haven't upgraded yet, you gotta. SP2 provides important protection against the Internet's e-thugs, and there are enough behind-the-scenes fixes and enhancements to make the SP2 upgrade hoop worth jumping through. For instance, Internet Explorer's new Information Bar alerts you whenever a site tries to download software onto your system. SP2's Security Center keeps a watchful eye on your antivirus and firewall programs, makes sure they're up to date, and faithfully—and automatically—downloads and installs any new critical patch or fix to XP.

In the following pages, you'll learn how to iron out the wrinkles in the upgrade process. (Before upgrading, wait until Scorpio is rising, Venus and Mars are aligned, and there's no full moon.) I also show you how to handle SP2's firewall, security alerts, and a plethora of annoyances that can crop up after you've upgraded.

INTERRUPTED SP2 DOWNLOADS

The Annoyance: Why doesn't Microsoft's Windows Update process let you resume a failed download? It's infuriating. I've tried twice now to download Service Pack 2, but my dial-up ISP disconnects me after six hours or so (I know, time to switch to broadband).

The Fix: Forget downloading—order the free CD. Even with my speedy broadband connection, I opted for the CD because it's far easier to upgrade several PCs this way. No downloading: just pop in the disc and go tend to your knitting. Go to *http://snipurl.com/SP2_CD*, scroll down a bit, and click the "order a CD" link.

YOUR XP SERVICE PACK 2 SURVIVAL GUIDE

Print this page and save this phone number. Most people survive the installation unscathed. But to its credit, Microsoft provides free chat, email, and phone support for any problems that make you cry. The toll-free number is (888) 772-4357; visit *http://snipurl.com/sp2_help* for other SP2 installation details from Microsoft.

Prepare your PC. Update critical applications, such as Microsoft Office and your antivirus, firewall, and anti-spyware software. Run 'em and clean out the junk: spyware and viruses can easily trip up an OS upgrade installation. Don't have antivirus software? Scoot over to *http://snipurl.com/house_calls* and try Trend Micro's free, web-based HouseCall antivirus scanner. For spyware, do a free online scan with CounterSpy at *http://snipurl.com/sunbeltscan*; on the same page you'll find a 15-day trial of the product. If you find viruses or spyware, remove them and then reboot your system. Before you run the SP2 upgrade, disable your firewall, antivirus and anti-spyware programs, and any other tool, such as WinPatrol, that watches for changes in

the Windows Registry. (Your free copy of WinPatrol is waiting for you at *http://snipurl.com/winpatrol*.)

Back up. I can't emphasize enough the value of backing up your system before you load SP2. If you don't already have a way to back up, buy Acronis's $50 True Image software (*http://snipurl.com/acronis*) and back up your hard drive to CD, DVD, an external USB drive, or other device. You might want to make your life easier by getting Maxtor's One Touch external USB drive, which comes with excellent backup software. The 80GB model costs about $110. Get details at *http://snipurl.com/maxtor_1touch* and pricing at *http://snipurl.com/maxtor_price*.

Take a snooze. Once you start the SP2 upgrade process, grab something to read or take a snooze. SP2 often takes its sweet time to install. Or maybe not. On my machine it took two hours; on my wife's PC, just 15 minutes. Don't panic if it seems the upgrade has frozen. SP2's shuffling a lot of data around, so it's critical you don't interrupt it.

BOTHERSOME UPGRADE ALERT

The Annoyance: I upgraded to SP2, so enough already with the annoying alerts about yet more upgrades!

The Fix: It's a good thing that you're being reminded. XP's Automatic Updates feature makes sure you don't miss an important security fix. Head to the Control Panel, double-click the Automatic Updates icon, and select "Automatic (recommended)". That way you won't be hassled with alerts, and the updates will be downloaded and installed in the background. However, if you're persnickety like me and want to see each and every downloadable upgrade, select "Download updates for me, but let me choose when to install them."

SP2'S ALERTS ARE SO, SO ANNOYING

The Annoyance: I did everything right. I installed a firewall, set Automatic Updates to download and install updates for me, and I have an antivirus program running. Yet I still get annoying Security Center alerts in Windows' System Tray. Make it stop!

The Fix: SP2 probably doesn't recognize your third-party firewall. (Then again, maybe it remembers you once threatened to switch to Linux.) Either way, if you're tired of looking at the alerts, get rid of them. Open the Security Center control panel and on the left, click the "Change the way Security Center alerts me" link. Uncheck the Firewall or Virus Protection boxes—provided you really know you're protected. (See Figure 2-25.) *Don't* uncheck Automatic Updates.

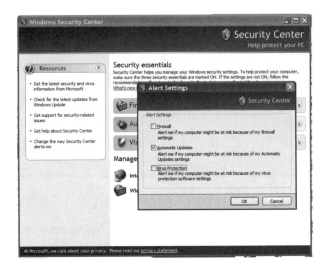

Figure 2-25. If you're sure your antivirus and firewall programs are working and up-to-date, go ahead and turn off XP's Security Center alerts.

AUTOMATIC UPDATE DUMBNESS

The Annoyance: I just read that an update to Outlook Express has been available for weeks. I have XP's Automatic Updates set to, well, automatically update my PC. But I just checked my Outlook Express and it's clearly not the latest and greatest version. What gives?

The Fix: The key word is *critical*. Automatic Updates only downloads critical updates. The Outlook Express update was optional. (Hey, this is Microsoft's design, not mine.) My strategy is to swing by the Windows Update site every so often. Not only can I avoid writing for a few minutes, but I may find an optional update worth downloading. What, you're not checking? Go to *http://windowsupdate. microsoft.com* or select Start → Help and Support, and under "Pick a task", click the "Keep your computer up-to-date with Windows Update" link. Then click Custom Install, let the site scan for updates, and in the left panel, click "Select optional software updates." (See Figure 2-26.)

Check the items you want to install, click the "Go to install upgrades" link at the top right of the page, and click the Install button.

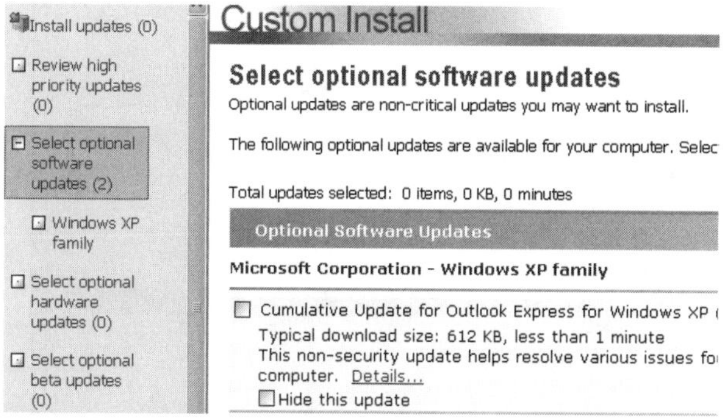

Figure 2-26. If you want to see all the optional upgrades you're missing, you'll have to do it manually.

AUTOMATIC UPDATE ERRORS

The Annoyance: I followed the above steps and was smacked in the face with an error message. Bottom line: I can't get any optional upgrades.

The Fix: I once encountered the dreaded 0x8024402C error message. (There are almost 100 others. See *http://snipurl.com/update_errors* to find yours.) It took me an hour to find the solution and, as with so many other computing problems, 15 minutes to fix. Your problem involves a proxy server (don't ask); the easiest course of action is to follow the instructions at *http://snipurl.com/XP_UpdateError* that start with "Remove invalid characters from the proxy exception list and then clear the proxy cache." It's at the top of the page.

BLOCKED IMAGES IN OUTLOOK EXPRESS

The Annoyance: Outlook Express was working just fine until I upgraded to SP2. Now images in some emails are missing. All I see is a little red "x" instead of a picture.

The Fix: This is a new option in Outlook Express, one designed to protect you. It's called the "Block images and other external content in HTML" email security option, and it protects you from web "bugs" or beacons embedded in email from spammers. (The bugs report back if your email address is valid.) Feeling overprotected? Open Outlook Express, click Tools → Options and select the Security tab. Uncheck the "Block images and other external content in HTML e-mail" box, click Apply, then OK.

DISTRESSED ABOUT ATTACHMENTS IN OUTLOOK EXPRESS

The Annoyance: I can't open attachments in Outlook Express now that I've upgraded to SP2. Heck, I can't even *save* 'em.

The Fix: It's another new Outlook Express "feature" that protects you from file attachments that might contain a virus or worm (or worse, a dumb video from your dumber brother-in-law). It's a good feature for novices and complete nincompoops. For the rest of us, it's okay to disable it. Head for Tools → Options, select the Security tab, and uncheck the "Do not allow attachments to be saved or opened that could contain a virus" box. Click Apply, then OK, and you're back in business.

POST-SP2 OUTLOOK EXPRESS FIXES

You say I haven't fixed your Outlook Express difficulty? Microsoft has a site that's just for you. It's stodgily entitled "Changes to Functionality in Microsoft Windows XP Service Pack 2," and it covers all that ails Outlook Express. Check it out at *http://snipurl.com/SP2_OE*.

SP2 BLOCKS SKYPE

The Annoyance: Skype, my super-duper, free make-phone-calls-over-the-Internet program is silent now that I've installed Service Pack 2. Help!

The Fix: Skype's trying to get on the Internet and SP2's firewall is blocking the connection. That's probably because you either didn't see, or blithely ignored, SP2's firewall dialog asking how you wanted to handle the Skype request. If the dialog appears again, click Unblock to let Skype get online. However, the dialog might not appear again (maybe just to teach you a lesson) and that might be your problemo. So you'll need to modify SP2's firewall setting manually, a two-minute job:

1. Open the Windows Firewall control panel. Click the General tab if it isn't on top.

2. Make sure the first setting—"On (recommended)"—is checked. "Don't allow exceptions" should *not* be checked.

3. Click the Exceptions tab.

   a) If Skype is in the "Programs and Services" list, make sure the box next to it is checked. (See Figure 2-27.)

   b) If Skype is *not* in the "Programs and Services" list, click the "Add Program" button and select it from the list offered up by Windows, or browse to Skype's folder and select its executable (*EXE*) file. Click OK. Skype will be added to the "Programs and Services" list and its box will be checked.

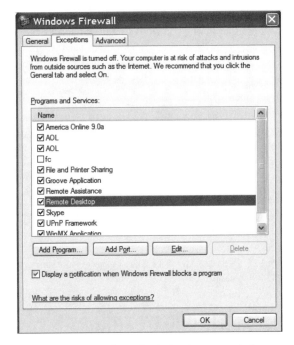

Figure 2-27. If Skype or another application is trying to access the Internet (and you recognize the program as safe), give it permission by clicking the checkbox.

Your Very Own XP Backup CD

Having SP2 on a CD is handy, but I encourage you go a step further: create an installation CD that holds both XP and the SP2 upgrade. You'll be grateful to have it if you ever need to reinstall XP. Check Tom's Hardware for instructions at *http://snipurl.com/Tom_CD*. The process is relatively straightforward—unless you're one of those unlucky users stuck with a restore disc that has an image of XP rather than the actual files. There's no harm trying your custom XP/SP2 restore CD; if it doesn't work, contact your PC's manufacturer and complain loudly and vigorously.

SP2'S FIREWALL TUTORIAL

The firewall built into SP2 is good, but I prefer ZoneAlarm from Zone Labs. Both are freebies, but ZoneAlarm offers lots more. ZoneAlarm automatically makes you invisible to hackers (it's called Stealth Mode). And unlike SP2's firewall, ZoneAlarm detects—and lets you stop—outbound communications, preventing a program, or worse, a Trojan or virus, from sending details about you and your PC back to God-knows-who.

I use ZoneAlarm Pro, a $49.95 product that's rich with extra features to protect you. For instance, it prevents you from accidentally clicking a virus-infested attachment, blocks ads and cookies, and won't let a virus send email via your PC. The Outbound MailSafe feature blocks outgoing mail if any of three virus-like conditions are met: too many emails are sent at once, a message has too many recipients, or the sender of the email isn't you . Grab a 15-day trial of the Pro version, or the freebie "lite" version, at *http://snipurl.com/ZAPro_trial*.

You might think that if one firewall is good, then two *must* be better. Wrong. Use *either* SP2's firewall *or* a third-party package. Otherwise the two will do battle and you'll have dueling dialog boxes popping up. It's not pretty, I assure you.

If you've decided to stick with SP2's firewall, kill a half hour and browse through Microsoft's valuable "Understanding Windows Firewall" tutorial:

* Introduction: *http://snipurl.com/SP_firewall1*

* Using the Exceptions Tab: *http://snipurl.com/ SP_firewall2*

* Adjust Your Firewall Settings: *http://snipurl.com/ SP_firewall3*

Internet
ANNOYANCES

There's no doubt that the Internet has revolutionized the world, but there are lots of things about it that tick people off—and rightly so. Like visiting a web site and discovering it's changed your home page without permission. Like launching Internet Explorer and having it sometimes open in a maximized window, and sometimes…not. Like dealing with pop-up ads, fiddling with bookmarks, searching, and more.

Put down that Valium and turn the page. You'll find over 40 tips that untangle and streamline browsing (both for Internet Explorer and Netscape), unleash Google, pound AOL into compliance, make IMing feasible and fun, and otherwise make your Internet experience nuisance-free.

BROWSING ANNOYANCES

GO FLASHLESS TO SAVE TIRED EYES

The Annoyance: Macromedia Flash allows web developers to create some really neat animations, movies, and interactive elements on a web page. It also allows developers to create really *annoying* stuff, including intrusive ads. How do I stop the Flash Player cold in its tracks?

The Fix: If Flash animations really make you want to hurl, you have a couple of options:

- You could uninstall Flash Player. But that's not as easy as you might expect; you won't find it in Add/Remove Programs. You'll find a Flash Player uninstaller at *http://snipurl.com/remove_player*. If the uninstaller doesn't work, *http://snipurl.com/remove* offers instructions for removing Flash Player manually, namely the Flash Player ActiveX control (if you're using Internet Explorer) and the Flash Player plug-in (if you're using Netscape, Opera, or Mozilla).

- A better solution is to use a web-filtering product like Proxomitron, a free program you can download from *http://www.oreilly.com/pcannoyances*. Proxomitron replaces Flash elements with a simple hyperlink, which you can click if you *want* the animation to play. Proxomitron does much more, including blocking pop-up windows, preventing animated GIF files from playing, managing frames, stopping scripts and applets, and so on. You can learn a lot more about the capabilities of Proxomitron at *http://snipurl.com/prox_scripts*.

NEAT-O FLASH VIDEO

XDude's Knowledge Emporioum offers some of the best Flash videos on the web. Check out XDude's titanic battle with the banking system in *The Dough*, and pay particular attention to his creativity and programming skills (*http://www.xdude.com*).

PUT FLASH ON HOLD

If the "Go Flashless to Save Tired Eyes" tip seems too complicated for you (or if you think Proxomitron sounds like something from Woody Allen's "Sleeper"), there's another solution. For quick relief, turn to TurnFlash. Whenever I hit a site with an annoying Flash ad, a quick click of the TurnFlash icon in Windows' System Tray disables the Flash component. There's no installation—just run the program and it appears in your System Tray, ready to work. (In Windows NT, 2000, and XP, you must have permission to write to Internet Explorer's Registry keys for TurnFlash to work.) One minor inconvenience—to see the change, you must open a new Internet Explorer window. Grab a copy of TurnFlash at *http://www.oreilly.com/pcannoyances*.

MAKE YOUR PC AN AD-FREE ZONE

The Annoyance: As I sit and wait for another web page to load, I'm left staring at a multitude of banner ads, which, of course, load first. I hate the way banner ads clutter up web pages, the flashing, blinking, and gyrating. Even more insidious, banner ads siphon off a fair-sized chunk of my Internet bandwidth, competing with everything else that a web site is trying to display.

The Fix: Many products block ads, and most work just fine. But I'm recommending two because I've used them and know they can do the job:

AdSubtract

This is my first line of defense against banner ads. The SE version is free, but limited to blocking ads on just five web sites you specify. I use the $30 version for lots of reasons. Besides stopping banner and pop-up ads on any number of sites, InterMute's AdSubtract also prevents windows from popping up, stops Java applets and JavaScripts, filters out two types of cookies, brings annoying animations to a halt, and stops background music. The utility's Filters tab, shown in

Figure 3-1, is where you set your preferences in the aptly named Annoyances section. I can set up an unlimited number of web sites, with each one configured differently. Download the free version from *http://www.oreilly.com/pcannoyances*.

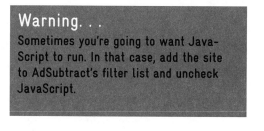

Figure 3-1. I've set AdSubtract Pro to globally block ads, animations, pop-ups, JavaScript, and cookies, but I can configure specific sites individually to allow certain annoyances.

> **Warning...**
> Sometimes you're going to want Java-Script to run. In that case, add the site to AdSubtract's filter list and uncheck JavaScript.

WebWasher

This program is absolutely free and has more features—and is more configurable—than AdSubtract. WebWasher zaps ads, bounces cookies, and blocks pop-up windows. At first glance, WebWasher is easy to use, but as you delve into the options and configure the tool for different web sites, you may need help. Check the WebWasher Workshop page for helpful tutorials at *http://snipurl.com/webwasher_help*. Download the program at *http://www.oreilly.com/pcannoyances*.

COUNTERESPIONAGE FOR SNEAKY SPYWARE

The Annoyance: I had an unpleasant surprise the other day. My friend stopped by and saw my colorful cursor. He said it was Comet Cursor and considered it spyware; he said I should uninstall it right away. Besides the annoyance of having spyware on my system, I now can't get rid of the Comet Cursor—it keeps reappearing.

DEFEAT BROWSER HIJACKERS

I hate it when SpyWare changes my home, default, or search page, or adds a malicious Browser Help Object to your system. Nail the hijackers before they touch your PC with Browser Hijack Blaster. This background tool watches for and alerts you to changes in Internet Explorer and lets you revert to your original settings. Grab a copy at *http://snipurl.com/hijack_blaster*.

> **BROWSER HIJACK BLASTER ALERT!**
>
> ⚠ **IE SETTINGS CHANGED!**
>
> Browser Hijack Blaster Alert
>
> ---
>
> **WARNING! Your IE search page has been changed!**
>
> Your Internet Explorer current user search page has been changed from
> *http://www.microsoft.com/isapi/redir.dll?prd=iear=iesearch*
> to the following
> *http://www.google.com*
>
> ---
>
> <u>WOULD YOU LIKE TO UNDO THE CHANGE?</u>
>
> (Select YES to change the setting back to its original value. Select NO to keep this new value.)
>
> [YES - UNDO CHANGE]   [NO - KEEP NEW]

The Fix: Spyware tracks your Internet behavior and files reports to goodness-knows-who with the sole purpose of profiling you, most likely for pushing more targeted advertising into your browsing experience. Someday, you too may encounter a site that tries to install Comet Cursor, a program that changes your cursor into a comet, a cat, or another animal. That's cute—but according to Richard Smith of the Privacy Foundation, it is also surreptitiously watching your web activity.

Worse are the dialers ("Connect2Party" and "The Dialer" are two common ones) that silently disconnect your modem and reconnect it via an international long-distance number. You get a nasty phone bill with phone rates that are high enough to make up a significant part of a third-world country's GNP.

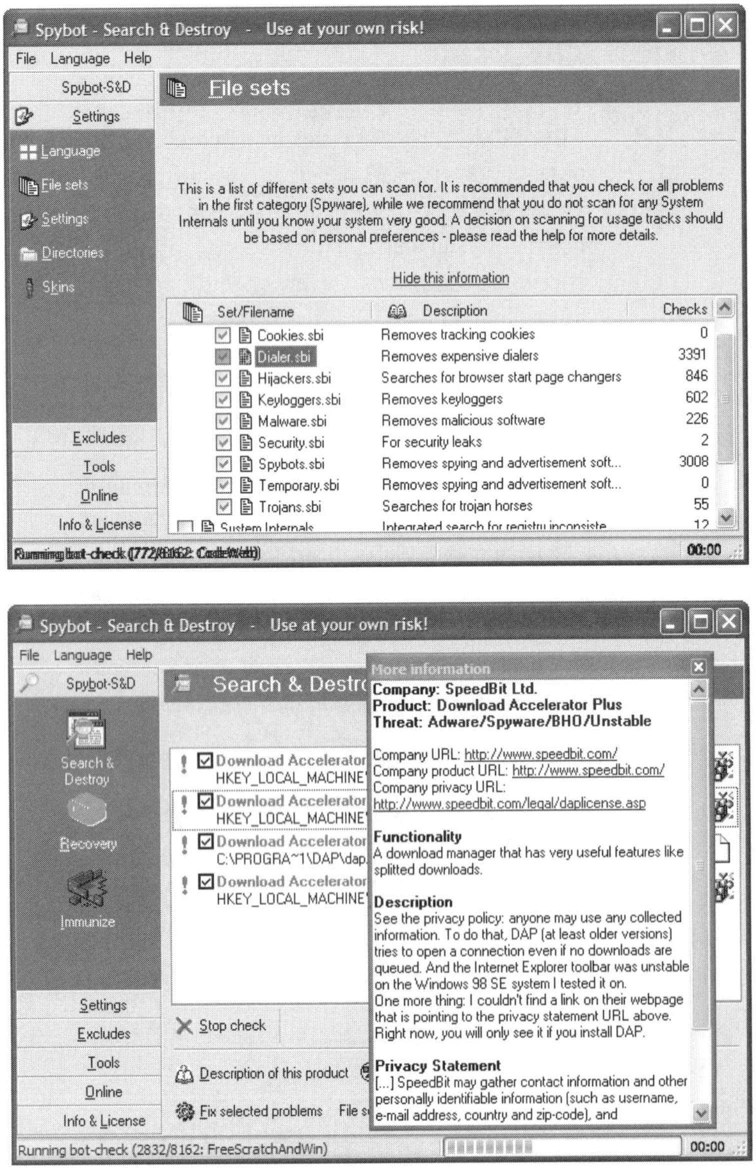

Spyware is a despicable business practice, but you have two nifty—and free—tools for fighting back.

Ad-Aware

This tool detects and removes spyware from your hard drive. The program is easy to use, and removes such spyware as Aureate/Radiate, Comet Cursor, Cydoor, Doubleclick, EverAd, Flyswat, OnFlow, TimeSink, and others. There's a copy available at *http://www.oreilly.com/pcannoyances.*

Spybot Search & Destroy

This is similar to Ad-Aware—it finds and removes spyware (see Figure 3-2, top). But Spybot offers many more advanced features, such as examining ActiveX, BHOs (browser helper objects), hosts files, and other esoterica. While I was writing this book, Spybot flagged SpeedBit's Download Accelerator Plus, a program I was trying. Imagine my surprise when I dug into Speedbit and found this statement: "SpeedBit may gather contact information and other personally identifiable information (such as username, email address, country and zip-code)." (See Figure 3-2, bottom.) You can download the Spybot program at *http://www.oreilly.com/pcannoyances.*

Figure 3-2. Top: Besides spyware, Spybot searches for and removes automatic dialers, keyloggers, Trojan horses, tracking cookies, and other malware. Bottom: In the course of writing this book, Spybot nailed a spyware tracking program on my PC and promptly dispatched it to the bit bucket.

OPEN NEW BROWSER WINDOWS YOUR WAY

The Annoyance: When I click a link on a web page, I sometimes have to peer under other windows to find the page. Sometimes a page opens in a maximized window, sometimes in a minimized window, and sometimes in a narrow line across the top of the screen. What's going on?

The Fix: Open Internet Explorer, hold down the Shift key, and click a link, which forces the linked page to open in a new or "child" window. Find the new window and set its position and size (but do not maximize the window). Switch back to the parent window and close it. Then close the child window.

So how does this help? When you close the last open Internet Explorer window, Windows stores its size and position in the Registry. Internet Explorer uses that information the next time you start it, and opens any child windows during the session. If child windows keep showing up in wacky positions, it's probably because the last window you closed before exiting IE was an oddly sized pop-up or pop-under window. Aside from using a pop-up blocker to prevent the blasted things from opening in the first place, you can make sure the last window you close is properly sized and placed.

If you want all of your windows maximized, here's another solution: open Internet Explorer and stretch the small window to fill the screen. (Don't click the maximize button.) Then close the browser window and in the future, Internet Explorer will open full-screen.

The best solution for keeping windows maximized? IE New Window Maximizer, a free utility that automatically maximizes every new Internet Explorer window. With a hotkey you designate, Maximizer also lets you hide or even close all Internet Explorer windows. Download a copy at *http://www.oreilly.com/pcannoyances*.

There's another solution to lost browser windows: use a browser that supports tabbed windows. Opera has this capability built in, but a number of third-party developers have created add-ins for Internet Explorer that

---

PUT A STOP TO POP-UPS

I want just five minutes with the imbecile who created pop-up web ads. Internet ads are annoying, but pop-up and pop-under ads are oh so much worse. They're everywhere and they don't take no for an answer. While it's true that one pop-up may be a fair price to pay for free content, some sites overdo it with tons of pop-ups, pop-unders—everything but Pop-Tarts.

One easy way to block these intruders is with Google's Toolbar Pop-up Blocker feature (see figure). Just click the Options button and check the Popup Blocker box.

There's also IHatePopups, a smart blocker than can differentiate between good and bad pop-ups on a page. For instance, a help site may have a legitimate link that opens another small window. IHatePopups recognizes it as a "good" pop-up box. Grab a copy of the trial version and make your own decision. If you're using Netscape, grab a copy of Pop-Up Stopper, a freebie from Panicware. Both are available at *http://www.oreilly.com/pcannoyances*.

Google's free pop-up blocker does an exemplary job at stopping all types of pop-ups and pop-unders. Get the toolbar at *http://www.oreilly.com/pcannoyances*.

give it a multiple-document interface, such as the free Avant Browser (available from *http://www.oreilly.com/ pcannoyances*), shown in Figure 3-3.

Figure 3-3. You can retrofit IE with tabbed windows, thanks to Avant Browser.

FLIP THROUGH JUST YOUR OPEN IE WINDOWS

Brett Bartholomew's IEScroll is like having Alt-Tab just for Internet Explorer. Install IEScroll, then tap the Scroll Lock key to jump to the next open Internet Explorer window. The free tool is available at *http:// www.oreilly.com/pcannoyances*.

TOGGLE YOUR BROWSER'S PROXY

When you take your notebook on a trip, you probably spend a lot of time fiddling with Internet Explorer's proxy settings so that you can connect to a client's LAN or a hotel's Internet line.

ProxyPal is a free utility you can add to Internet Explorer's toolbar to instantly toggle your browser's proxy on and off. For a proxy change to take effect, you must close and reopen Internet Explorer. Grab ProxyPal at *http:// www.oreilly.com/pcannoyances*.

OUTSMART OUTLOOK'S BROWSER CHOICE

The Annoyance: When I click a link in an Outlook email message, instead of opening a new browser window, it reuses an existing window. That's okay—I usually have too many windows open already—but it seems to pick an existing window at random. Or, worse, it perversely picks the window that I *least* want it to use! Nor does it bring the window to the front, so there I am, once again pawing through my Taskbar buttons looking for the right Internet Explorer window.

The Fix: Window selection isn't entirely random. Outlook normally chooses the last Internet Explorer window that was active. Armed with this tidbit of information, you can control which window it'll use, but only for the current session. Switch to the Internet Explorer window you want replaced, switch to Outlook, and then click the link in the message.

Users of Outlook 2003 don't have to deal with this annoyance; links open a new browser window instead of hijacking an existing window. Why did it take Microsoft so long to make this right?

PICTURELESS PAGES PREDICAMENT

The Annoyance: There are some great pictures available on the Web, but certain pictures don't appear on web pages I visit. Instead, I see a red X or a funny little icon where the picture is supposed to be.

The Fix: Several circumstances can keep pictures from appearing:

- There's a logjam at the web server or somewhere along the miles of wires between the web server and your browser. Try refreshing the page (press F5 or click the Refresh button on the toolbar). But you probably already tried that.

- Something's wrong with the web server. The picture might not be on the server, or the programmer who created the web page might have put in the wrong path to the picture.

- Internet Explorer may be configured so that it doesn't show pictures—a common setup for those with slow dialup connections who don't want to waste time downloading pictures. (If this option is set, you can selectively display pictures by right-clicking the X or the icon and choosing Show Picture.) To undo this setting in Internet Explorer, choose Tools → Internet Options. Click the Advanced tab, and in the Multimedia section, check the Show Pictures box to make your pictures appear.

- An invalid value in the Windows Registry is preventing pictures from appearing. It's an easy fix, even for those who are squeamish about poking around in the Registry. (Before you mess around with the Registry, back it up as per the instructions in the "What's The Registry?" sidebar in Chapter 2.) Select Start → Run, type in **regedit**, and hit Enter. In Registry Editor, navigate to *\HKEY_CLASSES_ROOT\.gif*. In the right pane, click the Content Type item; its value should be image/gif. Then check *\HKEY_CLASSES_ROOT\.jpg*; Content Type should be set to image/jpg or image/jpeg. For more information about this fix, see Microsoft Knowledge Base article 307239. (Don't know how to get to Microsoft Knowledge Base articles? Read the next topic.)

A SHORTER PATH TO MICROSOFT'S KNOWLEDGE

The Annoyance: Speaking of the Microsoft Knowledge Base, have you noticed how many steps it takes to dig up a particular document? Let's say you know the number of the article you want, and you go to *http://support.microsoft.com*. You have to find and click the Knowledge Base Article ID Number Search link, type the article number, and then click the green arrow. And because—surprise, surprise—the Microsoft support pages get tons of traffic, these pages always seem to load slowly.

The Fix: If you use Windows XP and Internet Explorer, there's a nifty trick you can use. Once you've set this up, you can go directly to a Knowledge Base article by typing **mskb**, followed by the article number in Internet Explorer's Address field, and pressing Enter. For example, you would type **mskb 307239** to go directly to the article about the big red X that appears instead of a picture.

First, download and install Tweak UI for Windows XP, one of Microsoft's free PowerToys you can download from *http://www.oreilly.com/pcannoyances*. Then follow these steps:

1. Choose Start → All Programs → Powertoys for Windows XP → TweakUI.

2. In the left pane, expand the Internet Explorer item and select the Search category.

3. Click the Create button on the right.

4. In the Prefix field, type **mskb** (see Figure 3-4).

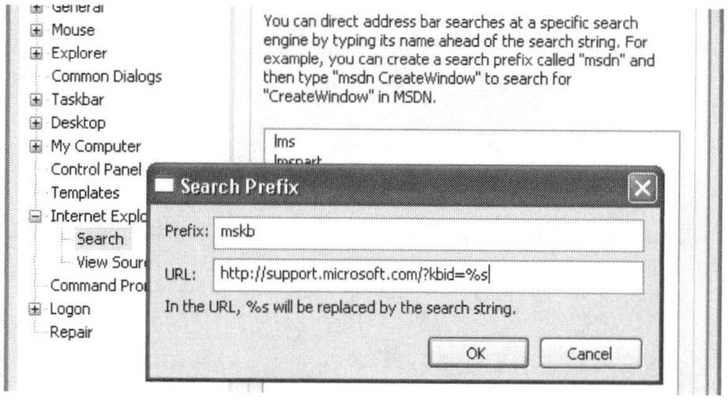

Figure 3-4. Setting up Tweak UI's Search Prefix lets you type an alias plus additional information into Internet Explorer's address bar, instead of a complicated URL. The additional info is substituted for the %s in the URL you've set Tweak UI to use for the alias.

5. In the URL box, type **http://support.microsoft.com/ ?kbid=%s**.

6. Click OK in the Search Prefix dialog box, and then click OK in the Tweak UI window to close the program and apply your changes.

This Tweak UI feature is really intended for sending queries to search engines. By performing a search on your favorite search engine and dissecting the URL that's generated, you can usually figure out how to create a convenient IE address bar shortcut. For example, you could create a basic Google search by entering `http://www.google.com/search?&q=%s` as the URL, and giving it a nice short prefix, like g. You could then find my Home Office columns by typing g `steve bass pcworld` in the address bar.

> **t i p**
>
> In Internet Explorer, use Alt-D to highlight the Address Bar without touching the mouse.

ALL YOUR FAVORITES, ALL THE TIME

The Annoyance: The Favorites menu in Internet Explorer is a wonderful place to store shortcuts to web sites, but some things about it drive me nuts. For example, Internet Explorer hides items on the Favorites menu that haven't been used lately. Also, there's no rhyme or reason to the order of items on the Favorites menu, which makes it harder to find the site I'm looking for.

FASTER FAVORITE WEB BROWSING

If you browse the Internet like I do, you probably visit the same half dozen web pages almost every day. Since I'm a keyboard kinda guy and would rather keep my hands on the keyboard than on my mouse, I use Chime Software's Hot Chime keyboard-macro utility. The free utility lets me hit the Pause key (it's in the upper right-hand portion of your keyboard, next to the Scroll Lock key) and type in a pre-selected key or phrase to get to the sites. For example, pressing Pause and then S gets me to SnipURL, the site I used to create all the shortcut links in the book. I also use Hot Chime to launch my most frequently used programs from the keyboard, by setting the letters "xl" to start Microsoft Excel on my PC. The program is available at *http://snipurl.com/chime*.

The Fix: To see hidden items, click the arrow at the bottom of the menu, or just be patient: in a few seconds Internet Explorer will realize your befuddlement and display all the hidden items. But you can also change IE's hide-and-seek behavior by selecting Tools → Internet Options and clicking the Advanced tab. Under Browsing, uncheck the Enable Personalized Favorites Menu box.

The order Internet Explorer places items on the Favorites menu might be a mystery, but it's pretty easy to dictate the order you want:

- To sort items alphabetically, open the Favorites menu (don't click the icon on the Explorer bar), right-click anywhere on the menu below the first two menu options, and choose Sort by Name. It doesn't matter which folder or link you right-click; Internet Explorer sorts all folders in alphabetical order, followed by all links in alphabetical order. Sort by Name acts only on the current menu level; it doesn't sort items in any subfolders. To do that, you need to open the subfolder in question, and then right-click an item within that subfolder.

- Just as you can with the Windows Start menu, you can drag links and folders around in the Favorites menu. A black bar indicates where the item will end up when you release the mouse button. With a little practice, you'll be able to drop items into subfolders, too. You can drag items by holding down the left or right mouse button; use the latter, and a pop-up menu lets you move or copy the favorite to the new location.

I usually do an alphabetical sort first to put things in a logical order, then move a few frequently used items to a more prominent position. It gives me—for a brief moment at least—a feeling of power over Microsoft. The victory may be short-lived, but I will not submit!

CLEAR DEAD LINKS FROM YOUR FAVORITES MENU

The Annoyance: My Favorites menu is as long as my arm. The problem is that a number of links point to sites that no longer exist. Checking and deleting them manually is tedious and time-consuming.

The Fix: A number of free and inexpensive programs can detect dead and duplicate links. One I've used with great success is AM-DeadLink (see Figure 3-5), which you can download from *http://snipurl.com/am_deadlink*. AM-DeadLink manages favorites (bookmarks) for Netscape and Opera as well as Internet Explorer.

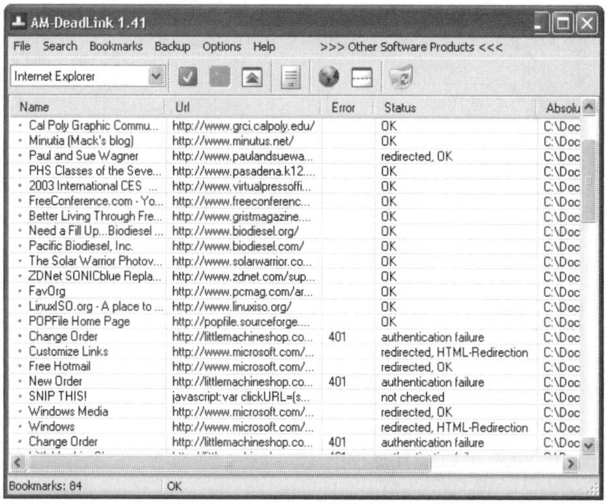

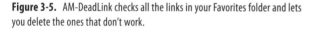

Figure 3-5. AM-DeadLink checks all the links in your Favorites folder and lets you delete the ones that don't work.

GET THE BIG PICTURE THE FIRST TIME

The Annoyance: Whenever Internet Explorer displays a large photo or other graphic, it shrinks the image to fit in the window. If I wait long enough and hold the mouse pointer in the right place at the right time, a button appears in the lower-right corner; clicking it enlarges the graphic. Why do I have to go through this silly dance every time I want to see the Big Picture?

The Fix: This alleged "feature," introduced in Internet Explorer 6, is reasonably useful for displaying large photographs; it automatically scales the image to fit within the window and continually resizes the picture as you change the window size. But it's a pain if you're looking at screen dumps or graphics that contain text, which become illegible when the image is reduced in size.

Before you tinker with IE, simply maximize the Internet Explorer window. Need more screen real estate? Press F11 (or choose View → Full Screen) to nuke all the window borders, the Taskbar, and other fillers. Gain even more space by right-clicking the toolbar and choosing Auto-Hide; the toolbar then drops into view only when you move the mouse pointer to the top of the screen.

If, after all this, you want to view the picture in its original size, place the mouse pointer on the graphic—and don't move. In a few seconds, a button appears in the lower-right corner; click it to enlarge the graphic to full size.

If you despise this feature, go to Tools → Internet Options and click the Advanced tab. Scroll down to the Multimedia section and uncheck the Enable Automatic Image Resizing box (see Figure 3-6).

Figure 3-6. Tired of having Internet Explorer shrink images to fit within the window? You don't have to stand for it. All it takes is unchecking Enable Automatic Image Resizing on its Tools → Internet Options → Advanced tab.

BOOT BORING IE ICONS

The Annoyance: Internet Explorer's Favorites icons are nothing more than Microsoft's dull blue "e" emblem. I'd prefer just about anything other than these tiny logos reminding me how much I've spent on Microsoft products.

The Fix: Right-click any icon in your Favorites list, select Properties, click the Change Icon button, then the Browse button, and click any *EXE* or *ICO* file. You'll likely see an icon (but maybe not; not all *EXE*s have icons). Find an icon you like and click OK, then OK again.

ONE CLICK RESTORES YOUR IE TOOLBARS

You're traipsing around the Internet when, out of the blue, your meticulously crafted Internet Explorer toolbar is jumbled. The address bar, links, buttons—even the Googlebar—have all changed places. Here's the fix: put your Internet Explorer toolbar back in order and save the settings with Toolbar Chest. Next time the toolbar gets hosed, smile as the utility restores it with one click. Grab a copy at *http://snipurl.com/bartdart*.

DISABLE IE'S IMAGE TOOLBAR

The Annoyance: Another feature that Microsoft added in Internet Explorer 6 is the small Image toolbar that pops up in the upper-left corner of pictures and other images when you point at them (shown in Figure 3-7). But the toolbar often obscures the most interesting part of the image.

THE END IS NEAR: THE INTERNET'S LAST PAGE

Do you spend hours each day browsing the Web? Want to stop? If so, visit this page: *http://snipurl.com/last_page*.

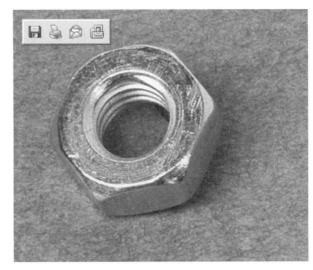

Figure 3-7. The Image toolbar that pops up in front of pictures can be very annoying.

The Fix: True—but the Image toolbar has some very useful functions. The first three buttons let you save, print, or email the image. (The fourth is kind of silly; it just opens the My Pictures folder.) However, all four functions are available from the menu that appears when you right-click an image, so banishing the toolbar is no great loss.

To get rid of the toolbar, choose Tools → Internet Options, click the Advanced tab, and uncheck the "Enable Image Toolbar (requires restart)" box. Exit and restart Internet Explorer.

THE VANISHING IMAGE TOOLBAR

So you like the Image toolbar but you're annoyed because it doesn't always show up? Call it discrimination, but the Image toolbar is finicky and doesn't appear unless the image is least 200 by 200 pixels. Right-click the image to access the same functions from a pop-up menu.

But that's the hard way. I mention it only so you'll appreciate the following nifty tip even more. If the image toolbar pops up, right-click the toolbar and choose Disable Image Toolbar (see Figure 3-8). Internet Explorer then asks whether you want to lose the toolbar forever or only for the current session. If you choose Always, you can restore the toolbar with a visit to Internet Options, as described above.

Figure 3-8. Top: Does the Image Toolbar distract you? Right-click it to disable it. Bottom: When the dialog appears, decide whether to send it into the bit bucket for this session—or for good.

WHAT YOU SEE IS NOT WHAT YOU GET

The Annoyance: When I print a web page from my browser, the result is often unusable. The text and graphics are clipped off on the right side, and I invariably end up with an extra page that has only the menu from the bottom of the web page.

The Fix: Most web pages are designed for on-screen display, not for printing. Depending on how the page is coded, text and other elements might adjust to fit the page width, much like the word-wrap feature that's part of every word processing program. But many web pages use fixed-width columns; they retain their width even if it means printing beyond the edge of the paper. There's no easy way to tell if a web page is going to print out right. But there are several workarounds:

- Look around the web page for a link to a "printer-friendly version." (You'll typically see this on newspaper and magazine sites, such as *PCWorld.com*.) The printer-friendly version typically omits banner ads, navigation bars, and unprintable colors; consolidates all parts of a multipage article into a single web page; and is coded to wrap the text to fit your page margins.

- Use the browser's print preview feature so you can quickly spot blank or useless pages. Once you have, click the Print button and enter the proper range to print in the Pages field.

You can also force a web page to conform to the printed page:

- In the Print Preview screen, click the Page Setup button (or press Alt-U). If you need to gain a little bit of width, adjust the margins. To gain more width, switch to landscape orientation. This usually eliminates most problems with truncated text.

- If the page has frames, a drop-down menu appears to the left of the Help menu at the top of the preview window and lets you print each frame on a different page. (Choose "All frames individually" instead of "As laid out on screen.") Then scroll through the document and figure out which pages you really want to print. Click the Print button, and specify the page range to print.

QUICK FIX FOR MULTIPAGE ARTICLES

The Annoyance: I often see articles on web sites I'd like to print out. But some articles go on for two or three pages, forcing me to find and then click the "next page" link to continue reading. I know it's just a gambit to make me look at more ads, right?

The Fix: Having to go through the printing rigmarole for each page when you're ready to print is a royal pain. Worse, the glitzy ads on each page suck your printer's ink or toner cartridge dry. Although it's not always available, look for a "printer friendly" link on the page. This link will generate a single long page (often minus many of those annoying ads) that you can print out.

GET RID OF IE'S AUTOMATIC "YOUR FILES ARE ATTACHED"

The Annoyance: Internet Explorer insists on adding "Your files are attached and ready to send with this message" to my message whenever I try to email a web address to someone using Tools → Mail and News → Send a Link (see Figure 3-9). Worse, it makes the subject "Emailing:" followed by a partial name of the link. Can I make Internet Explorer a little less helpful?

The Fix: There's a quick Registry fix from Kelly's Korner (see the sidebar "Kelly's IE Tweaks") that adds an "Email Page" option when you right-click a URL in Internet Explorer. The text in the message is now simply the name of the web site along with its URL, and the subject line is just the name of the site.

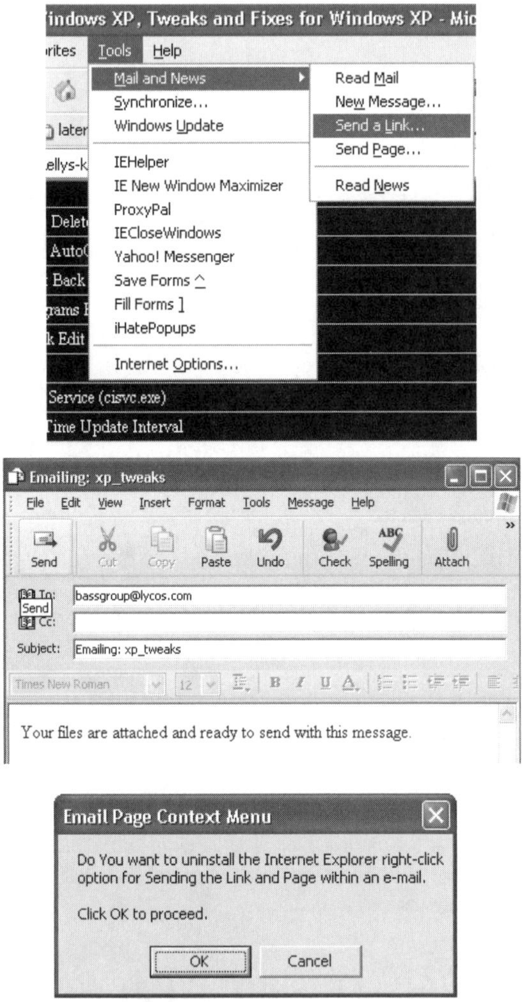

Figure 3-9. Top: If you find a Web page you'd like to send to a buddy, Internet Explorer makes it easy with "Send a Link." Middle: The problem is that Internet Explorer automatically adds the unnecessary (and annoying) "Your files are attached and ready to send with this message" to the message. Bottom: Click OK to run Kelly's script, and you'll see a difference next time you try to email a link from Internet Explorer.

KELLY'S IE TWEAKS

Some sites are good, but Kelly Theriot's is outstanding (see *http://snipurl.com/kellyskorner*). It's filled with over 200 tweaks, tips, Registry changes, and utilities for XP and Internet Explorer—small programs (actually VBScript files) that will make your computing life easier and slicker. (See "Get Rid of IE's Automatic 'Your files are attached'" for an example.) Kelly also provides terrific tweaks, such as:

- If you use Microsoft's Knowledgebase often, add it to Internet Explorer's Toolbar. Find the tweak on line 176 of *http://snipurl.com/xp_tweaks*.

- Prefer Google as your primary search engine for Internet Explorer? The tweak is on line 18 of *http:// snipurl.com/xp_tweaks*.

REVIVE IE'S DISABLED BACK BUTTON

The Annoyance: Sometimes when I browse a site with Internet Explorer, neither the Back button nor the Backspace key will return me to the previous web page. Instead, the current page keeps reappearing. How loopy is that?

The Fix: Some sites are programmed to put you in a loop that lands you right back where you were. To escape these "redirects," click the down arrow to the right of the Back button to display a list of the last nine pages you have visited, and select one of these earlier entries. The alternative: click the Back button twice in quick succession.

FORCE IE TO REFRESH THE PAGE

The Annoyance: When I refresh a web page in IE, I expect it to be updated with the latest version. But sometimes the same page remains on screen, even when I *know* the page has changed on the web server.

The Fix: You can refresh a page by pressing F5 or Ctrl-R, by clicking the Refresh button on the toolbar, or by choosing View → Refresh. This reloads the page into the browser. But to improve speed, Internet Explorer doesn't immediately download the page anew when you ask it to refresh a page. Instead, it checks the timestamp of the page on the web server; if it matches the timestamp of page cached on your PC, Internet Explorer reloads the page from your hard disk—not from the web server.

To force Internet Explorer to reload from the web server, press Ctrl-F5 or hold down the Ctrl key when you click the Refresh button.

HOW OLD IS THAT WEB PAGE?

Have you ever wondered when the web page you're visiting was last updated? Here's a neat Internet Explorer trick for finding out. Go to the site, type `javascript: alert(document.lastModified)` into your browser's address field, and press the Enter key. The time and date of the last update will appear in a pop-up window (see below).

THE CASE OF THE DISAPPEARING STATUS BAR

The Annoyance: I like having the status bar at the bottom of the screen so that when I hover my mouse over a link, I can see where it leads to. For some unknown reason, the status bar disappears in IE 6.0—sometimes when I go to a new page, other times when I open another Internet Explorer session. I have to keep going back and selecting View → Status Bar to bring it back. Any suggestions?

The Fix: This is a known bug in Internet Explorer (and, because they're interrelated, Windows Explorer). There's a

two-minute fix, and you'll never be bothered by the problem again—well, not until Microsoft releases a new version of Internet Explorer!

1. Load Internet Explorer, making sure just one session is open. Click View and select the Status Bar (if it's not already selected) to turn it on.

2. Right-click a blank spot on Internet Explorer's toolbar and select "Lock the Toolbar" (if it's not already selected) to lock the toolbar.

3. Hold the Ctrl key and click Internet Explorer's close button, the "X" in the upper-right corner of the window.

4. Open Windows Explorer, click View, and select Status Bar (if it's not already selected).

5. Right-click a blank spot on Windows Explorer's toolbar and select "Lock the Toolbars" (if it's not already selected).

6. Click Tools → Folder Options → View tab and click the "Apply to All Folders" button. Click Yes to confirm and OK to close the dialog box.

7. Hold the Ctrl key and click Explorer's Close button.

8. To test it, open Internet Explorer, right-click a link, and select "Open in New Window" or "Open Link in New Window."

Take pride in combating—and fixing—an Internet Explorer 6.0 bug.

MAKE NETSCAPE BLOCK THOSE POP-UPS!

The Annoyance: I'm happy with the way Netscape 7 blocks most pop-ups. Unfortunately, the emphasis is on *most*, because I still get annoying pop-ups from AOL, AIM, and even Netscape itself. What a crock!

The Fix: Don't you love it when a vendor touts a product's great feature, but turns it off by default? And in this case, even when you've changed the setting to suppress pop-ups, the scoundrels leave you with a stack of exceptions (see Figure 3-10). It's no surprise; many of the exempted sites are part of the AOL/Time Warner conglomerate. Here's how to get truly free of pop-ups.

Select Edit → Preferences, and expand the Privacy & Security item on the left. Click Popup Window Controls (Popup Windows in 7.1), and check the "Suppress popups" ("Block unrequested popup windows" in 7.1) box; then click the Exceptions ("Allowed Sites" in 7.1) button to display the Allowed Web Sites dialog box. Click "Remove All." If there are some sites you'll accept pop-ups from, add them to the Exceptions list. Click OK to close each dialog box.

World Clock Time-Waster

When I get email from someone in New Zealand, I wonder, "What time is it there?" Instead of speculating, I turn to TimeTicker (*http://www.timeticker.com*), a nifty, albeit loud, site that calculates the time anywhere in the world. (Uh duh question: if it's tomorrow in New Zealand, could someone there tell me how the stock market did in the States today?)

Figure 3-10. Netscape 7.0 does a good job of blocking advertising pop-ups—except from companies it seems to have a relationship with.

NETSCAPE CAN GOOGLE, TOO

The Annoyance: I'm a Netscape user, and I'm fully aware that the Google Toolbar is available only for Internet Explorer. That's irritating, and I want a fix.

The Fix: I can't argue—Google has ignored Netscape users, and that's blatantly discriminatory. Here are a few options:

- Sue Google for ignoring Netscape users (and see how far that gets you).

- Drag and drop Google buttons onto Netscape's toolbar (see *http://snipurl.com/google_buttons* for instructions).

- If you pine for the Google Toolbar and won't settle for anything less, ignore everything I just said and simply install the Googlebar, a free Google Toolbar clone for Netscape and its open source cousin Mozilla. Find it at *googlebar.mozdev.org*. If you don't like the Googlebar, download GGSearch, a third-party plug-in for Google that works with Netscape (see Figure 3-11). It's available at *http://snipurl.com/ggsearch*.

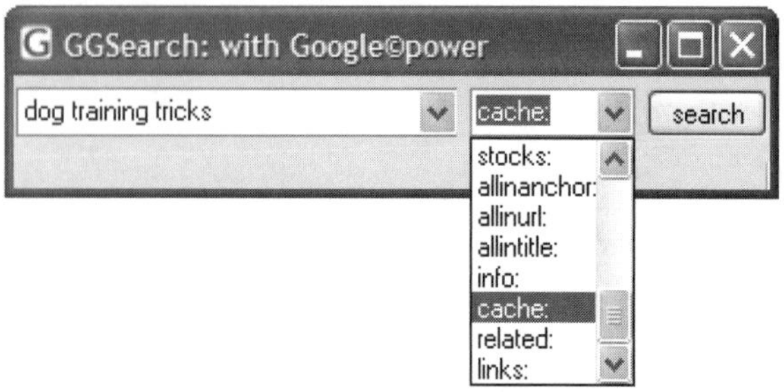

Figure 3-11. Netscape users rejoice! You can have access to a Google Bar that's just as good as Google's original.

> **tip**
>
> Have you ever mistyped a web address or realized that you don't really want to go to a site after all? Press the Escape key to stop Netscape and Internet Explorer in their tracks.

GIVE ME BACK INTERNET EXPLORER

The Annoyance: I experimented with a new browser, didn't like it, and uninstalled it. Later, when I clicked a link in an email message, that (now absent) browser tried to open the link instead of Internet Explorer.

The Fix: This browser confusion is common. The good news: the fix is straightforward. To reset Internet Explorer as your default browser, open the program and click Tools → Internet Options. Choose the Programs tab and find the "Internet Explorer should check to see whether it's the default browser" box near the bottom. Check this box, restart IE, and that should be that.

This trick might not work with some third-party Internet Explorer shells, such as Maxthon (formerly MyIE2). If that's

the case, download Jem Berkes's SetBrowser from *http://snipurl.com/setbrowser* (see Figure 3-12). It's a free utility that uses brute force—actually, a Registry setting—to quickly make Internet Explorer your one and only.

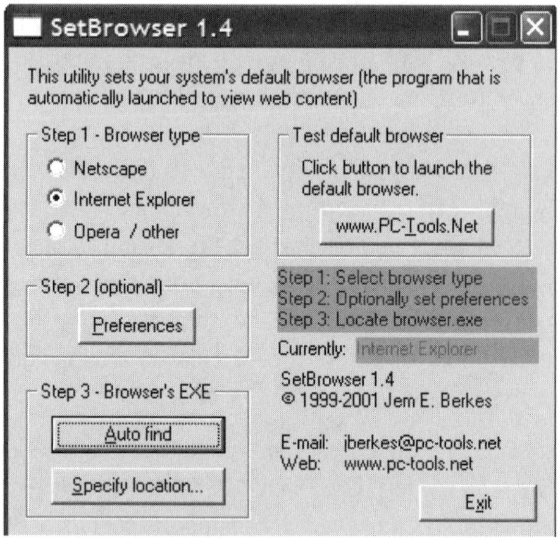

Figure 3-12. Is your favorite default browser no longer the default? Use SetBrowser to change it back.

PULL THE PLUG ON NET2PHONE

The Annoyance: I launch Netscape to browse the Web, not to make phone calls over the Internet. Yet Netscape has both a Net2Phone toolbar button and a Net2Phone item in the Tasks menu that sit there, taking up space.

The Fix: To nuke a toolbar button in Netscape 6 or 7, choose Edit → Preferences, click Navigator in the Category window, and uncheck the Net2Phone box under "Select the buttons you want to see in the toolbars."

Killing the Net2Phone menu item takes more elbow grease. First, close Netscape if it's open. Go to the Netscape folder (it may be in *\Program Files\Netscape\ Netscape 6*, even if you're using Netscape 7), open the Chrome folder, then the Overlayinfo folder, then the

Communicator folder, and finally the Content folder. Find the *overlayinfo.rdf* file and back it up just in case. Then open it up in Notepad or another text editor and find the line `chrome://net2phone/content/Net2PhoneTaskMenu.xul` and delete. Save *overlayinfo.rdf*, and launch Netscape. The toolbar should now be Net2Phone-less.

VEXING AOL CONNECTIONS

The Annoyance: I've had an AOL account for ages, and even when I got cable modem service I kept it—mostly because I'd never get half my relatives to remember that I switched e-mail addresses. But all too many times I can't connect to AOL, or I get disconnected for no apparent reason at all.

The Fix: AOL has been responsible for more botched connections than all the planet's airlines combined. If it's dropping yours, try another AOL access number, since AOL adds new (and hopefully, more stable) ones all the time. Enter keyword **Access**, click the Search button, and search your area code. Newer numbers are at the top of the list.

If you're using AOL 7.0 or earlier, time to upgrade. Version 8.0 seems less prone to muck up otherwise healthy Internet connections. Go to keyword **Upgrade**.

A few other fixes for most common AOL connection hobgoblins:

AOL tries to dial when it shouldn't. If you've got a cable or DSL connection, you want your AOL software to talk to the service via that connection, not dial-up. But the software may still be configured to dial your old modem—or try to, anyhow. To connect via broadband, launch AOL and click the Setup button in the Sign On dialog box. Then click the Edit Numbers button and double-click the first item under "Numbers (Connections) for this Location." In the "Connect using" drop-down menu, choose "TCP/IP; LAN or ISP (Internet Service Provider)" or "Broadband (High-Speed, Cable, DSL, or other ISP)" or whatever similar choice your version presents. Then make sure Automatic Connection Script is selected and choose your connection

type (Cable Modem or DSL) in its menu. Click OK twice to back your way out to the main menu, and sign on as usual.

AOL disconnects due to inactivity. The AOL software likes to boot dialup users offline if too much time passes without them doing anything. But many users like to keep the connection going and there are a bevy of utilities that will answer AOL's nag messages for you and keep you connected. One pick: TPA Software's Terminator (*http://www.tpasoft.com*) is free to try, $10 to buy. Just remember such utilities violate AOL's Terms of Service, so use at your own risk. Better fixes: upgrade to AOL 8.0 or 9.0, which have autoreconnect features; or move up to broadband Internet access, which isn't affected by AOL's idle/autologoff "feature."

Call waiting can disrupt a dialup connection. You could dial *70 on your phone keypad before connecting, but here's a more permanent solution: at the AOL Sign On dialog box, click the Setup button, then the Edit Numbers button. Select each dialup number in turn and double-click it. Check the "Dial *70, to disable call waiting" box and click OK twice to back out. Sign on as usual.

Still frustrated by connection woes? Try AOL's Computer Check-Up feature, which diagnoses and fixes common problems. Go to Keyword: **Check-Up**, click the "No, continue to Computer Check-Up" link, then click the Check My Computer button and follow the instructions. Check-Up checks for various Internet and PC troubles, so don't be startled if it tells you about computing ailments you didn't even know you had.

KEEP AOL FROM OVERSPINNING YOUR HARD DRIVE

AOL can sometimes obsessively flush its disk buffer. There's a free patch that not only disables this "feature," but also boosts hard drive performance. Download AOLSpeed at *http://snipurl.com/aolspeed*.

Still tearing your hair out? AOL has a whole section devoted to connection hassles and how to cure them. Keyword **Connect** gets you there.

VANISHING FORM DATA

The Annoyance: I spend an hour filling in a lengthy form on a web page, only to be told after I submit it that it's missing an item. When I hit my browser's back button—zap!—everything's gone. Now I have to start from scratch.

The Fix: Instead of growling, fix your browser's cache settings to hold on to the information. In Internet Explorer, click Tools → Internet Options, select the Settings button on the General tab, and check "Every time you start Internet Explorer." In Netscape 6.0 and 7.0, click Edit → Preferences, expand Advanced, and click Cache. Set the memory cache to at least 1024 KB, and the disk cache to a minimum of 7680 KB. Then clear both caches. Note that you may have to click your browser's refresh button to see a revisited page's dynamic data.

Another option? Check out the upcoming sidebar "Fill Forms Automatically," and discover the joys of RoboForm.

SKIP THE REGISTRATION

The Annoyance: I really dislike giving my personal information to every online news site I visit. Not only does it invade my privacy (I know, I could fib), but it irritates me and takes too much time.

The Fix: The ethical considerations of entering faux information aside (pause here for laughter), I don't get bogged down with such matters anymore. Instead I use *BugMeNot.com*, a nifty site that offers a database of valid passwords and user IDs that you can use to visit all sorts of sites that require registration. At BugMeNot (*http://snipurl.com/BugMeNot*), just enter a site address (such as *http://www.nytimes.com*) and click the Show Logins button, and the site spits out an ID and password you can use.

FILL FORMS AUTOMATICALLY

If filling out forms is a chore, you *must* download Siber Systems' AI RoboForms, a free form-filling tool that I never browse without. Provide RoboForm with all the vitals you might need to fill in on a web site form, such as name, address, phone numbers, web site—even credit card numbers. Then click the "Fill Forms" button, and the program will fill in any blanks using the information you've provided. Click a web site from the RoboForm's Passcard screen, and your browser's transported to the site; if the site needs you to log in, RoboForm does it for you. RoboForm works with most browsers, including Internet Explorer, Netscape 7, Firefox, Mozilla, and AOL. And don't worry about security: RoboForm is itself password-protected. There's a free copy at *http://www.oreilly.com/pcannoyances*.

tip

> Occasionally a site may reject multiple users logging in with the same info. Not to fear—BugMeNot.com often has multiple IDs and passwords to choose from.

BUYING ONLINE? PLAY IT SAFE

The Annoyance: I would like to shop on the Internet, but no matter how secure I'm told a site may be, I'm still leery of using my credit card online.

The Fix: If you want to buy online, get a single-use credit card number. The number is generated on the fly, and it's good for a set amount and a specific length of time. It works just like your regular credit card—you'll see the charges on your next statement. Want to use it again? Just go to the site and generate another number. I use MBNA's ShopSafe and word is that Citibank and Morgan Stanley's Discover Financial Services will be adding this service. Your credit card company or bank might offer a similar free service. You can see my intentionally expired example card in Figure 3-13.

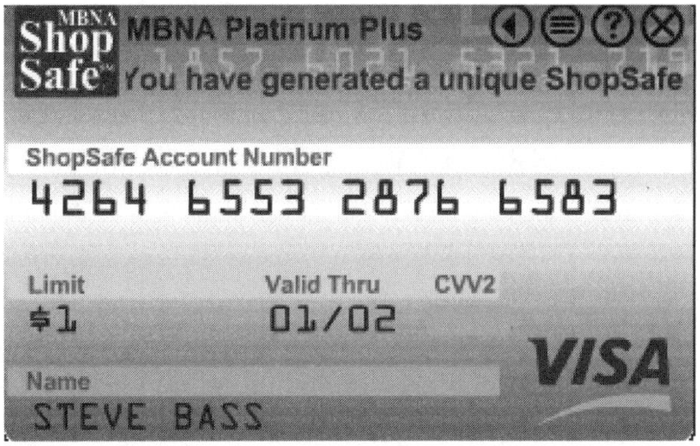

Figure 3-13. MBNA's ShopSafe generates a new, single-use credit card number for each purchase. You can set a dollar amount and an expiration date. Use it if you're leery of using your real credit card number online.

KEEP YOUR PRIVATE DATA PRIVATE

Way too many web sites push me into filling out lengthy forms with info I don't want to share. I use a bookmarklet (yep, that's a real word), a small JavaScript program that fills in every field with the word "anonymous." It's one of dozens of useful bookmarklets, such as stopping the music on a web page, jumping backward three pages, or resizing the window to full screen.

Installation is a snap. Go to *http://www.bookmarklets.com/tools/misc/index.phtml* and scroll down to the AutoFill Anonymous item. Right-click the link and add it to your Favorites list, or better yet, drag the link to your browser's toolbar. Now go surfing. When you encounter a site with a form that demands info, click the AutoFill Anonymous toolbar button you created, and it'll fill in the blanks.

One potential problem: this has become a pretty popular bookmarklet, and the word "anonymous" has been overused. If you use this trick on a site visited by other savvy users, "anonymous" could already be registered.

The fix is easy. Change "anonymous" to another word. Right-click the AutoFill bookmarklet (either the toolbar button you created or the Favorite), and click the Web Document tab. In the "URL:" field you'll see a lo-o-n-n-ng string that starts off like this:

```
javascript:function%20ROIoiW(){var%20i=0,j,A=
'anonymous',D,
```

Just sneak the cursor into the field and use the right arrow key to slide down to `'anonymous'` **and change it to something else, such as** `'anonymous66'`**. Click the OK button and you're done. If you want to see the entire code in this field—with the** `'anonymous66'` **modification—go to *http://snipurl.com/anonm*.**

ZAP MICROSOFT'S PASSPORT

The Annoyance: I just bought a new PC and don't plan to leave the country. So how in the world do I stop that annoying icon from asking me if I want to sign up for a Passport?

The Fix: By now it's probably stopped—Microsoft's perky Passport account.net Messenger appears only the first few times you access the Web. If it's still there—or you're impatient—click the Passport message and when the window appears, select Cancel.

BOOST INTERNET SPEED

The Annoyance: I finally got a fast DSL connection. But guess what: it's not all that great. Downloads are still slow, and browsing is often sluggish.

SPEED-UPS THAT DRAG YOU DOWN

I get ticked off whenever a web accelerator program slows me down—or even stops me from visiting some pages. The reason this happens is that many speed-up utilities fiddle with your PC's Hosts file, which substitutes an IP address for a web site name (your browser can get to the IP address faster than to the name). If the site's IP address changes, you get an error when you try to access the page.

My cut-the-Gordian-knot approach: click Start → Search or Start → Find (depending on your version of Windows) → For Files and Folders; click "All files and folders" in the "All or part of the filename" field, type hosts and click the Search button. Select the file in the search results pane and delete it—Windows will rebuild it from scratch.

The Fix: A number of factors may be affecting your DSL performance. For starters, you may be too far away from the phone company's central switching office (called the CO); the further away you are, the lower the speeds. Even if you're in range, performance can vary due to line quality problems: the wires from the CO to your telephone pole, from the pole to your house, and the phone wiring inside your house. At the very least, call your DSL vendor and have them inspect the outside lines and, if need be (this can be a little expensive), your internal wiring.

You might also be suffering from interference. Make sure any equipment sharing the line with your DSL modem—such as a phone or fax machine—is connected to appropriate filters, which minimize the interference between phone calls and DSL signals. Likewise, keep the DSL modem away from sources of intense electromagnetic fields, such as 900MHz to 2.4GHz portable phones, security alarms, digital phone systems, and PBXs.

Bits still dragging? You can boost your Internet connection speed by tweaking your Registry. One cool way to goose your connection—whether dialup or broadband—is by using the free CableNut utility (*http://snipurl.com/cablenut*) to fine-tune the Internet settings in the Windows Registry. After you install CableNut, use its Registry backup feature for insurance. With the backup in place, choose the profile that matches your Internet connection, save the settings, and reboot your PC. I found a moderate improvement in the DSL speed of my XP system, and a significant boost when using dialup on a Windows 98 PC.

> **Warning. . .**
> Choosing the right profile is important, so visit *http://snipurl.com/cablenut_help* to read CableNut's Help file first.

For still more tweaks, check out the Navas Cable Modem/DSL Tuning Guide (*http://snipurl.com/navas*).

DOWNLOAD MORE THAN TWO FILES

The Annoyance: I was in a frenzy and I tried downloading a bunch of files at once from a freeware site. No matter how many files I try to download, Internet Explorer limits me to just two at a time. How can I open this pipe?

The Fix: For some reason, IE limits you to two simultaneous downloads by default (crazy, I know, especially if you have a high-speed Internet connection).

There's a very easy Registry tweak that increases the number of IE download streams in Windows to 10. Better yet, you don't have to fiddle with the Registry to make this happen. Instead, go to *http://snipurl.com/xp_tweaks* and scroll down to line 55. In the righthand column, you'll find a link labeled "Increase Internet Explorer Downloads to 10." Click this link and run the small *.vbs* file. If you've upgraded to Service Pack 2, the file may cause Windows XP's Security Warning to pop up. Don't be surprised if your computer's firewall or antivirus software also balks; in most cases, you'll have the option to let the download continue. And it's okay to download—it's safe tweak. Once you're done tweaking, restart IE.

Turn Off the Internet

Be careful, boys and girls, you may be responsible for a disaster....

[Warning: I was going to let you muddle your way out on your own, but my O'Reilly editor nixed the idea. So after you create the disaster, just close the browser session by pressing Alt-F4.]

See *http://snipurl.com/turnoff*.

MODEM SPEEDUPS

Here's an example of what it's like to switch from a a 56k dialup modem to a broadband connection: *http://snipurl.com/fastmodem*.

THE PASSWORD BEHIND THE ASTERISKS

The Annoyance: I visited a web site I haven't been to in months, and Internet Explorer automatically inserted my password into the right field. I'd really like to write down the password, just in case, but I can't remember it. Why does Microsoft make it so hard to figure it out?

The Fix: Webster's defines a password as a "secret word that one uses to gain admittance or access to information," so I'm not surprised it's hard for you to retrieve. But it's your password, so use Asterisk Key, a freebie that can show all the passwords hidden behind practically any row of asterisks. Use it wisely, okay? It's available at *http://www.oreilly.com/pcannoyances*.

FIX YOUR BROWSER'S FONT SIZE

The Annoyance: Every other web page I visit has a different font size: one's too small, and the next one's too big. Is it too much to ask to keep the font sizes uniform?

The Fix: In Internet Explorer, select Tools → Internet Options; the General tab should be on top by default. Click the Accessibility button (near the bottom of the dialog box), and check "Ignore font sizes specified on Web pages" box (the wording varies depending on your Internet Explorer version). In Netscape 6 and 7, choose Edit → Preferences, expand Appearance, and select Fonts, then either check "Use my default fonts," check "Always use my font settings," or uncheck "Allow documents to use other fonts," depending on your version.

OPEN ACROBAT READER SEPARATELY

The Annoyance: I just hate it when I try to read a PDF (Portable Document Format) file on a web page and Adobe Acrobat Reader insists on opening right in my browser. On top of that, a small Acrobat applet loads into memory, taking up system resources. Still more grating, that applet doesn't unload when I close the reader.

The Fix: It's simpler, more efficient, and just as fast to open Acrobat Reader separately. First, launch the reader from your Start menu, select Edit → Preferences, choose Options (Internet in Acrobat 6.0), and uncheck the "Display PDF in Browser" box (see Figure 3-14). Now when you select a PDF file while browsing, you'll see a File Download box. The reader starts automatically when you choose Open.

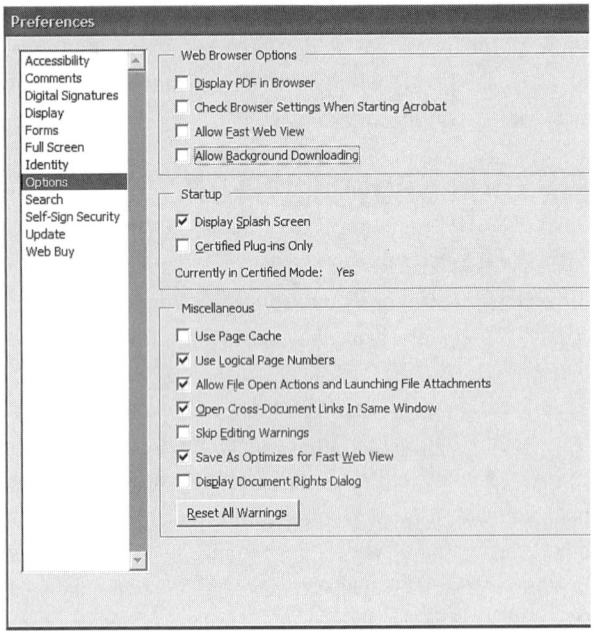

Figure 3-14. You can stop Adobe's Acrobat Reader from opening in your browser with just a few clicks.

On the other hand, if you use the reader integrated with your browser, you can unload the applet after closing your browser: in Windows 98 and Me, press Ctrl-Alt-Delete, select Acrord32, and click End Task. In Windows XP and Windows 2000, right-click the Taskbar, select Task Manager, choose the Processes tab, select Acrord32, and click the End Process button.

GOOGLE ANNOYANCES

GET BACK WHERE YOU STARTED WITH GOOGLE

The Annoyance: When I do a Google search and click a result, it generally leads me to another page, then another, and so on. A half hour later I'm done and want to go back to my original search page and start over, but it's nowhere to be found. (OK, I can find it in my Internet Explorer History, but who needs that hassle?)

The Fix: There's a better way to do this, and it's easy to set up. First, go to *http://www.google.com*. To the right of the search field, click the Preferences link. Scroll down to the very bottom of the Google Preferences page and check "Open search results in a new browser window." Click the Save Preferences and OK buttons to return to the Google home page. Now when you click one of Google's hits, it will launch a new browser window, leaving the original search results untouched.

VIEW GOOGLE'S PDFS IN HTML

It's fairly common to run a Google search and discover the page with the best result is an Adobe PDF file. If you click the PDF link, a copy of Adobe Acrobat Reader opens—a waste of time if you discover the site isn't terrific. A faster way is using Google's "View as HTML" link. The view isn't always pretty, but you can get a quick look at the PDF file's content before deciding to open it in the Reader.

TRACK DOWN SEARCH TERMS IN GOOGLE

The Annoyance: Sometimes, when I search Google and click a result, the term I searched for is nowhere to be found on that page. It's annoying.

The Fix: I've found one solution that works at least half the time: Look in the Google cache. On the last line of each Google search result is a "Cached" link. Clicking it will bring up an older copy of the page that Google has archived. Odds are you'll find the term you were looking for on this page. (To find it, press Ctrl-F, type in the search term, and click the Find Next or Find button.)

But there's one catch. If you followed the instructions in "Get Back Where You Started with Google," you'd expect clicking the cache to open a new browser window. But for reasons understood only in Googleville, it doesn't, no matter what your Preferences say. To open the cached page in a new window, hold down the Shift key while you click the "Cached" link.

GET BETTER RESULTS WITH THE GOOGLE DIRECTORY

The Annoyance: Sometimes Google is a little too good at searching. Who wants to wade through 2.2 million results? There's gotta be a way to pare things down.

The Fix: If I'm looking for a site primarily about my search term—not one that merely mentions or links to it—I use the Google Directory instead. Just click the Directory tab above the search term field, then enter your terms as you normally would. You're also a little more likely to turn up sites created by official associations and organizations, not an obsessive fan site. (Whether that's a good thing is entirely up to you.)

GO MONOLINGUAL WITH YOUR GOOGLE SEARCHES

The Annoyance: I search for a common term and get a zillion results, half of them in Urdu, Klingon, or some other character set I can't read. How can I avoid all the gibberish?

The Fix: Two ways: temporary and permanent (more or less). Here's the temporary one: click the Advanced Search link to the right of the Google search field, fill in your search terms, and in the "Return pages written in" menu, select your native tongue. Then click the Google Search button. The downside: Google will search only part of the Web, so you may miss some pages that have the information you're looking for.

But the next time you do a search, Google will continue to look at pages written in all tongues. If you want Google to always search for pages in a particular language, you'll need to change the Google Preferences page. Click the Preferences link on Google's home page. In the Search Language section, select "Search only for pages written in these language(s)" and check the ones you want Google to look at.

While you're there, you might want to change a few other preferences. For example, I like Google to display 50 results at a time instead of the usual 10. (Go to the "Number of Results" section of the page, click the down arrow or the list box, select 50, and click "Save Preferences.") The extra time it takes to display those results on one page is a fraction of the time it would take to click through five pages of hits.

GOOGLE NEWS YOUR WAY

The Annoyance: In my opinion, Google News supplies the most current news on the Internet. What doesn't make sense is that the News page can't be customized. For instance, I'm not interested in business or sports and don't want to see them.

The Fix: You can indeed have it your way:

1. Click the category link (the headings at the top left of the page), such as Entertainment.

2. Drag and drop the URL in the address field onto an empty spot on an Internet Explorer toolbar, or bookmark it, or put it on a toolbar.

Now you can use that link instead of Google's News tab to launch right to your favorite section. You'll still have access to the other categories listed on the left side of the page.

TWO GOOGLE ANNOYANCES WITHOUT A FIX

No one's perfect, not even Google, the champ of search engines. I'll save you some time because these two annoyances don't have a workaround.

Old is new again. **Want to find only content published in the last three months? Sorry, can't do it. Although the Advanced Search page lets you winnow results by the last three months, six months, or year, Google only looks at the date the page was updated, not the date the material was posted. So the page may have been updated three minutes ago, but the article could still be four years old.**

No news is bad news. **So the summary of a news story appears on your search results, but clicking the link brings you to a dead page, with no way to look at a previous copy of it. Solution? Sorry, there ain't one; Google does not cache news stories.**

INSTANT MESSAGING ANNOYANCES

MAKE AOL INSTANT MESSENGER AN AD-FREE ZONE

The Annoyance: Call me a Web geezer, but I can remember when the online world was virtually ad-free. Now it looks more like a NASCAR event, and AOL Instant Messenger is no exception. My Buddy List sports a little blinking ad window that does nothing but hog space. Worse yet, many of the ads it plasters on my screen are for AOL itself!

The Fix: Erasing ads from AIM is something of a national pastime—type "REMOVE AIM ADS" into a search engine, and you'll get links to a bevy of approaches, including firewall tricks, configuration-file tweaks, and software tools. Problem is, many of these techniques are needlessly complicated, or so long in the tooth they don't work with the current version.

My AIM ad zapper of choice is James Dennis's DeadAIM, which works with AIM 4.8 and up. DeadAIM doesn't just eradicate ads; it also gives you an array of options for tweaking AIM's look and features, including the ability to log chat sessions and make windows semitransparent (two features I like in AIM competitor Trillian). DeadAIM isn't freeware, but it's close enough: at $4.99 (payable in advance via PayPal), it provides loads of bang for your sawbuck. Download DeadAIM from *http://www.jdennis.net*.

An even better deal is Freddy's No Ads for Yahoo! Messenger. Not only can you block ads, you can substitute something in the ad's space. Download *noads.zip* from *http://snipurl.com/noads*.

FIGHT OFF MESSENGER SERVICE ADS

Messenger Service Ads, sometimes known as DirectAds, are the latest craze in spamming. Spammers shower a range of IP addresses, and if you're within that range, you get blasted with an ad. Messenger Service Ads are seen mostly on broadband systems—cable or DSL—and increasingly, dialup connections.

Despite the name, the pop-ups have nothing to do with MSN Messenger or other IM software. This facility has long been used by network administrators to broadcast these messages to others on a LAN. If you're using Windows 95, 98, or Me, don't worry, be happy—you don't have this feature. But if you're using Windows NT, 2000, or XP without a firewall, you may see the ads. There are three free, easy fixes:

* Get a free firewall. It's crazy to be using a computer without one, and as a computing guru said to me, "if you're receiving Messenger Service ads, they're really a symptom of a larger problem easily resolved with a firewall." Zone Labs gives away ZoneAlarm, a firewall that will give you all the protection you'll need. Download a copy at *http://snipurl.com/free_zonealarm*.

  If you don't want a firewall, download Shoot The Messenger, Gibson Research Corporation's Windows Messenger spam elimination freeware utility, from *http://snipurl.com/grc_1*. The site (*http://grc.com*) also has a great explanation of how the ads are broadcast. (And if you're curious about who generates these ads, check out IP-Direct Broadcasting at *http://snipurl.com/ip_broadcast*.)

* Another quick way to stop the ads: select Start→Run, type `services.msc`, and press Enter. In the right pane, scroll down, right-click Messenger, and choose Stop.

BLOCK INSTANT MESSAGING CHAT INVITATIONS

The Annoyance: It's bad enough that my brother-in-law keeps bugging me with instant messages, but I'm frustrated with strangers sending IMs with links to nasty "adult" sites. I often get two or three an hour when I'm using AOL's Instant Messenger, and even more through Microsoft's Messenger. It's enough to make me turn off instant messaging altogether.

The Fix: I used to get annoying chat invites until I changed my IM settings to block everyone except people on my list. The downside is that you'll have to take an extra step and add new contacts to your "allow" or no-block list (or miss out if your long-lost cousin tries to reach you through IM). The following instructions tell you how to change your privacy settings in several different IM clients:

MSN Messenger

Select Tools → Options and click the Privacy tab. Select "All others" in the "My Allow List" pane and click Block.

Yahoo! Messenger

Press Ctrl-P, select Privacy in the Category pane, choose "Ignore anyone who is not on my Friend List" in the top pane, and click OK. Then select Tools → Manage Friend List → Add a Friend (or press Ctrl-A) and add only those people you really want to hear from.

AOL's AIM

From the Buddy List Window, select the Prefs icon or press F3, select Privacy in the Category pane, and select "Allow only users in my Buddy List" (see Figure 3-15).

Trillian

On the default (Cordillera 2.1) skin, click the Earth-like button on the lower left of the window and choose Connection → Connection Manager. You'll need to set chat preferences for each service you're using within

Trillian by highlighting the service and clicking Preferences. Trillian emulates the options you'd find in the original instant messaging service (see Figure 3-16).

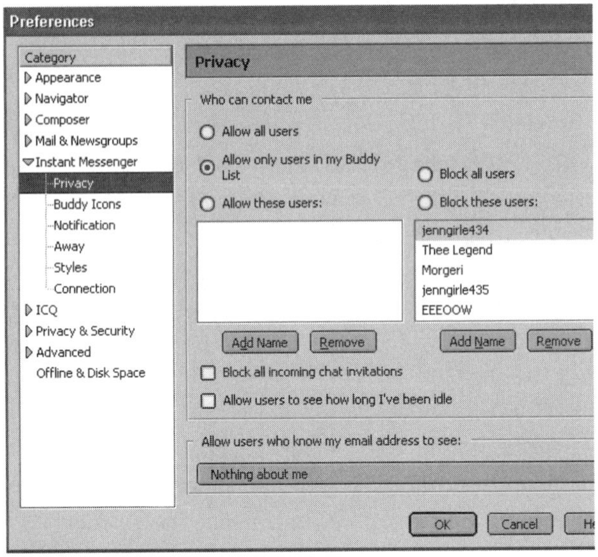

Figure 3-15. Tired of chatty AIM strangers bothering you with inane requests? Block them out using the Preferences dialog box.

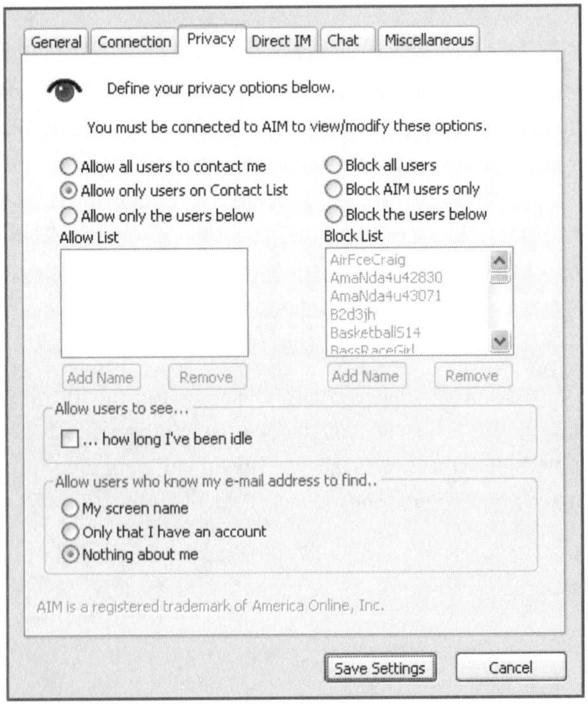

Figure 3-16. Trillian emulates the preferences or options screens from AOL, Yahoo, MSN, IRC, and IRQ.

WHEN AIM OVERSTAYS ITS WELCOME

The Annoyance: I'm hunkering down to get some real work done, and want to shut down AIM for the moment. I click the X to close the Buddy List window, assuming it will shut down AIM. And if this were anything but an instant-messaging program, it would. But all it does is minimize AIM; I'm still signed in and prone to receive IMs from anybody who notices I'm online.

The Fix: On your Buddy List Window's menu, select My AIM → Sign Off. Unless you've changed the default, you'll get a message asking if you're sure; click Yes. You're now logged out, although AIM is still loaded and sitting in the System Tray, sucking up resources. To remove it from the systray, right-click its icon (the little AIM guy) and choose Exit and Yes if you haven't previously checked the "Do not ask me this again" box.

REMOVE UNWANTED ENTRIES FROM YOUR SCREEN-NAME LIST

The Annoyance: Ever mistype your AIM screen name into the logon screen? The misspelled name sticks around and shows up whenever you launch AIM, reminding you that you're a lousy typist.

The Fix: This is one of those annoyances that a truly smart software package should handle itself. If you type in a name that doesn't let you successfully log into AIM, why does the program bother to remember it at all? But at least you can remove it manually.

In the Sign On window, open the Screen Name menu and click the name you want to remove. Then press Delete. Goodbye to bad spelling. This also works with other screen names you want to deep-six—like Uncle Bernie's, who used your PC six months ago without asking permission.

YAHOO! MESSENGER COMES WITH UNWANTED EXTRAS

The Annoyance: I thought I was downloading and installing Yahoo! Messenger. And I was—but I also got the Yahoo! Experience (also known as Yahoo! Essentials), which by default installs a passel of Yahoo-related buttons and bookmarks in Internet Explorer and rewires Internet Explorer's search features to take you to Yahoo!. How can I get rid of this "Experience"?

The Fix: If you haven't installed Yahoo! Messenger yet, sidestepping the Yahoo! Experience is easy: in the install program's Install Options screen, select "Install Yahoo! Messenger only."

If you did install the Experience, getting rid of it is a multi-step pain. First, open the Add or Remove Programs control panel. Scroll down and select Yahoo! Companion; click the Change/Remove button. Use the same process to remove Yahoo! Internet Mail and Yahoo! Messenger Explorer Bar.

Next, undo the changes Yahoo! made to Internet Explorer's search features. If Yahoo!'s Search Explorer Bar isn't open, press Ctrl-E. Click the Customize button on the Search pane's toolbar, and in the dialog box, click Reset. Then click "Autosearch settings" and choose the search provider you had used for Address bar searches—where you type a question mark, a space, and your search term(s)—before you installed Yahoo! Messenger, and click OK. Choose your desired Search interface (Search Assistant, one search service, or Search Companion) and any settings it needs, then click OK. Close and reopen Internet Explorer.

Finally, if you want to erase the favorites (a.k.a. bookmarks) that Yahoo! added, click Favorites, then right-click any Yahoo-related item (such as My Yahoo!) and select Delete. Click Yes to shuttle it to your Recycle Bin.

WINDOWS MESSENGER FILE TRANSFER

Windows Messenger has this really cool-sounding feature that lets you instantly send a file to someone else. You can do this while you're chatting, or you can choose Actions→Send A File Or Photo. You don't have to mess with attaching a file to an email message. (Admit it: half the time you send an email that's supposed to have an attached file, you follow it up a minute later with one that says "Oops, this time I remembered to attach the file!") You aren't constrained by file-size limits imposed by your mail provider or the recipient's mail provider. And the recipient doesn't have to figure out how to save an attached file or work around an email program that blocks certain attachments.

However, sending a file in Windows Messenger sometimes doesn't work. The transfer is probably being blocked by a firewall, either yours or one at the other end. Windows Messenger uses ports 6891 through 6900 for file transfers, and with most firewalls these ports are closed by default. (Actually, Windows Messenger uses only one port to transfer a file, but you can transfer up to ten files simultaneously by opening all the ports in this range.)

How you open the ports depends on the firewall you're using. If you're using the Internet Connection Firewall included with Windows XP, follow these steps:

1. Open the Network Connections control panel.

2. Right-click the Internet connection and choose Properties.

3. On the Advanced tab, click Settings. (If you're connected to the Internet through another computer using Internet Connection Sharing, you'll find the Settings button on the General tab.)

4. On the Services tab, click the Add button.

5. In the description field, type `Windows Messenger file transfer`. In the next field, type the name of your computer. In the two port fields, type `6891` and select TCP.

Repeat the last two steps using different port numbers in the 6891–6900 range if you want to be able to transfer multiple files simultaneously.

DUMP WINDOWS MESSENGER

The Annoyance: Windows loads Windows Messenger every time I run Outlook Express. It drives me nuts! Can I decide when to run Messenger? Or if need be, can I remove it?

The Fix: The answer to both questions is yes. I have a dozen ways to remove the product, none terrific—and they're not always 100% successful. And, of course, some users don't want to blast Messenger off their PCs—they want to load it every so often, but not every time they launch Outlook Express. The omnibus solution is WinMessControl, a handy and free utility available at *http://snipurl.com/WinMessControl*.

Using the program is a no-brainer—just choose one of the following settings:

Disable Windows Messenger Completely
If you select this option, Windows Messenger is disabled completely, and you won't be able to use it in any way. In short, it's uninstalled.

Enable Windows Messenger Without Interfering With Outlook Express
If you select this mode, Windows Messenger is simply enabled. It's available on a menu somewhere, but it's not loaded in the background when you use Outlook Express.

Enable Windows Messenger Completely
This option sets Messenger to its (annoying) default mode.

IM Password Recovery

Now you've done it—you lost the password that gets you into your favorite Instant Messaging program. You lucked out, though, because MessenPass can dig out the encrypted passwords stored on your PC for nearly a dozen IM apps, including AIM, Yahoo Messenger, MSN Messenger, and Trillian. Download the freebie at *http://snipurl.com/mspass*. And yes, MessenPass works only for the person who's logged onto your PC (that's you, right?), so snoopers can't get at your passwords.

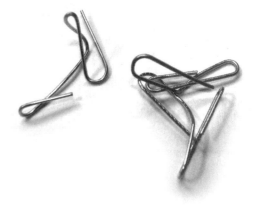

INSTANT MESSAGING NETIQUETTE

1. Just because you see I've come online, you don't have to say hello. Just bask in the pleasure of knowing we're both sitting next to each other in cyberspace.

2. I know you have 3 million happy face variations to choose from. Try not to use them all in one chat session.

3. When I've gotta go, I'll say just that—"gotta go," "c'ya," or maybe just "later." It's annoying when people don't respect that. Don't feel obligated to reply with "goodbye."

4. If you have a lot to say—and it's going to take time for me to digest—put it into email.

5. Did you try chatting and receive my automatic reply that says "busy writing," or "I'm out to lunch"? (And no smart remarks about my being out to lunch for years, okay?) This isn't an answering machine—don't keep blasting away asking if I'm really there. I'm not. If it's really, really urgent, call my answering machine.

6. Maybe you have some of the abbreviations down—BRB (be right back), TTYL (talk to you later), and WTF (what the #&@!), for example—but some of them still stump you. If you don't know what something means, ask; that's what I do.

7. Let someone know if you have to leave the conversation to, say, answer the phone or run to the restroom.

8. If you make a typing error, unless it's really egregious, don't spend time correcting it.

9. Most programs let you see that the other person is typing. Wait until what they're typing pops up on screen before responding.

10. Here's a startling revelation—I may not want to enter a three-way chat room. Ask me before you send the invite, okay?

11. I know that my cousin Judy doesn't like to IM. So even though I know she's online, I never annoy her. It's good netiquette, right Judy?

12. Keep your status current and respect other people's status (I'm not always good at this).

13. If you're IMing with me, avoid popping up a new message every five minutes. If I think the conversation's done, I usually close the IM window.

Microsoft Office
ANNOYANCES

If Windows is the King of Annoyances, Microsoft Office is the Queen. In this chapter, I'll guide you through the strange things that can happen in Word's find feature, design flaws using styles, and printing problems. And I'll help you conquer Public Enemy #1: numbering in Word. I'll also give you nifty workarounds, well-buried Microsoft tricks, and some of the coolest tools and utilities available to help you make Office work smarter.

WORD ANNOYANCES

A FAVORITES MENU FOR WORD

The Annoyance: The recently opened documents list at the bottom of the File menu provides a quick way to pick up where I left off on a file. But there are five specific documents I need to use quite often—just not frequently enough to keep them on that list.

The Fix: You've probably already figured out that you can increase the number of recently used items shown at the bottom of the File menu (if not, see the "Lengthen the List" sidebar on the next page).

If you're looking for a better solution, Word has it. You can add a Work menu to your menu bar or a toolbar that stores those five documents you always need. It works a lot like the Favorites menu in Internet Explorer.

I use the Work menu all the time (see Figure 4-1). For example, I have a document where I jot down ideas and notes for columns or books—and it's always available on the Work menu. It's also really handy for keeping shortcuts to online reference documents. And when I have a flurry of projects and one of the documents I'm working on keeps sliding off the File menu, I add it to the Work menu.

Figure 4-1. In addition to shortcuts to documents I use often, I've customized this Work menu by adding a Remove Menu Shortcut command so that it's easy to remove documents from the menu.

Before you set this up, though, a word of caution: don't let anyone borrow this book. It's a killer to remove files from the Work menu. You'll want these instructions close at hand.

1. To set up a Work menu, select Tools → Customize and click the Commands tab.

2. In the Categories box, scroll down and select Built-In Menus.

3. In the Commands box, scroll down and drag Work to your menu bar or a toolbar (see Figure 4-2). Click the Close button.

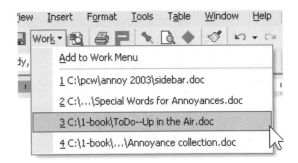
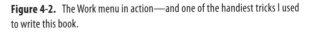

Figure 4-2. The Work menu in action—and one of the handiest tricks I used to write this book.

Easy so far, right? To add a document name to the Work menu, open the document and choose Work → Add to Work Menu. To open a document in the Work menu, just click Work and select the document from the list.

To remove a document name from the menu (here's where it gets tricky), press Ctrl-Alt-Hyphen (use the hyphen key next to zero at the top of the keyboard, not the minus sign on the numeric keypad), open the Work menu, put the enlarged hyphen on the name of the document you want to remove, and click it (Figure 4-3).

> **Warning. . .**
> The big hyphen can delete *any* menu command you click—not just an item on the Work menu. If you press this key combination and change your mind about deleting an item, press Esc.

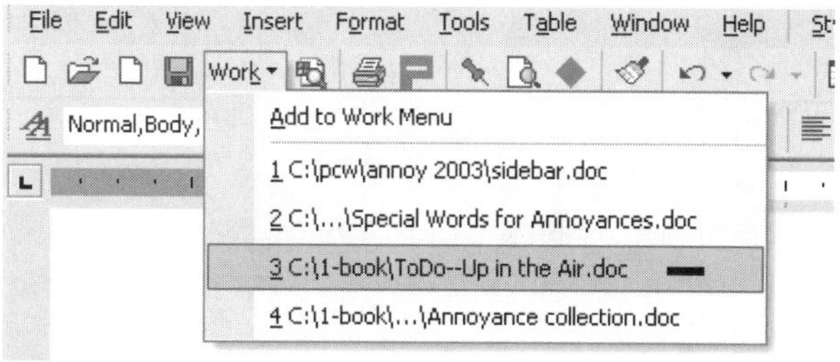

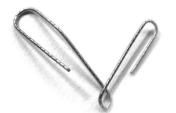

Figure 4-3. Removing an item from the Work menu uses a heretofore unknown keystroke.

With an extra few minutes work, you can bypass the Ctrl-Alt-Hyphen trick by adding an option for removing documents to the Work menu.

1. Select Tools → Customize and click the Commands tab.

2. In the Categories box, scroll down to and select All Commands (see Figure 4-4).

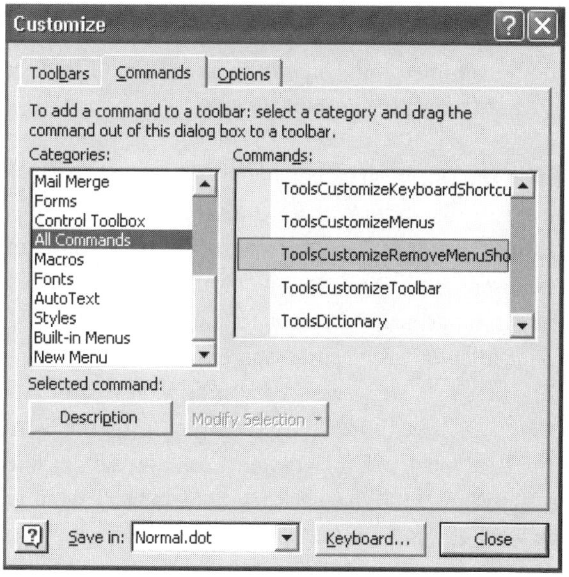

Figure 4-4. Adding the Remove Menu Shortcut option to the Work menu takes a few minutes, but you'll find it convenient if you use the Work menu fairly often.

3. In the Commands box, scroll down to Tools → Customize → RemoveMenuShortCut and drag it to your Work menu. Hover for a moment so that the Work menu opens, then drop it in the menu as the second option.

4. To shorten the command to Remove Menu Shortcut and change its hotkey from T (as in Tools) to R (as in Remove), right-click the new option. In the text box of the Name option, use the mouse to highlight the text between the ampersand (&) and "Remove Menu Shortcut," press Delete and Enter, and click the Customize dialog box's Close button.

LENGTHEN THE LIST

To extend the list of your recently opened documents, go to Tools→Options, click the General tab, and bump up the number in the "Recently used file list" spinner; the maximum is nine.

WHEN WORD'S FIND FEATURE CAN'T SPELL

The Annoyance: One day, out of the clear blue sky, Word's Find started finding incorrect words, like "leave" when I asked for "live," and "tool" for "tell." What's going on?

The Fix: It sounds like you accidentally activated the "Sounds like (English)" feature, which tells Word to find similar-sounding but differently spelled words. To fix the problem, select Edit → Find or press Ctrl-F to open Find, click the More button, and uncheck the "Sounds like (English)" checkbox (Figure 4-5).

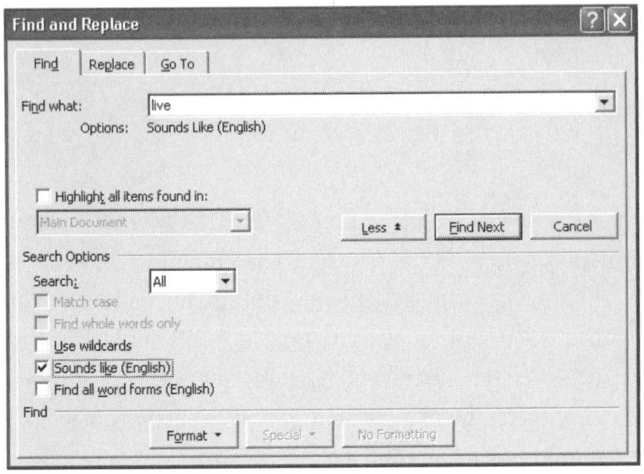

Figure 4-5. Uncheck "Sounds like (English)" (or French if you're in France) to stop Word's Find feature from presenting you with words that sound similar but are spelled differently.

TAKE CONTROL OF YOUR FORMATTING

The Annoyance: I have a handful of words I want to italicize scattered throughout a paragraph. You'd think I could change all the words at once, but I can't figure out how, and I'm going gray changing each individually.

The Fix: Here's an easy solution: hold down the Ctrl key and highlight individual words, sentences, or even paragraphs. Then change the formatting of the highlighted items to anything your heart desires (see Figure 4-6). (Note that this works only in Word 2002 and 2003.)

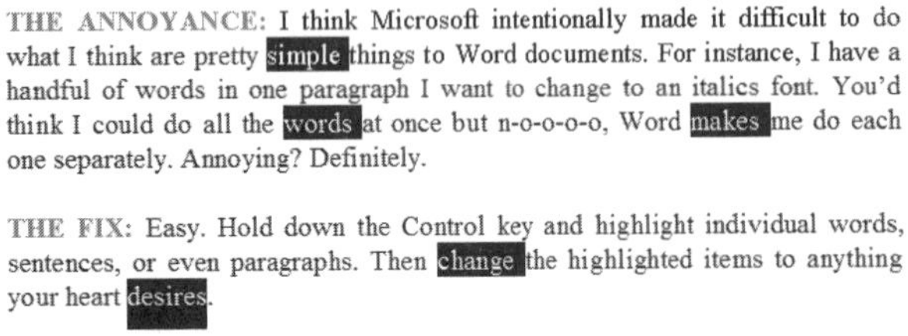

Figure 4-6. Hold down the Ctrl key and highlight the words you want to change, and keep holding it until everything you want is highlighted. Then click the Italics button on Word's Formatting toolbar or change the font using the other font controls on the toolbar.

REMOVE WEIRD LINES IN WORD

The Annoyance: Whenever I type underscores (_) in a Word 2000, 2002, or 2003 document, they're automatically transformed into solid, thick horizontal lines. That's not what I want! Is this a bug?

The Fix: One man's bug...is Bill G's feature. Basically, you're suffering from Word's overly ambitious AutoFormat feature, which turns certain repeated characters into borders. Every time you type more than three asterisks, hyphens, underscores, or equals signs in a row, Word applies a character or paragraph border style (see Figure 4-7). There's an easy—dare I say, gratifying—fix. In Word 2002/2003, select Tools → AutoCorrect, click the "Auto-Format As You Type" tab, and uncheck the "Border lines" box. (In Word 2000, uncheck the Borders box.) Word will now leave these special characters as is.

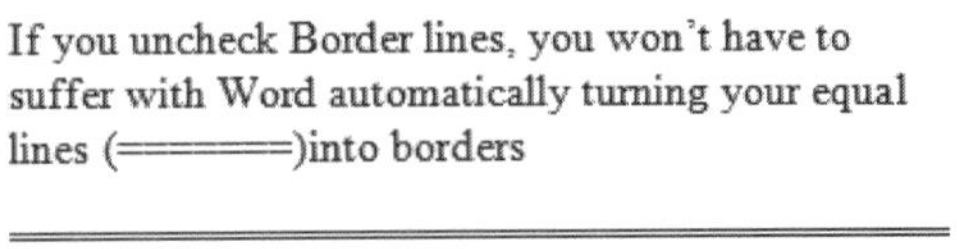

Figure 4-7. Word's alleged feature turns a bunch of equals signs into an annoying border. You can turn this behavior off in a jiffy.

Me, I *like* the way Word turns these characters into borders. But I also occasionally want Word to butt out. The trick: press the magic Undo keyboard shortcut—Ctrl-Z—right after Word creates the border and presto, the border vanishes and turns back into plain characters.

PASTE EMAIL TEXT, NOT WHITESPACE

The Annoyance: Is there a way to slice off a section of whitespace that appears on the left side of a document when I cut and paste an email message?

The Fix: You bet—just use Word's column select mode. Place the cursor at the top of the paragraph and hold down the Alt key. Drag the mouse down and to the right to adjust the size of the marked-off area (you'll see it as a black box or rectangle), and let go of the mouse button when you've marked off what you don't want. Press the Delete key and say adios to the excess (see Figure 4-8).

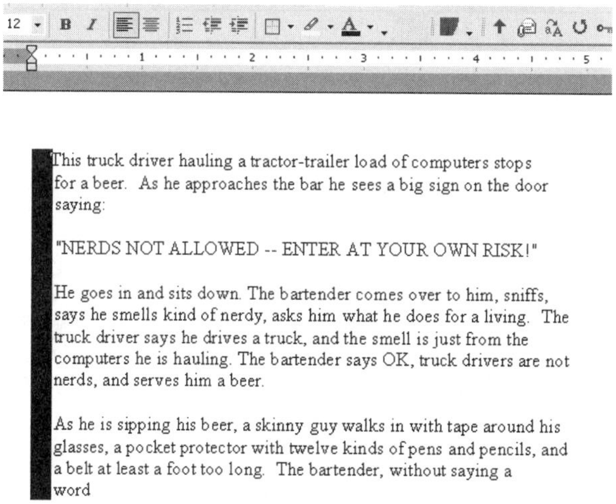

This truck driver hauling a tractor-trailer load of computers stops for a beer. As he approaches the bar he sees a big sign on the door saying:
"NERDS NOT ALLOWED -- ENTER AT YOUR OWN RISK!"
He goes in and sits down. The bartender comes over to him, sniffs, says he smells kind of nerdy, asks him what he does for a living. The truck driver says he drives a truck, and the smell is just from the computers he is hauling. The bartender says OK, truck drivers are not nerds, and serves him a beer.
As he is sipping his beer, a skinny guy walks in with tape around his glasses, a pocket protector with twelve kinds of pens and pencils, and a belt at least a foot too long. The bartender, without saying a word

Figure 4-8. While holding the Alt key, drag your mouse cursor over the area you want to delete.

SPELLCHECK ONE WORD AT A TIME (AND TURN OFF THE RED SQUIGGLES)

The Annoyance: I'm merrily typing away in Word and notice a spelling error. So I bring my cursor back to the word and press F7 to bring up Word's spelling checker. The typo's identified, I correct it, and—here's where I get grumpy—Word insists on spellchecking the entire document.

The Fix: Don't bother with Word's spelling and grammar checking feature unless you really want it to check the entire document. A better approach is to right-click over the misspelling (see Figure 4-9). Word will let you check the individual word—and even let you add it to your AutoCorrect dictionary. By the way, hate those squiggly lines? If they bother you, look at the upcoming sidebar "Dump the Red Spelling Squiggles" to see how to turn them off.

n't bother with Word's spelling
ar chcking feature unless you
it to check
A much be
ight mouse
. Word's
checking
chucking
chocking
choking
cocking
Ignore All
Add to Dictionary
AutoCorrect
Language
Spelling...
ClickStamp Online - Internet Postage
Cut
Copy
Paste
checking
chucking
chocking
choking
cocking
AutoCorrect Options...

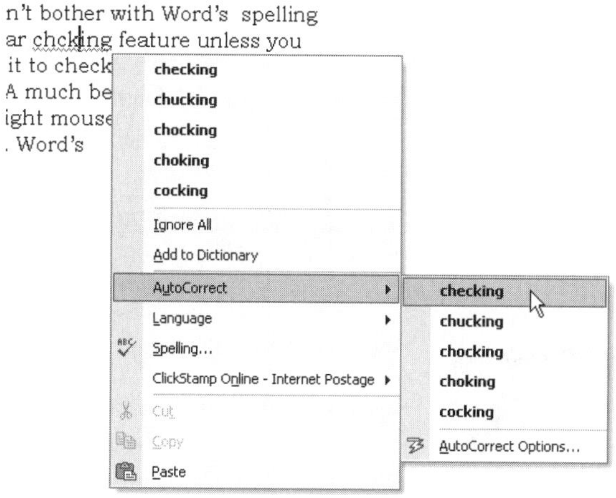

Figure 4-9. If you're checking the spelling of just one word, it's easier to access Word's AutoCorrect feature with the right mouse button.

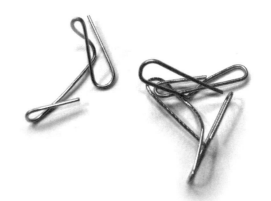

DUMP THE RED SPELLING SQUIGGLES

Do you find the red squiggly underlines pointing out your undernourished spelling skills a little distracting? If so, head for Tools→Options, choose the Spelling & Grammar tab, and uncheck the "Check spelling as you type" box.

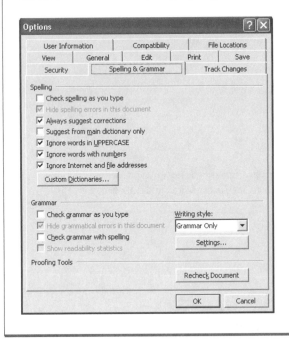

BACK UP YOUR AUTOCORRECTIONS

The Annoyance: I've accumulated eight years of AutoCorrect entries in Word. How can I save it as a file, both for safekeeping and to transfer to the copy of Word on my notebook?

The Fix: Microsoft has a way to move the AutoCorrect file to another PC, but it keeps the feature under wraps on its web site.

- If you use Word 2000, grab a copy of Microsoft's free Word 2000 Supplemental Macros, Macros9.dot, which contains the AutoCorrect backup tool (see Figure 4-10), at *http://www.oreilly.com/pcannoyances*. Download *Macros.exe* from the site, double-click it, and follow the prompts. (Macros9.dot should be installed in *C:\Program Files\Microsoft Office\Office\Samples* or *C:\Samples*. If not, search for Macros9.dot using Windows Explorer.) To use the Macro, open Word, select File → Open, and change "File of Type" in the pull-down menu at the bottom of the dialog to "Document Templates (*.dot)." Select Macros9.dot and click the Open button. In the Security Warning dialog box, check the "Always trust macros from this source" box, and click to Enable Macros. To run the backup macro, click Sample Macros in the little macros box and select AutoCorrect Utility. Click the Backup button and you're ready to roll (Figure 4-11).

Figure 4-10. To back up your AutoCorrect entries, open *support.dot* and click the AutoCorrect Backup button at the bottom of the page to bring up the AutoCorrect Utility tool.

Figure 4-11. The AutoCorrect Utility tool lets you easily back up or restore your AutoCorrect entries.

- If you use Word 2002 or 2003, there's a good chance the file you need is already on your PC. Use Window's Search feature and dig around for *support.dot*.

If it's not on your PC, you can install it through the Control Panel's Add/Remove Programs tool ("Add or Remove Programs" in Windows XP):

1. First, close all your Office applications.

2. Next, open the Add/Remove Programs control panel, click the Install/Uninstall tab (in Windows 98 or Me) or the "Change or Remove Programs" button at top left (in Windows 2000 or XP), and select the entry for Office XP (or Word).

3. Now click the Add/Remove (98 and Me) or Change (2000 and XP) button. (This is tedious, I know, but the payoff's great.) Choose "Add or Remove Features" (see Figure 4-12), click the Next button, find and expand the "Microsoft Word for Windows" entry, and then the "Wizards and Templates" entry.

4. Click the little downward triangle on "More Templates and Macros," choose "Run from My Computer," and click Update (see Figure 4-13).

5. Now that *support.dot* is installed, find it, open it, and follow the directions noted earlier.

If you want to go blind reading Microsoft's lengthy explanation of how the AutoCorrect backup tool works, go to *http://snipurl.com/autocorrect_howto*.

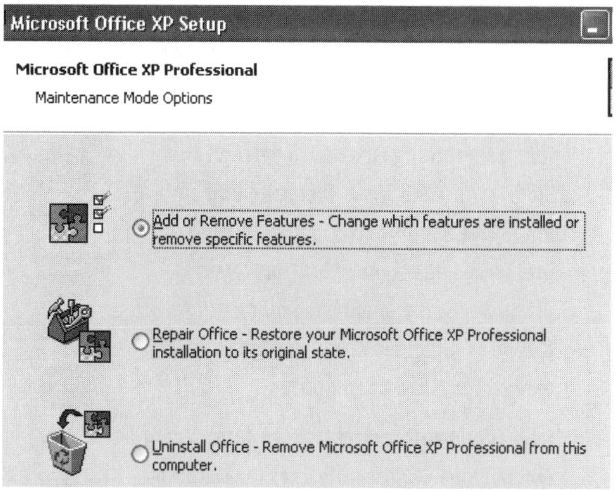

Figure 4-12. Choose "Add or Remove Features" to install more Word templates, including *support.dot*, the file you'll need to run the AutoCorrect backup utility.

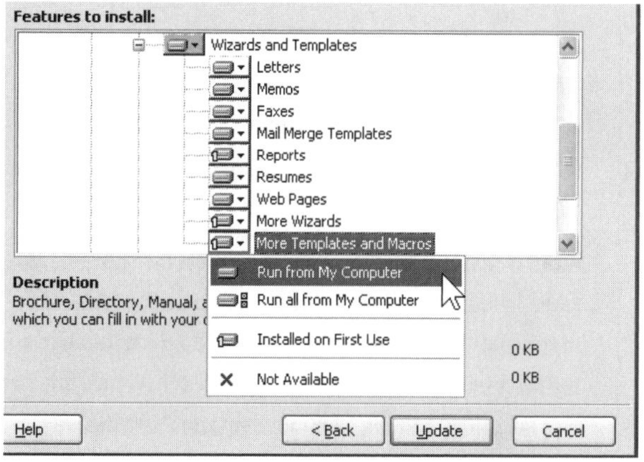

Figure 4-13. Under Wizards and Templates, click the drive icon next to "More Templates and Macros" and select "Run from My Computer."

OUTFOX WORD'S AUTOCORRECT

The Annoyance: When I create an AutoCorrect entry, such as "del" for "DeltaTree," the full text appears whenever I type "del" at the beginning of any word. How do I stop this?

The Fix: Put an "x" in front of any abbreviation you create in AutoCorrect to prevent AutoCorrect from expanding real words that it thinks are abbreviations. For instance,

TURN OFF WORD'S SPELLCHECKER AND USE AS-U-TYPE

Word's spell check does a good job, but I found something I like much better: Fanix Software's $49.95 As-U-Type. Shelling out money for a feature that's already built into Word—heck, most text-processing products—may sound like lunacy, but As-U-Type's features give me an edge in nearly everything I do on a computer.

As-U-Type's autocorrect feature doesn't care where I am—it instantly fixes the spelling errors I make every place I type words: chat rooms, forms on web pages, Internet forums, accounting apps, and dialog boxes in any program.

Some of As-U-Type's tricks are similar to Word's AutoCorrect features. For instance, when I'm frantically typing a mile a minute, As-U-Type corrects any words that have two initial capital letters instead of just one.

It can transform specific letter sequences into phrases, so when I email my editor, I only have to type the letters "ila" to tell him "I'm late again, but we had a 7.5 earthquake and the driver of an 18-wheeler lost control of his truck, plowed into my office, and ran over my computer!" (By the way, As-U-Type imports Word's existing AutoCorrect list. Details are at *http://snipurl.com/asutype_export*. If you use Word's AutoCorrect, turn it off when you use As-U-Type, to prevent conflicts.)

As-U-Type is so smart that it can track not only common mistakes—spelling "receive" as "recieve," say—but also misspellings that are beyond belief. An example? Thanks to As-U-Type, you can forget about being embarrassed by typing "imbearissed," "embraissed," "emgarrassek," or any of the other variations As-U-Type corrected for me. (See the figures for a sample of my incredible misspellings.) Try out As-U-Type by downloading it from *http://www.oreilly.com/pcannoyances*.

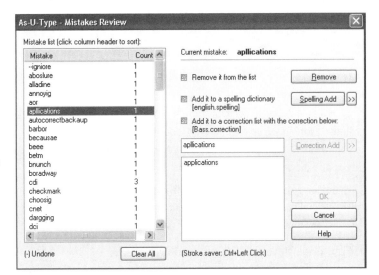

Top: As-U-Type corrects errors no matter where you're typing—in chat rooms, dialog boxes, and even Word. It takes a few minutes to correct errors, and from then on As-U-Type automatically corrects the misspelling. Bottom: How many ways can you spell embarrassed? I'm dyslexic, so I think I hold the record.

"xat" expands to "Altadena", and "xmd" becomes "Maryland", but if you type "MD" or "at", they're ignored. (See Figure 4-14.)

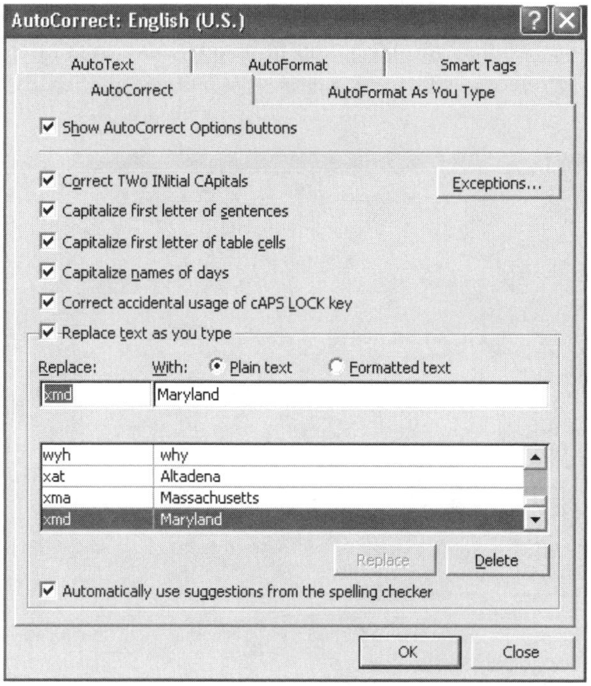

Figure 4-14. If you add the letter "x" in front of any abbreviation you create, you'll avoid the problem of AutoCorrect expanding real words that look like abbreviations.

Give Word's Dictionary the Boot

One of my favorite utilities is WordWeb, a free thesaurus and dictionary combo that surpasses Word's by a long shot. WordWeb can check a word for antonyms as well as synonyms, and it also lists similar words and checks whether the word can be used as a noun, verb, adjective, or adverb. Grab a copy of the freebie from *http://www.oreilly.com/pcannoyances*. You can install WordWeb as a standalone tool for when you're, say, writing email, or as a Word toolbar. Head to the Word-Web site at *http://snipurl.com/wordweb_word* and check the Unsupported Extras section for instructions.

GET THERE SOONER WITH BOOKMARKS

The Annoyance: Shift-F5 lets me jump to previous spots I've revised in a Word document, but it's an inefficient way to move around in a document over 10 pages long. I tried adding asterisks to the document and jumping to them using Find, but that's not a great workaround.

The Fix: Use bookmarks.

To add a bookmark anywhere in your document:

1. Place the cursor where you want the bookmark. (And yes, you can bookmark a single, contiguous selection.)

2. Select Insert → Bookmark, enter a name for the bookmark, and click the Add button. (You can also press Ctrl-Shift-F5 to enter a new bookmark or jump to an existing one.)

To find a bookmark:

1. Press F5 to open the Find and Replace dialog box with its Go To tab on top.

2. If you know the name of the bookmark, just type it in and press Enter, ignoring the default Page selection.

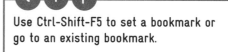

> **t i p**
> Use Ctrl-Shift-F5 to set a bookmark or go to an existing bookmark.

If you need to pick the name from a list, select Bookmark in the "Go to what" pull-down menu, and in the "Enter bookmark name" pull-down menu, select your bookmark. Click the Go To button or press Enter, and you're immediately transported to your bookmark.

> **t i p**
> Don't start the name with a number or use a space in the name—Microsoft is adamant about this. But you can use an underscore, as in *last_chapter*.

REMEMBERING WORD SHORTCUTS

The Annoyance: I know Word has a scazillion keyboard shortcuts, and I can rarely remember them all. Is there a trick to learning them without resorting to—gasp!—writing them on a piece of paper?

The Fix: If you have trouble remembering what Word's Function keyboard combinations do, the program itself can help. In all versions since Word 2000, just choose Tools → Customize, click the Toolbars tab, check the Function Key Display box, and click Close. Now when you hold the Alt, Shift, or Ctrl keys, individually or in combination, a Function key toolbar on the bottom of the screen changes, listing the functions. Click any item in the toolbar to run it (see Figure 4-15). If the toolbar takes up too much screen real estate, grab the vertical bar at the left end, and flip and drag it elsewhere on the page.

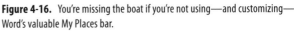

Figure 4-15. If you can't remember Word's scazillion keyboard shortcuts, get yourself a free cheat sheet.

FAST JUMPS TO FAVORITE FOLDERS IN OFFICE

The Annoyance: I know about changing the five favorites on the left in a File → Open dialog box for most Windows applications. (See the sidebar "End Annoyances with Tweak UI" in Chapter 2.) How about a way to do the same thing in Office's File and Open dialogs?

The Fix: Starting with Office XP, you could add up to 256 items to the My Places bar—the panel on the left side of the Open and Save As dialog boxes. (And no, I haven't added 256 items to the My Places bar; 13 entries is more than enough. See Figure 4-16.) These items are tremendously handy for navigating to folders you access often; you can also add, remove, and rename items in a flash.

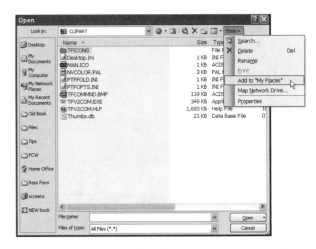

Figure 4-16. You're missing the boat if you're not using—and customizing—Word's valuable My Places bar.

To add an item to the My Places bar:

1. Select File → Open in any Office program. (Or select File → Save As and follow the steps below.)

2. In the Open dialog box, select the item—a folder, file, or even a drive that you want to add in the contents pane.

3. In the "Look in" list, click, say, My Documents.

4. In the contents pane, click My Received Files.

5. In the Open dialog box, add it to My Places bar by selecting Tools → Add to "My Places."

The Items You Can't Change

You can't rename or delete Office XP and 2003's default items—History, My Documents, Desktop, Favorites, My Network Places, My Computer, and My Recent Documents—unless you want to go through a convoluted Registry hack. A simpler way? Move 'em out of the way. Just right-click an item and select Move Up or Move Down.

PLACES BAR WITH PIZZAZZ

If you want a faster, far easier way to customize the Office Places bar, get the WOPR Places Bar Customizer at *http://snipurl.com/placesbar*. Granted, it's $15, but navigating to folders is speedy and you can change the item's icon. (See the figure to see how I've set up my Places Bar.) Different versions of WOPR support Office 2000 through 2003.

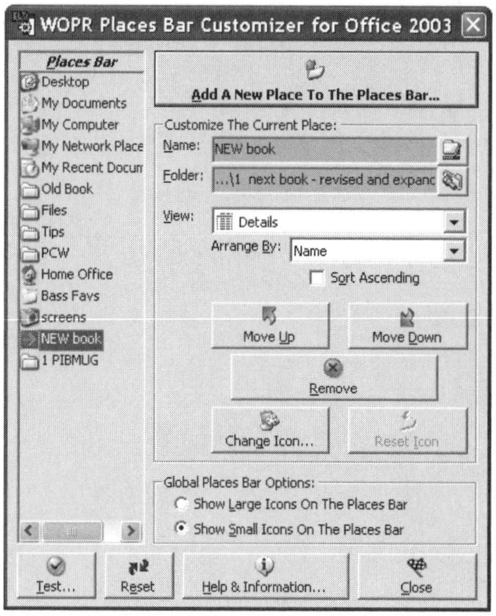

OPEN WORD FILES—ALL IN A ROW

The Annoyance: I often have 10 Word documents open, and navigating among them isn't fun. I can use Word's silly Window → Arrange All feature or just head for the Windows menu and pluck the docs from there. But there's gotta be a better solution.

The Fix: You probably already know about Windows XP's "Group similar taskbar buttons" function. (If not, right-click the Start button, choose Properties, click the Taskbar tab, and check the "Group similar taskbar buttons" box.) Word lacks this logical equivalent feature, but the free DocuBar template can line up all your open documents in one horizontal toolbar, so switching among multiple docs takes a single click. (See Figure 4-17.) With another click, you can tile and un-tile documents. Want to hide DocuBar? Click a button added to Word's toolbar and it's out of sight.

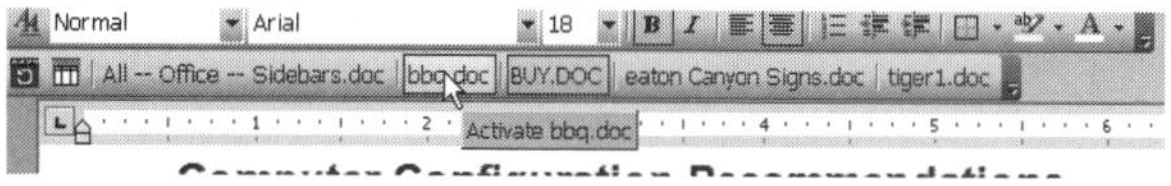

Figure 4-17. DocuBar is a free Word add-in that gives you what Word doesn't—an easy way to work your way through multiple open documents.

Installing DocuBar is pretty straightforward. First, download the *.dot* file at *http://snipurl.com/docubar.*

1. Copy the template to your Word Startup directory.
2. To find out what Word's Startup directory is, choose Tools → Options (in Word) and select the File Locations tab. Look at the Startup line to see which folder to use. Select the Startup line and click the Modify button if you can't see the entire path. (It's probably *C:\Documents and Settings\<username>\Application Data \Microsoft\Word\Startup.*)
3. If you don't see DocuBar after launching Word, you may have to copy the *.dot* file to *C:\Program Files\Microsoft Office\Office\Startup.*

The next time you open Word, DocuBar will be waiting to serve you.

REVEALING CODES

The Annoyance: Word, no matter what the version, embeds unseen fonts, strange commands, and heaven knows what else all over my document. If I cut and paste from one document to another, the pasted text's attributes are often changed. The source is 12-point Times New Roman, but when I copy a section to another file, it's set in 10-point Arial.

The Fix: I'll bet you're frustrated, *especially* if you know about WordPerfect's Reveal Codes, the super feature that lets you see every trace of formatting in a document. It's an indispensable tool for finding the bizarre, picayune formatting problems that can turn parts of your document into gibberish. For fun, first try Format → Reveal Formatting, Microsoft's half-baked try at the feature in Word 2002 XP. Disappointing, isn't it?

Take one look at what Levit & Jones' CrossEyes add-on reveals and you'll be blown away. (Check Figure 4-18 for a taste of what CrossEyes does.) The $49.99 program takes you behind the curtain in Word. Click the CrossEyes

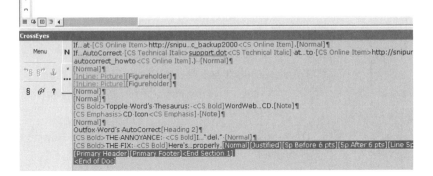

Figure 4-18. CrossEyes is miraculous at revealing all of Word's idiosyncratic formatting codes. Unlike Word's undernourished Reveal Formatting, CrossEyes pulls back the curtains and shows you every nitty-gritty detail.

icon on Word's Toolbar to split the screen horizontally into two windows—the document above, corresponding text and formatting codes below. You see tables, sections, field codes, and all character, paragraph, and style formats. The two windows work in concert: move the cursor in either window, and you go to the corresponding location in the other.

CrossEyes lets you do more than just view the formatting. You can excise misbehaving formats in the code-revealing window, or copy and paste to apply formatting elsewhere in the document. You can even enter and edit text in the code window. CrossEyes is a little pricey, but it's vital for power Word users. It works with Word 97 through Word XP, and with Windows 95 and up. There's a trial version at *http://www.oreilly.com/pcannoyances*.

PASTE THE TEXT, NOT THE FORMATTING

The Annoyance: I often grab text or the URL from a web page and copy it into a Word document. When I paste, I want to get only the text, *not* all the formatting junk from the web page.

The Fix: There's not one, not two, but three slick ways to get around what I think is one of Word's biggest annoyances:

- The least elegant but totally effective method is to insert the text using Edit → Paste Special and click Unformatted Text, as shown in Figure 4-19. You'll paste in text with no formatting at all. This trick is *very* handy, and without it, writing this book would have been a horror.

- A slicker approach is to create a Paste Special macro. Mine's assigned to Alt-F1. Check the "Make a Macro in a Minute" sidebar (a little later in this chapter) to create a macro. It'll save you lots of keystrokes.

- If you're using Word 2002 (a.k.a. Word XP) or later, you're going to love Paste Options. Enable it from Tools → Options: choose the Edit tab and the "Show Paste

Options buttons" box. Now whenever you paste—either with Ctrl-V, with the right mouse button, or by dragging and dropping—a little clipboard button will appear. (Careful: if you keep typing, the button vanishes.) Click the button, and you can choose to keep the copied text's original formatting, match the destination formatting, or paste the text only. (See Figure 4-20.) You can even apply a style.

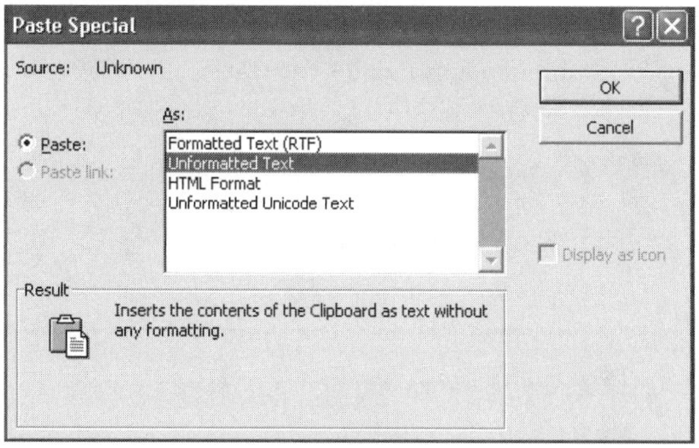

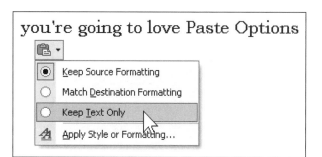

Figure 4-19. Make sure you choose Unformatted Text to strip out the fonts and formatting codes you don't want when you paste web text into a document.

Figure 4-20. Word's Paste Options is a cool tool available only since Word XP. Take advantage of it for quickly converting font-and HTML-ridden data into plain text.

INSIDE A MACRO

You may be unfamiliar with macros. Want to see a weird photo that shows how a macro works? Sure you do: *http://snipurl.com/neat_macro.*

FIND FASTER WITHOUT THE DIALOG BOX

The Annoyance: I'm using Word's Find function, plowing through a humongous document, trying to see where I've used the word "Windows". But Word's Find dialog box keeps blocking the part of the document I want to see.

The Fix: That used to happen to me, too, until I found Word's Previous Find and Next Find buttons. Start a search the usual way: open the Find dialog with Edit → Find (or with Ctrl-F), enter the word or phrase you want to find, and press Enter. Close the Find dialog with Esc and head for the double triangles at the bottom of the vertical scrollbar (see Figure 4-21). Click the lower one to search down in the document; the upper icon searches up. Ctrl-PageDown and Ctrl-PageUp do the same thing.

Figure 4-21. Click the upper or lower double triangles to repeat a previous word or phrase search without opening the Find dialog.

TURN OFF AUTOMATIC HYPERLINKS

The Annoyance: When I type a URL or email address into a document, Word automatically creates a hyperlink. I know many people like this feature, but can the default be no hyperlink?

HYPERLINKS EXPOSED

If you need to see an embedded URL right away, press Alt-F9, which prefaces all URLs with {HYPERLINK.

You can turn off the hyperlink feature in WordPerfect, too. Click Tools → Quick-Correct, select the SpeedLinks tab, and uncheck the "Format words as hyperlinks when you type them" box.

The Fix: In Word, click Format → AutoFormat and click the Options button. Under Replace, uncheck "Internet and network paths with hyperlinks." Click OK and then Close or Cancel (unless you want to autoformat the document).

MAKE A MACRO IN A MINUTE

Word macros can capture—and play back—a combination of keystrokes and mouse-issued commands, automating any number of dreary operations.

The quickest way to create a macro is to have Word record what you do:

1. Choose Tools → Macro → Record New Macro. In the Record Macro dialog box, type a name for the macro in the "Macro name" field (don't use spaces), as shown at the top of the figure (see right).

2. Assign the soon-to-be-recorded macro to either a toolbar button or, in this example, a keystroke combination. In the latter case, click the Keyboard button and actually press the keys you want to use (see bottom left). If the shortcut keys are already in use, you'll get a warning; unless you want another big Word annoyance, use a different set of keystrokes (see bottom right).

3. Click OK. The Record Macro dialog box vanishes, and a small floating toolbar with the Stop Recording button appears. The Macro Recorder keeps track of your mouse clicks and keystrokes. Click the Stop Recording button when you're done, and your keystrokes and mouse clicks (but not mouse movements) are saved for posterity.

AVOID INADVERTENT BROWSING

The Annoyance: My boss sends me Word documents filled with embedded URLs. They look like plain text except they're blue and underlined, and when I inadvertently click one, Word turns into a quasi-browser, adds things to the toolbar, and heads for the site.

The Fix: There are two ways to get rid of irritating hyperlinks:

- In Word 2000, move the cursor over the hyperlink, right-click (careful—don't left-click), and select Hyperlink → Remove Hyperlink.
- The same thing works in Word 2002 and later. But try this trick instead. Open Tools → Options, click the Edit tab, and check the "Use CTRL + Click to follow hyperlink" box (see Figure 4-22). If you Ctrl-click a URL, Word will hop online and find the site. Just click a URL, and nothing happens. When the checkbox is not selected, you get the old annoying behavior.

![Options dialog box with Edit tab selected, showing the "Use CTRL + Click to follow hyperlink" checkbox checked]

Figure 4-22. If you check the "Use CTRL + Click to follow hyperlink" box, you'll be able to see URLs in a Word document, but you won't turn Word into a browser if you click one.

SMARTER PRINTING WITH MACROS

The Annoyance: Sometimes I want to print only the page I'm viewing; other times, I want to print just a few lines I've selected on that page, such as a shopping list. But either way, Word prints the whole document when I click the printer icon on the toolbar.

The Fix: Create a macro for each task. The step-by-step instructions in the sidebar "Make a Macro in a Minute" (earlier in this chapter) will show you how to do this in less than, well, a minute. Name the macros "A_PrintPage" and "A_PrintSelect" to make them easier to find later.

When the macros are created, assign them to their own toolbar buttons. Here's how:

1. Right-click a blank area of a toolbar in Word, choose Customize, and click the Commands tab.
2. In the Categories list, click Macros, find the two macros in the Commands list (see why those naming conventions were valuable?), and drag them (one at a time) to the toolbar. Make sure you drop the macro in the active toolbar area; if you don't, no button will be created.

SEE ALL YOUR MENU OPTIONS

The Annoyance: Office 2000 and Office XP insist on hiding menu options that I haven't used for a while. They call it a feature. I call it a pain.

The Fix: "Custom" menus are the default in Office, but if you change this setting in one Office application, it affects every other installed Office program in one fell swoop. In Word, select Tools → Customize, select the Options tab, and check the "Always show full menus" box. Voilà: no more à la carte Office menus.

SET PREFERRED VIEW ONCE AND FOR ALL

The Annoyance: Word always opens documents in Normal view, but I prefer Preview (in Word 2002, Print Layout view).

The Fix: You can switch views with shortcut keys: Ctrl-Alt-P gets you to Preview or Print Layout view, and Ctrl-Alt-N takes you back to Normal view. I hardwired the view I like best by editing *normal.dot* (Word's Global Template) as follows:

1. Close Word and use Start → Find → Files or Folders (Start → Search → For Files or Folders in Windows XP) to locate *normal.dot* on your hard disk. Right-click it (or the appropriate filename if more than one are found) and select Open Containing Folder.

2. Back up the original *normal.dot* file. Hold down the Ctrl key, drag *normal.dot* to a blank spot in the same folder, and release the mouse button. The file is named "Copy of normal.dot". Press F2 and name the copy *default.dot*.

3. Right-click *normal.dot* and choose Open; don't double-click the file, because that just opens a new document.

4. Make whatever modifications you want: change the fonts, remove toolbar items, or even—ta-da!—make Preview the default view.

5. Save *normal.dot* and close it.

The next time you open Word, the program will have all your new settings.

ZOOM IN WORD AND EXCEL

The Annoyance: I often get Word documents from a buddy who sets the fonts on his 15-inch CRT at a space-saving 10 points. On my high-end LCD, the fonts look minuscule. Of course, the opposite occurs, too: when he opens my Word docs the fonts are humongous. What's the solution?

The Fix: The standard toolbar in Word (and Excel) has a Zoom box with a percentage setting. Simply increase or decrease the number to zoom in or out as you please. A quicker way: press the Ctrl key as you roll your mouse wheel up (for zooming in) or down (for zooming out). This trick doesn't actually change the font size, merely the way it appears onscreen. By the way, if the Ctrl-mouse wheel combination doesn't work, you may need to change an existing setting, such as Pointer Speed or Pointer Acceleration. Upgrading your mouse driver may also do the job.

GET THE INSIDE SCOOP ON YOUR SOFTWARE

Buried deep within Windows is System Information, a cool diagnostic tool that helps me unearth gazillions of details about my PC. For instance, I can review Word's settings and learn which file converters are installed; I can also scrutinize a comprehensive list of my system's hardware resources and components. System Information's Tools menu gives me access to five more diagnostic tools, including Dr. Watson and Network Diagnostics. The tool also gives you quick access to Win XP's System Restore. It may be buried in Windows (select Start→Programs→System Tools→System Information), but Word pops it open with just Ctrl-Alt-F1.

MAKE OFFICE DOCS PRIVATE

The Annoyance: I sent a Word document to a coworker and was stunned when she somehow figured out exactly who else edited the file. How'd she find out?

The Fix: Privacy paranoiacs take note! When you save a Word, Excel, or PowerPoint document, all sorts of your personal baggage goes along with it (depending on your version of Office): Smart Tags, hidden text, a list of everyone who worked on the document and how long, and more. For example, open up a Word doc and select Files → Properties and browse through the tabs. Scary, huh?

The good news is that you can make your Word, Excel, and PowerPoint XP and 2003 documents slimmer and safer by removing hidden information, thanks to Microsoft's free Remove Hidden Data add-in at *http://snipurl.com/Office_data*. Close all your Office apps before you install the tool, and when you reopen them, you'll see a new entry on the File menu about a third of the way down—Remove Hidden Data. You'll have to run this add-in for each file and in each application. The tool creates a new document, so your original is preserved. Be careful, though. If you open and edit this new document, you'll have to run the Remove Hidden Data tool again.

Quick Word Privacy Tip

To save Word XP and 2003 files with all your tracked changes, comments, and personal data stripped out, select Tools → Options, choose the Security tab, and make sure both the "Warn before printing, saving, or sending a file that contains tracked changes or comments" and "Remove personal information from this file on save" boxes are checked. Note that this option doesn't remove as much hidden information as Microsoft Office's Remove Hidden Data add-in, but it is a lot quicker.

SOMETHING ABNORMAL ABOUT NORMAL.DOT

The Annoyance: When I create a new, blank document, I expect it to be blank. But clicking the New Blank Document button on the toolbar (which is equivalent to choosing File → New and selecting Blank Document) sometimes opens a new document that already contains text or graphics. What is this stuff? Where did it come from?

The Fix: When you request a new blank document, Word creates a new document based on the *normal.dot* template file. A template can contain text and graphics (many templates include common elements, such as a letterhead, basic contract text, and so on). A template can also include macros. The most likely cause of your woes is something in the *normal.dot* file.

But wait, there's more! Word can be configured to load one or more "global templates"—templates that always load, such as *normal.dot*. These templates can contain text, graphics, styles, macros, toolbar buttons...you get the idea.

The quick-and-dirty solution is to start Word using the Run command (select Start → Run). Starting Word with the command `winword /a` causes it to start with a new document that's truly blank. No global templates—including *normal.dot*—are loaded.

NEW SPEAK

Looking for help writing snappy sentences that make you sound e-commerce savvy? Or maybe you need to write a meaningless report packed with New Economy nonsense? Just use The Web Economy BS Generator at *http://snipurl.com/BS_generator*.

A more lasting solution is to clean up (or re-create) your *normal.dot* file and remove any global templates. First, find your *normal.dot* file, which is buried in the folder *Documents and Settings*. Right-click it, choose Open, delete the stuff you don't want, and save it. An easier alternative is to simply rename *normal.dot* (call it *xnormal. dot* or *normal.xdot*, for example). The next time you start Word, it'll create a new, clean *normal.dot*.

To remove global templates, start Word and choose Tools → Templates and Add-Ins. In the list of global templates, select each item and then click Remove. (If the Remove button is grayed out, the selected item is in the *\Documents and Settings%UserProfile%\Application Data\Microsoft\Word\ Startup* folder; the only way to banish such items is to move them from that folder.)

FOR FONT FANATICS ONLY

Bembo's Zoo is a must-see web site for font fanatics. (Besides, you were ready for a break.) See *http:// snipurl.com/bembo*.

A BETTER VIEW OF YOUR PRINT LAYOUT

The Annoyance: I like Word's Print Layout view, but the space between the bottom of one page and the top of the next is considerable, and a good chunk of screen space is wasted. It doesn't leave much room to admire my clever prose.

The Fix: If you have Word 2002 or Word 2003, click the gray area between two pages while you're in Page Layout view. The headers, footers, margins, and gray space between all the pages in the document disappear and are replaced by a bold black line. You're still in layout view, but with a lot more usable stuff visible, as shown in Figure 4-23.

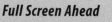

Full Screen Ahead

Another way to make better use of your screen real estate (and this one works in all versions of Word) is to choose View → Full Screen. This view takes some getting used to because the menu bar, all toolbars (except for a floating Full Screen toolbar, which contains a single Close Full Screen option), and the scrollbars disappear, leaving almost the entire screen for your document. While in Full Screen view, you can access menu commands from the keyboard or by moving the mouse pointer to the top of the screen. To exit Full Screen view, simply press Esc.

To restore the full Page Layout view (which you'll need to do if you're editing the headers and footers, for example), click the line separating the pages. When you save the document, the last page layout setting (full or scrunched) is saved with the document. You can change this feature's default setting by visiting Tools → Options, clicking the View tab, and setting or clearing the White Space Between Pages checkbox.

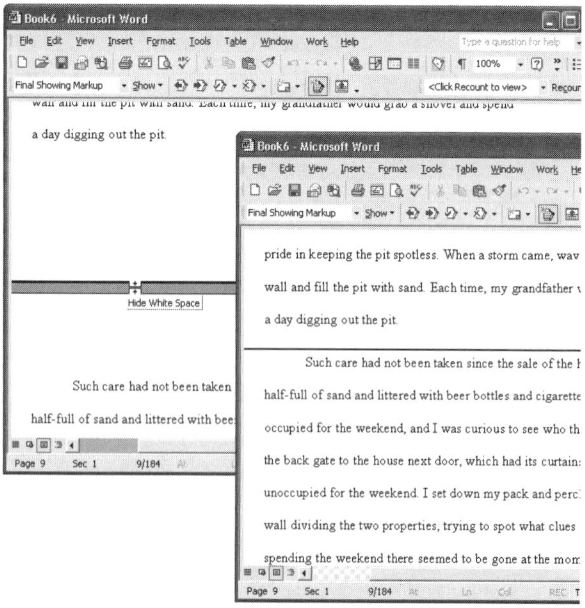

Figure 4-23. Clicking between pages compresses all the space between margins to a single line.

WHEN AUTOCORRECT GETS CARRIED AWAY

The Annoyance: I sometimes need to type Latin plant names, and as soon as I hit the spacebar, Word has this nasty habit of changing the arcane words without so much as a warning. For example, if I type "Purshia tridentata" (that's bitterbrush, in case you're wondering), Word almost imperceptibly changes the last letter to an "e". Usually, if Word doesn't recognize a word, it applies a red squiggly underline, and I'm okay with that. But I don't like these sneaky changes.

THE MYSTERIOUS "SAVE CHANGES" DIALOG BOX

Every time I open a document just to print it, Word asks if I want to save changes when I close it. But I didn't *make* any changes! What's going on?

Word prompts you to save changes even if *it* made the changes, not you. What's going on here is that Word is updating the fields in the document before it prints. A *field* is a code that is replaced by text. Fields are commonly used to print the page number on each page, to print a date, and many other items that can change. The mere act of updating fields counts as a change, even if no field results change; hence the reminder to save the document before closing it.

The easiest way to avoid the problem is to ensure that your document contains no fields—a totally impractical solution for many documents. You can try going to Tools → Options, clicking the Print tab, and clearing the Update Fields checkbox; doing so is supposed to prevent Word from updating the fields before printing (and, therefore, your document won't change), but in my experience this doesn't always work. You could automatically blow off the "Save changes?" dialog box in various ways, but that would be pretty dangerous, since it would also discard changes you intended to save.

Bottom line? Get used to it.

The Fix: To stop this nonsense, open Tools → AutoCorrect (AutoCorrect Options in Word 2002) and uncheck the "Automatically use suggestions from the spelling checker" box. This feature corrects typing mistakes when the word you type is very close to a word in the dictionary, but it's often too smart for its own good, particularly with foreign terms. Turn it off.

You have an alternative solution if you're using Word 2002 or later. Whenever Word makes a correction like this, it adds a "smart tag," which appears as a small blue bar underneath the word when you hover the mouse pointer over the word. Click the blue bar and a small menu appears (as shown in Figure 4-24), allowing you to correct the "correction" or tell Word to stop changing a particular word. (If you later change your mind, go to Tools → Auto-Correct Options, click the Exceptions button, and on the Other Corrections tab, remove words that you want Word to correct.)

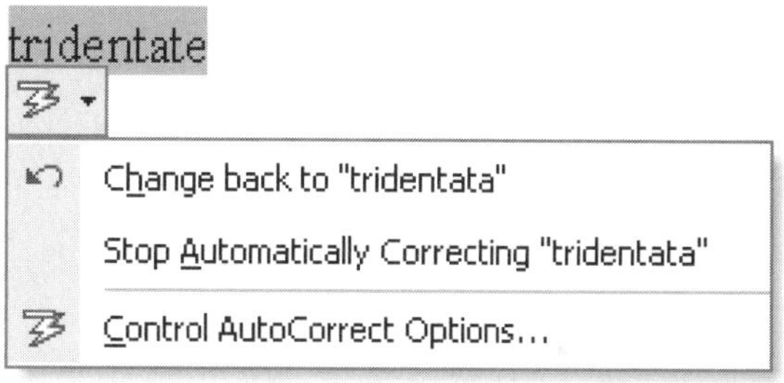

Figure 4-24. If you happen to catch Word in the act of improperly correcting a word, you can click the smart tag to rein it in.

A STAR IS BORN

If you're feeling nostalgic about word-processing programs, check out "A Potted History of WordStar" at *http://snipurl.com/wordstar*.

DELETE TEXT WITHOUT THE CONFIRMATION

The Annoyance: I hate programs that are so cautious that they ask for confirmation for every little change, supposedly to protect me from myself. The only time I want to see "Are you sure? Y/N" is if I'm about to do something truly drastic and irreversible. That certainly doesn't apply to deleting text in Word, which I can easily undo. But all of a sudden, Word now refuses to delete highlighted text until I press Y in response to its annoying prompt (see Figure 4-25). What gives?

Figure 4-25. Is Word asking you to confirm even simple text deletions? You've accidentally turned on "Help for WordPerfect users."

The Fix: Word is channeling WordPerfect. In some versions of WordPerfect, if you highlight some text and press Delete, WordPerfect asks if you want to "Delete Block?" Microsoft Word mimics this behavior when the user turns on "Help for WordPerfect users." It's easy to unintentionally turn on, and just as easy to fix: choose Tools → Options, click the General tab, and uncheck the "Help for WordPerfect users" box.

A FIX FOR WORD'S WACKY LIST NUMBERING

The Annoyance: Most of the time, the automatic numbering feature in Word works great. I type some paragraphs, select them, and click the Numbering button on the toolbar. Even easier, I start the list by typing a number before the first item, and Word magically starts applying numbers to successive paragraphs. But too often Word becomes numerically challenged, proving that it is, in fact, a word processor, not a spreadsheet program.

For example, if I have an unnumbered paragraph between two numbered paragraphs, Word will number following paragraphs in the proper sequence, but will sometimes restart at 1. If a document contains more than one numbered list, the same thing happens: subsequent lists sometimes pick up numbering from the end of the previous list. Worst of all, the numbering sometimes changes spontaneously. Everything looks just right, and the next time I open the document, my list starts with 6. Aaaargh!

The Fix: I must give Microsoft credit; the numbering foul-ups in Word 2002 are fewer than in previous versions. But they still happen, and I avoid using the automatic numbering feature whenever possible because I just don't trust it. I still create numbered lists, but I use a much more reliable counter: the Seq (sequence) field. Here's how:

1. At the beginning of the first numbered item, press Ctrl-F9 to insert an empty field code, which looks like a pair of curly braces.

2. Between the braces, type `SEQ numlist \r1`. (The last character is the number one, and it specifies the starting number for the list.)

3. Click outside the braces to the right, type a period, press Tab, and enter the text for the first item. Press Enter to start the next item.

4. At the beginning of the next item, press Ctrl-F9 and type `SEQ numlist \n` between the braces. Click outside the braces, type a period, press Tab, and type away.

Now, I know this sounds *way* too complex, and if you do it manually as described above, it *is* too complex. But turn these two field codes into AutoCorrect items, and creating numbered lists is a piece of cake. Here's how:

1. If you see the field codes—the cryptic text between curly braces—instead of numbers, press Alt-F9, which toggles the display between field codes and field results. (A field result is what prints in place of the field code.)

2. Select the number "1", the period, and the tab character that follows.

3. Choose Tools → AutoCorrect (AutoCorrect Options in Word 2002).

4. In the Replace box, type `1]`. Next to With, select "Formatted text." Then click OK.

5. In your document, select the number "2", the period, and the tab character.

6. Choose Tools → AutoCorrect (AutoCorrect Options in Word 2002).

7. In the Replace box, type `n]`. Next to With, select "Formatted text." Then click OK.

Once you've created these two AutoCorrect entries, which are now available whenever you use Word, creating numbered lists is easy. You need to remember only three things:

- At the beginning of the first item in a list, type `1]` followed by a space. When you press the space bar, Word replaces the text with the AutoCorrect entry: a field code that displays the number 1 followed by a period and a tab.

- At the beginning of all subsequent list items, type `n]` followed by a space. Word will enter the appropriate number in sequence.

- You can add, remove, and move items any time—but the field results don't change automatically. If the displayed numbers are incorrect, press Ctrl-A to select them all and then press F9 to update the fields.

THREE WAYS TO GIVE TABLES THE BOOT

The Annoyance: To delete something from a Word document, you select it and press Delete, right? That works for most things, but, annoyingly, not for tables. If you select a table and press Delete, Word deletes the contents of the table but leaves the empty table in the document.

MIND READING SUPREME

You'll love the Flash Mind Reader—and you'll spend hours trying to figure it out (*http://flashpsychic.com*).

The Fix: I offer not one, not two, but *three* easy work-arounds. Take your pick:

- Place the cursor anywhere in the table and choose Table → Delete → Table.

- Include the table as part of a larger selection—even if it's just a single character or an empty paragraph mark before or after the table. Then press Delete.

- Select the table and press Shift-Delete. There are a number of fast ways to select the entire table. If the cursor is in the table, press Alt-Shift-NumPad 5 (the 5 on the numeric keypad). Or you can place the mouse pointer to the left of the table's first row, and when it points to the right, hold down the mouse button as you drag the pointer down, highlighting the table's rows. If you're using Word 2000 or later, you can simply click the "table move handle" (the square with the four arrows in it that appears at the table's upper-left corner when you move the mouse pointer over the table).

GIVE CLIPPY HIS WALKING PAPERS (REALLY)

The Annoyance: When I use Office's help system, I'm often confronted by Clippit (a.k.a. Clippy), the smarmy talking paperclip. How can I scrap him permanently?

The Fix: Switch to WordPerfect. Or suggest Clippy take his own life. Or take your own: Clippy can help (see Figure 4-26). Just kidding. You can dump Clippy with a few quick clicks:

- If you're still using Office 97, Clippy and his cohorts are located in the *\Program Files\Microsoft Office\Office\ Actors* folder. The quickest way to banish them is to simply change the name of that folder—to *NoActors*, for example.

- If you have Office XP or 2000, open the control panel and (depending on your version of Windows) double-click Add/Remove Programs or Add or Remove Programs.

In Windows XP, Me, or 2000, select either Microsoft Office or a specific Office program in the "Currently installed programs" list and click the Change button. Click the Add or Remove button, expand the Office Tools item, select Office Assistant, and then "Not available." Confirm your choices and exit. In Windows 98, select the item for Office or a specific application under the Install/ Uninstall tab, and click Add/Remove Program. Then follow the wizard to remove the Office Assistant (it may be called "Clippit"); change its setting to Not Available. (The wizard may ask for the Office CD-ROM; I hope you keep better track of yours than I do.)

Figure 4-26. David Deckert's humorous take on Clippy's demise.

PROBLEM RESOLUTION FLOWCHART

This is a flowchart for problem resolution in the workplace. It's ideal if your boss resembles Dilbert's. See *http://snipurl.com/flow_chart*.

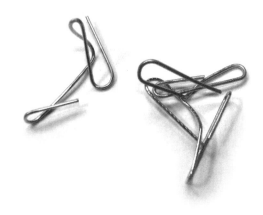

EXCEL ANNOYANCES

TABLES PASTE BETTER IN EXCEL

The Annoyance: I copy and paste lengthy tables of sports schedules and stats from web pages into Word, mostly without success. Word can't seem to import tables correctly and things just never look quite right.

The Fix: Don't even consider using Word. Excel is the premier tool for handling tables. Here's how:

1. Highlight and copy info on the web page (see Figure 4-27).

2. In Excel, right-click the cell where you want to start the table.

3. Select Paste Special and—here's the important part—select HTML format.

4. The data pours beautifully into the cells to form a perfect table. While the data's still selected, choose Format → AutoFormat, and you can fiddle for countless hours choosing a style to display the data (see Figure 4-28).

Thoroughbred Poll: Week 15
Week 15 of the 2003 NTRA Thoroughbred Poll conducted by the National Thoroughbred Racing Association(NTRA), covering racing performances through **June 8.** Rankings based on the votes of Thoroughbred media on 10-9-8-7-6-5-4-3-2-1 basis with first-place votes in parentheses, 2003 record and total points. A-S: Age-Sex, Sex: C-colt, G-gelding, H-horse, F-filly, M-mare.

	Horse	A-S	St-1-2-3	Pts	Pvs
1.	Azeri (16)	4-F	2-2-0-0	206	1
2.	Mineshaft	4-C	5-4-1-0	166	3
3.	Medaglia d'Oro (3)	4-C	2-2-0-0	163	4
4.	Empire Maker (2)	3-C	5-3-2-0	154	9
5.	Funny Cide (2)	3-G	6-2-2-1	134	2
6.	Aldebaran	5-H	4-3-1-0	109	6
7.	Milwaukee Brew	6-H	2-1-1-0	83	5
8.	Congaree	5-H	5-3-1-0	60	7
9.	Harlan's Holiday	4-H	2-2-1-0	56	8
10.	Denon	5-H	2-1-1-0	32	-

Figure 4-27. If you're into thoroughbred racing, you'll recognize this table. Copy the section of the table you want to export into Excel.

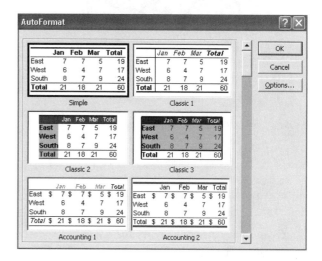

Figure 4-28. Top: The table from the Web pours smoothly into Excel using the "Paste Special'" HTML format. Bottom: Use Excel's AutoFormat tool to tweak the table so it looks just right.

AUTOMATE TEDIOUS DATA ENTRY

The Annoyance: I often need to enter a bunch of repetitive data in a worksheet. Sometimes it's a column of numbers that are all the same; other times it's a row of numbers or dates that increment. I often need to do this across a row, such as when I have a series of dates at the top of each column.

The Fix: You're probably vaguely aware of the Auto Fill feature in Excel, which is designed to relieve the tedium of entering repetitive data. But I'll bet you haven't used many of the capabilities that make it a truly useful and convenient tool. Here are some of the things you can do with Auto Fill:

- Select a single cell that has a numeric value. Place the mouse pointer on the *fill handle*—the tiny black square in the lower-right corner of the active cell indicator (see Figure 4-29). Drag in the direction you want to repeat the data.

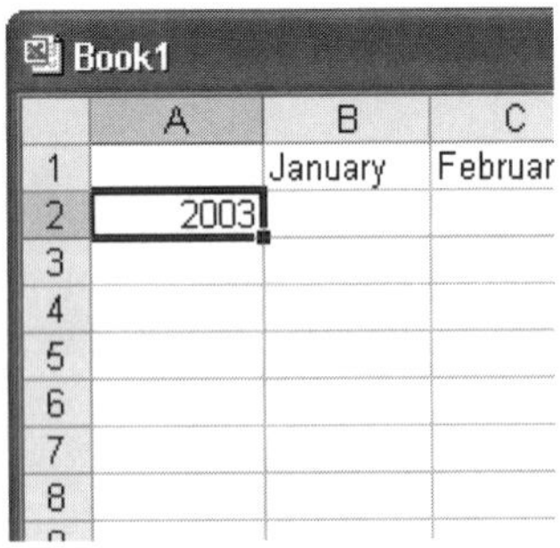

Figure 4-29. Dragging the fill handle (the black square in the lower-right corner of the active cell) downward repeats a value or increases it, depending on whether or not you hold down Ctrl as you drag.

As you drag, a tooltip shows the value that will be placed in each cell as you pass over it. Excel tries to guess whether you want to repeat the data (put the same value in each cell) or enter a series (increase the value in each cell by one if you're dragging to the right or down, or decreasing it if you're dragging up or to the left)—and it often guesses wrong. If that's the case, hold down the Ctrl key before you release the mouse button to finish dragging; if Excel thought you wanted to repeat data, it changes to a series, and vice versa.

If you're using Excel 2002 or later, you can switch between repeated data and a series even after you finish dragging: click the tiny Auto Fill Options box that appears by the cell where you ended and choose either Copy Cells or Fill Series.

- You can enter a series that increases or decreases by amounts other than one. For example, if you want to

create a series that increases by five, enter the first two values in the series. Select both cells, and then drag the fill handle.

- Excel can enter a series of month names or day names. Simply enter the first value you want (for example, February or Monday) and drag. Excel fills the cells you drag over with successive months or days. When doing so, Excel maintains the style you used in the first cell; if you abbreviate the month or day name, Excel abbreviates the ones it creates.

By default, the only text series that Excel generates are for months and days and their three-letter abbreviations. But you can create your own custom series, whether it's the order of planets in the solar system, a list of your store locations, whatever. To do this, choose Tools → Options and click the Custom Lists tab. In the "Custom lists" box, select NEW LIST, and then type the values in your new series in the "List entries" space to the right, as shown in Figure 4-30. Click the Add button when you're done. If you've already typed the series into a worksheet, you can import it to the "Custom lists" box without retyping; select the cells, select Tools → Options, and click the Import button.

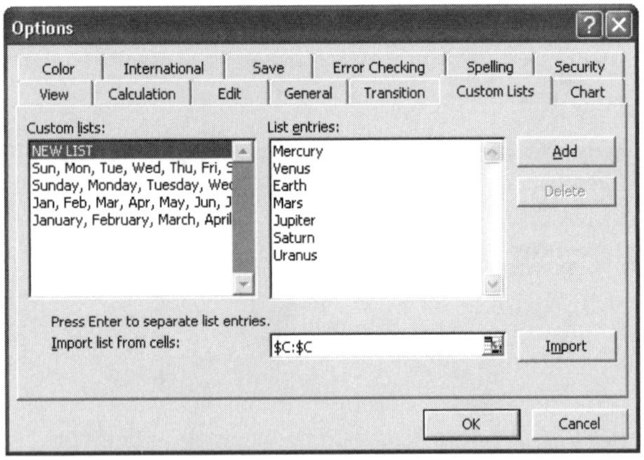

Figure 4-30. Excel comes with only a few predefined lists, but you can create a custom series just by typing in the values—like a sequence of planets.

- Don't like dragging? Then you'll love this one: double-click the fill handle. If there are values in an adjacent column, Excel fills cells downward until it reaches a cell without a value in the adjacent column.

- If you haven't had your fill of Fill, there's more: select a cell with a value and choose Edit → Fill → Series. You'll find all kinds of options for creating series with much more complex progressions.

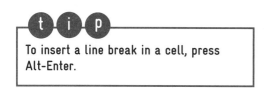

To insert a line break in a cell, press Alt-Enter.

LET ME COUNT THE DAYS

The Annoyance: I know you can do date calculations in Excel, whether it's to find how many days late I am on a car payment or to see how long it's been since my last haircut. It's pretty easy to determine the number of days between two dates; just subtract one from the other. But when I do that, the result is another date! Huh?

The Fix: In a blank worksheet, try this little exercise, which should show your age in days:

1. In cell A1, enter your birth date in MM/DD/YYYY format.

2. In cell B1, enter the formula =today() to display the current date.

3. In cell C1, enter the formula =b1-a1.

You'll notice that the result of the formula in C1 is some other date, which appears to have no correlation to either of the first dates. How come?

When you enter a formula, Excel matches the formatting of the formula's inputs. This works well, when you're doing calculations on dollar amounts or percentages; the result comes out formatted just the way you'd want. But in our example, Excel formatted the formula result—a number of days—as a date.

The solution is simple: select the formatted result cell (C1 in the example) and choose Format → Cells or press Ctrl-1. On the Number tab, select General in the Category box, and click OK. Now your age (in days) is displayed as a huge integer. Hmmm, I think I liked the result better before I fixed the problem.

PROTECT FORMULAS FROM ACCIDENTAL DELETION

The Annoyance: A carefully crafted worksheet might be full of formulas that calculate all kinds of important things. But if the result of the formula is zero or blank (depending on how the cell is formatted), the cell that contains the formula appears to be blank, unused, empty, devoid of data—and ready for me to put something else in its place. And too often, I do just that; I type something or copy into a cell, wiping out the formula that was there. Even when the formula results are visible, it's all too easy to assume that it's just a normal, typed-in value, and to inadvertently overwrite it.

The Fix: Excel has several features that prevent you or someone else from messing up your worksheet. The first method has been available in just about every spreadsheet program since VisiCalc (for you youngsters, that early spreadsheet was the "killer app" that led to the widespread acceptance of personal computers), but lots of spreadsheet users still don't know about it. Here's how you use it:

1. Select the cells that do *not* have formulas or fixed information that you want to keep. Hold down Ctrl to make multiple selections.

2. Choose Format → Cells, click the Protection tab, uncheck the Locked box, and click OK. This tells Excel that these cells are okay to edit. But Excel enforces this restriction only when you protect the worksheet, which you do in the next step.

3. Choose Tools → Protection → Protect Sheet. You can enter a password if you like, but it's not required. If

you enter a password, you (or anyone else using the worksheet) won't need it to enter data in the unlocked cells. But you will need it if you want to unprotect the worksheet so you can make changes in the locked cells. Click OK when you're done.

You can now enter anything in the unlocked cells, but if you try to change the content of a locked cell, Excel pops up an error message. If you need to change those cells, choose Tools → Protection → Unprotect Sheet; you'll need to provide the password if you originally specified one.

If you're using Excel 2002 or 2003, you have another, more powerful option for protecting parts of your worksheet from accidental or malicious changes. You can even enforce varying restrictions for different users on each part of the worksheet:

1. Choose Tools → Protection → Allow Users to Edit Ranges, then click New.

2. In the Title box, type a descriptive name for a cell or range of cells in which you want to allow data entry (that is, the cells that do *not* have formulas or fixed information you want to protect).

3. In the "Refers to cells" field, type a cell range or click the range button at the right end, which lets you select the range on the worksheet. When you're done selecting the range, click the box again. (If you select the cells first, as in the first fix, those cell names will already be in the "Refers to cells" box.)

4. In the Range password box, enter a password, click OK, confirm the password, and click OK again.

5. Back in the Allow Users to Edit Ranges dialog box, click the Protect Sheet button. Then click OK.

When you attempt to enter data outside of the range (or ranges) you specified, Excel displays an error message and prevents you from making changes. When you attempt to enter data within the range you specified, Excel asks for the password; provide it once and you can keep making entries. You can avoid the password prompt in two ways:

• Don't specify a password.

• In the Allow Users to Edit Ranges dialog box, select a range, click the Permissions button, and specify which

users can edit the range. When one of these users logs on and opens the worksheet, Excel will allow the user to edit cells in the specified range without asking for a password.

To disable or modify this type of protection, choose Tools → Protection → Unprotect Sheet.

PROTECT YOURSELF FROM YOURSELF

The Annoyance: I've protected my worksheet so that I don't accidentally wipe out formulas and other entries. Unfortunately, when I enter data I'm not always paying attention, and I end up typing the wrong values into cells. Excel then gives me bogus answers, which leads to my making stupid decisions that result in financial ruin. How do you prevent *that*?

WHEN PASSWORDS ARE NO PROTECTION

Specifying a password with Tools → Protection won't prevent snoops from viewing your worksheet and learning your super-secret information; the purpose of this feature is to keep someone from *changing* the data. To keep a file from prying eyes, turn to the File→Save As command, which has a well-hidden feature that can require a user to provide a password before he or she can open the file. In the Save As dialog box, click Tools → General Options and create your passwords for opening and modifying a worksheet. Even with the advanced encryption options available in Excel 2002 and 2003, don't rely on this method to provide absolute protection. With enough time and some password-cracking tools readily available on the Internet, anyone who has access to your file can eventually get into it. Don't believe me? One day you'll password-protect an Excel file and forget the password. Annoying, yes, but for the cost of a download—and if it strikes you, a donation to the author—there's a way to crack it. Try the Excel Password Remover at *http://www.oreilly.com/pcannoyances*.

The Fix: Excel can force you to enter only appropriate data in certain cells. To enable these restrictions:

1. Select the cell (or cells) where only one type of input should be accepted.

2. Choose Data → Validation. On the Settings tab, you can choose from Whole Number (integers), Decimal (real numbers), List (a defined list of allowable entries, which you can display to users as a drop-down list), Date, Time, Text Length, or Custom (allows you to use formulas to calculate acceptable values).

3. Enter values in the remaining boxes, which change depending on your choice in the Allow pull-down menu. See Figure 4-31.

4. (Optional) On the Input Message tab, you can create a text message that appears when you select a cell with data validation restrictions.

5. On the Error Alert tab, enter a message that appears when you make an entry that doesn't match the criteria specified for the cell. (If you don't enter text, Excel issues a default message.)

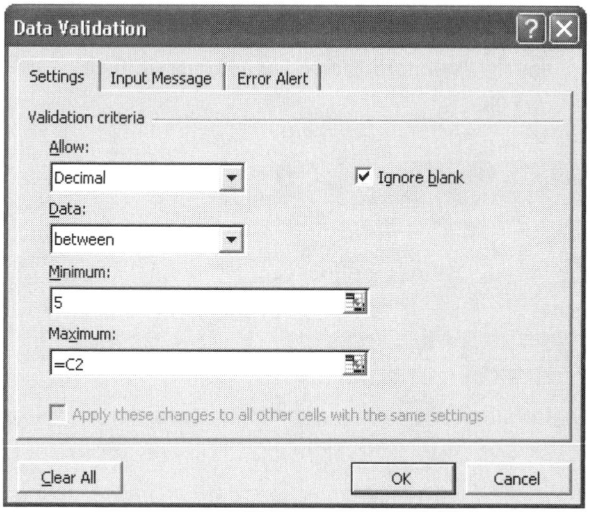

Figure 4-31. You can enter absolute values (as shown in the Minimum box), cell references (as shown in Maximum), or formulas.

The Style menu offers three icons. Your selection here affects more than just the icon that appears in the error message box:

- If you choose Stop, the message box includes Retry and Cancel buttons. You can retry all day if you like, but Excel won't accept a value outside the prescribed range.

- If you choose Warning, the message box includes Yes, No, and Cancel buttons. Clicking No is the same as clicking Retry in the Stop box; it gives you another chance to enter a valid value. Clicking Yes, however, tells Excel to accept the out-of-range value you've given it.

- If you choose Information, the message box includes OK and Cancel buttons. Clicking OK is like clicking Yes in the Warn box: it accepts the invalid value.

If you uncheck the "Show error alert" box on the Error Alert tab, you might expect Excel to reject any nonconforming data entry. Instead, Excel ignores the condition and accepts any entry, effectively disabling this command. Oy!

THE FAST WAY TO FIGURE PARTIAL SUMS

The Annoyance: Often when I'm in a worksheet, I need a quick total. I sometimes want to sum all the numbers in a column, but often I want to sum just a few values. Sure, with Excel, I could create a formula to calculate just about anything, but there's got to be an easier way!

The Fix: Excel can add selected numbers and perform certain other common functions on the spot, and you don't have to mess with formulas. First, make sure the status bar is showing—that's where the answers will appear. Choose Tools → Options, and on the View tab, be sure "Status bar" is selected.

Next, select the numbers you want to add. You can select a single range of adjacent cells, or you can select nonadjacent cells by holding down the Ctrl key as you click each one.

(You can also extend a range by holding down Shift as you click. Practice a bit with Ctrl, Shift, and click, and you'll be able to select any combination of cells you like.)

The sum of the selected cells now appears in the status bar below the worksheet, next to "Sum=". If it doesn't, right-click the status bar and choose Sum. The right-click also displays the other results you can show in the status bar:

Average
Displays the mean (average) of the selected cells

Count
Displays the number of nonblank cells in the selection

Count Nums
Displays the number of numeric values in the selection

BRING AUTOFILTER BACK TO PROTECTED SHEETS

AutoFilter is one of Excel's slicker features. If you have a bunch of data in a worksheet set up like a database—that is, you have column headings with your data below, one record per row—try choosing Data → Filter → AutoFilter. It adds a drop-down arrow next to each column heading. You can then filter your database so that only certain records (rows) are shown, as in the figure. It's a lot easier than trying to figure out Access, right?

But here's the rub: you can't use AutoFilter on a protected worksheet. If you protect the worksheet and then try to use the AutoFilter command, you'll find that the command is unavailable. If you set up the AutoFilters and then protect the worksheet, the drop-down arrows no longer work.

Although they still appear on the worksheet, clicking them does nothing. If the list is already filtered, it stays filtered; if it's not filtered, you can't filter it.

If you're using Excel 2000 or earlier, you're out of luck. You have to choose either protection or filtering. But if you're using Excel 2002, you can employ AutoFilter in a protected worksheet. Here's what you do:

1. Choose Tools→Protection→Protect Sheet. (If the sheet is already protected, you must first choose Tools → Protection → Unprotect Sheet.)

2. In the Protect Sheet dialog box, scroll down until you find the Use AutoFilter checkbox and select it. Then click OK.

Max

Displays the highest (maximum) numeric value in the selection

Min

Displays the lowest (minimum) numeric value in the selection

Sum

Displays the sum of the numeric values in the selection

COLUMNS AND ROWS DO A FLIP-FLOP

The Annoyance: Occasionally, after I've set up column headings and row names, and started entering data, I realize the arrangement isn't going to work out. The column headings should be row titles, and the row titles should be column headings. The prospect of retyping or cutting and pasting or dragging to rearrange everything is daunting.

The Fix: Fret not. Excel has this cool ability to copy a vertical set of cells and then paste them horizontally, and vice versa. And it's easy to do if you know where to find this feature.

1. Select the cells that you want to turn on their ear. Don't select cells across more than 256 rows; turned on its side, your selection has to fit within Excel's 256-column limit (A through IV). Also, you can't paste the range you're copying, so you may want to paste into a new sheet. To quickly transpose an entire worksheet, press Ctrl-End and then Ctrl-Shift-Home to select all the cells that have been used.

2. Copy the selected data by pressing Ctrl-C, clicking the Copy button, or right-clicking the selection and choosing Copy.

3. Right-click the destination cell—the cell in the upper-left corner of the range where you want the data to end up—and choose Paste Special.

4. Select Transpose and click OK.

Each row from the selected area becomes a column in the new area, with the first (top) row becoming the first (leftmost) column of the destination area, as shown in Figure 4-32.

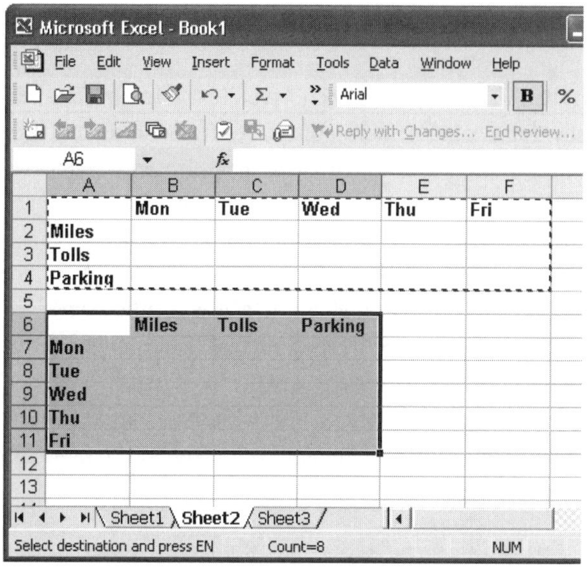

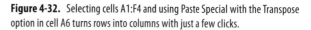

Figure 4-32. Selecting cells A1:F4 and using Paste Special with the Transpose option in cell A6 turns rows into columns with just a few clicks.

EXCEL HYPERLINK HELL

The Annoyance: Storing hyperlinks in Excel worksheets is a pain—I'm always clicking one by accident and launching my browser. How can I select the contents of a cell holding a hyperlink?

The Fix: The quick and dirty way to select a cell in Excel 2000, 2002, and 2003 without triggering the link it contains is to click the cell and hold the mouse button until the cursor changes to a plus sign, and then let go. The cell is highlighted and your browser stays closed. Now you can do the usual cell tasks, such as moving the cell's contents to another location.

On the other hand, if you want to remove a link, right-click it and choose Hyperlink → Remove Hyperlink. If you never, *ever* want to see a hyperlink created in Excel 2002 and 2003 when you enter a web address in a cell, stop the program from automatically converting them: choose Tools → AutoCorrect Options, click the AutoFormat As You Type tab, and uncheck the "Internet and network paths with hyperlinks" box.

TYPE A LIST IN EXCEL

The Annoyance: When I type text into an Excel cell, say, for a label or heading, the text goes in as one long line. I'd really like to type in a short list, with numbered entries on separate lines. Is this possible?

The Fix: What? You're not happy with a mile-long line of text? Try this trick: click the cell where you want the text to appear, enter the desired text, and then press Alt-Enter whenever you want a sentence to start on a new line. (Typing Alt-Enter essentially enters a carriage return in the cell.) When you're done typing, press the Enter key to close the cell (see Figure 4-33).

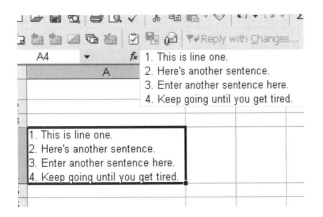

Figure 4-33. Want to type a short list in a cell? Alt-Enter is the magic keyboard combo that lets you do it.

EXCEL'S ENTER ALTERNATIVES

The Annoyance: The way the Enter key works in Excel drives me nuts. I want it to take me one cell to the right, but it always takes me down one cell in the column instead.

The Fix: After doing a little digging, I discovered you can make the Enter key move the cursor to any adjacent cell—up, down, left, right, or even not at all. To change the Enter key's setting, click Tools → Options, click the Edit

tab, and go to the Direction drop-down menu. Or uncheck "Move selection after Enter" to keep the current cell active when you use Enter.

THE WORKSHEET CONSERVATION SOCIETY

The Annoyance: When I create a new, blank workbook, Excel creates three blank worksheets, labeled Sheet 1, Sheet 2, and Sheet 3. (Don't confuse this phenomenon with "three sheets to the wind," which is something else altogether.) Most of my quick-and-dirty workbooks use only a single worksheet, and if I need more worksheets, it's easy to add them. So why does Microsoft always clutter my screen and hard drive with worksheets I don't need?

The Fix: I can't answer that last question, but I can offer a solution. Open Tools → Options and click the General tab. In the "Sheets in new workbook" field, pick the number of sheets you want in each new workbook you create. I set mine to 1, but this box accepts values up to 255.

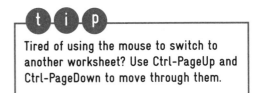

Tired of using the mouse to switch to another worksheet? Use Ctrl-PageUp and Ctrl-PageDown to move through them.

Since I've called your attention to those tabs at the bottom of the workbook, here are a few things you can do with them:

Change the name to something more meaningful than "Sheet1". Double-click the tab, or right-click it and choose Rename.

Create one or more new worksheets in the same workbook. Right-click the tab of a sheet near where you want a new one. (If you want to insert more than one worksheet, hold down Shift and click another sheet to highlight the two sheets and all the sheets in between them.) Choose Insert, and select OK to accept the default "Worksheet" selection. A number of new sheets equal to the number that were highlighted will appear.

Change the order of the tabs. You can reorder tabs in a workbook or move or copy selected tabs to another workbook. Select the first tab, then hold down Ctrl and click the other sheets, if any. Right-click a highlighted tab, choose "Move or Copy," and answer the dialog box as desired. You can also just drag a tab to a new location; watch for the downward-pointing black triangle.

Apply a color to one or more tabs (Excel 2002 and 2003 only). Right-click the tab(s), choose Tab Color, select a color from the palette, and click OK.

Print multiple worksheets. Select the tabs (using Shift and Ctrl) and in the Print dialog box, ensure that "Active sheet(s)" is selected.

Finally, here's a really cool trick that can speed data entry and impress your friends:

Enter data or apply formatting to multiple worksheets simultaneously. Select multiple tabs. Entries you make and formatting you apply affect all selected (active) worksheets. This trick makes it a snap to reformat all the worksheets in a workbook if you want to change their appearance, for example.

POWERPOINT ANNOYANCES

LOOKING GOOD IN BLACK AND WHITE

The Annoyance: My color PowerPoint presentations look smashing on-screen. But when I print them out on my trusty monochrome laser printer, they're downright atrocious. My vibrant colors get turned into icky grays I can barely tell apart.

The Fix: Ask your boss to buy a color laser printer. And after the old tightwad's done laughing in your face, try a cheaper solution: PowerPoint's extensive features for making grayscale printouts look good. They work well; they're just tucked away where you might not stumble across them.

If you're using PowerPoint 2002, you'll find these features by selecting View → Color/Grayscale → Grayscale. You'll get a little floating window with no fewer than nine different grayscale print options; pick one and you'll see exactly what your printout will look like. For instance, if your problem is due to light text on a dark background, the Inverse Grayscale setting can work wonders. Once the presentation looks more presentable, click the Close Grayscale View button, and it will be restored to vibrant on-screen Technicolor.

Credit where credit is due: PowerPoint often does a perfectly good job of figuring out appropriate grayscale choices by itself, so try its default printout before you futz with the grayscale features.

You'll run into one related annoyance if you do have a color printer but want to print in grayscale (an intelligent move if you plan to distribute black-and-white photocopies of that printout): just because you're in grayscale mode on-screen doesn't mean PowerPoint will print in shades of gray. When you print, make sure Grayscale is selected in the Print dialog's "Color/Grayscale:" section.

WHEN AUTOFORMATTING MUCKS THINGS UP

The Annoyance: When I paste or insert graphics onto a slide, all the other elements are pushed aside. My carefully organized slide becomes an eyesore, and undoing the damage gets old real fast.

The Fix: PowerPoint is trying to rearrange elements to accommodate the new object. Turn off this feature—which for some odd reason is in Tools → AutoCorrect Options. Click the "AutoFormat as You Type" tab—even though this annoyance doesn't happen when you type—and uncheck the "Automatic layout for inserted objects" box. Click OK, and your PowerPoint layouts will fall into place.

One other thing: PowerPoint 2002 lets you leave this automatic layout feature on and undo it selectively. After a slide has been rearranged, a little lightning-bolt icon appears below the pasted item; click it, and select Undo Automatic Layout. The slide's elements will return to their original places.

PUT YOUR PRESENTATIONS ON A DIET

The Annoyance: If your PowerPoint presentations are anything like mine, they have a weight problem. My slide shows are way too fat to stick on a floppy, and emailing them takes eons (if it works at all).

The Fix: File size will balloon when you add anything other than plain text and simple colors to a presentation—and I'm not talking humongous video clips here. Just a photo or two can really pack on the pounds, and compressing the show into a zip file usually doesn't help much.

The good news is that several tricks can squeeze down those slides. The first one's painless: open your presentation and choose File → Save As. Unless you have a specific reason to save the presentation in a format other than the default, make sure the "Save as type" drop-down menu lists Presentation (*.ppt), rather than a variant such as PowerPoint 95 (*ppt). Then click Save. This should shave at least a few kilobytes off the file. (In certain cases, it's slimmed down my presentations by 90 percent.) Try *that*, Jenny Craig.

Still too portly? Select any picture in your presentation, then go to Format → Picture and click the Compress button. In the "Apply to" section, choose "All pictures in document"; under "Change resolution", choose Web/Screen (if you don't plan to print the slides) or Print (if you do plan to print them, and image quality is essential). Click OK; if you get a warning message about this reducing the quality of your pictures, click the Apply button. Then save your presentation. Depending on the original resolution of your images, this tip can work wonders. (Strangely, it can *increase* the size of the slideshow if image resolution was low to begin with, so keep a backup of the original version just in case.)

PAY ATTENTION TO POWERPOINT

The Annoyance: I have to create a PowerPoint presentation that contains lots of images. I'm not looking forward to it, because PowerPoint makes you insert images one at a time. Is there some way to insert images en masse?

The Fix: If you're using PowerPoint 2002 or 2003, you can add fistfuls of images at once to a presentation—if you first store them in PowerPoint's Photo Album. First, fire up PowerPoint but don't load any presentations. (You may be forced to load a blank presentation, then press Ctrl-F4 to remove it.) Click Insert → Picture → New Photo Album, choose File/Disk, navigate to a folder, and select all the pictures you want to import. Click Insert and press Ctrl-A to highlight all the photos (see Figure 4-34). In the Photo Album dialog, highlight all the images in the "Pictures in Album" panel and click Create (see Figure 4-35). All your images are now in a brand new PowerPoint album. When you're later building a presentation, you can quickly import multiple images by simply dragging them from the album into your presentation.

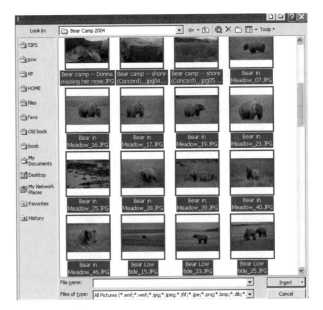

Figure 4-34. To pull a lot of images into a presentation, first import them into a PowerPoint photo album.

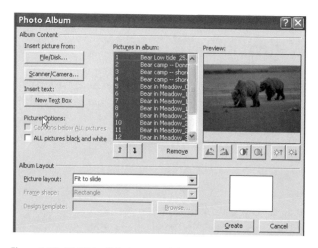

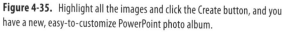

Figure 4-35. Highlight all the images and click the Create button, and you have a new, easy-to-customize PowerPoint photo album.

FIX POWERPOINT'S OPEN DIALOG BOX

The Annoyance: When I select File → Open in Power-Point, I see a panel on the right showing me a PowerPoint sample. Why? I also notice that the directories and files are reverse-sorted. How can I get them to sort from A to Z?

The Fix: Ah, it's the old PowerPoint "I know what's best for you" problem. By default, PowerPoint 2000 through 2003 opens in Preview mode, displaying folder and file names on the left and a preview on the right (see Figure 4-36).

To banish the preview, click the View icon—it's second from the right in the upper-right portion of the dialog. This changes the (duh) view in the dialog. Choose the one you like the best. (Me, I like Details.)

GETTYSBURG IN POWERPOINT

You're not the only one who has to sit through long-winded and boring (and annoying) PowerPoint presentations. I have proof that it happened as early as 1863. But don't take my word for it; get ready to doze through "The Gettysburg PowerPoint Presentation" at *http://snipurl.com/getty.*

To change to A to Z sorting (but only in PowerPoint 2002 and 2003), look for the Name field in the dialog above the list of folders and filenames. Click the down arrow to the right of "Name" to change the sort order. This preference should be remembered the next time you select Open.

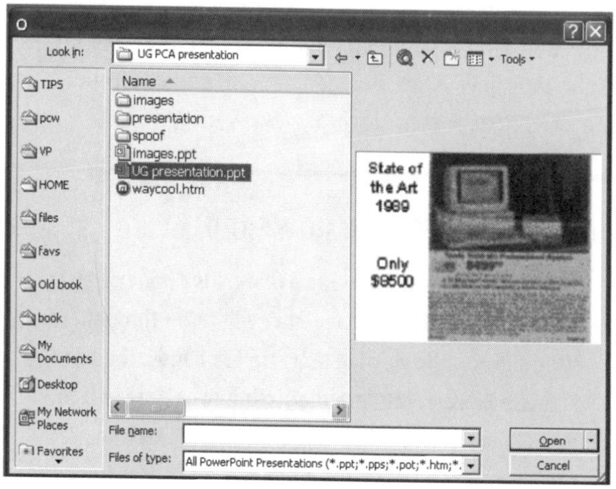

Figure 4-36. Annoyed by PP's preview mode? You can change it with a click of a button in this dialog box.

VIEW POWERPOINT FILES WITHOUT POWERPOINT

The Annoyance: I occasionally receive PowerPoint files from coworkers. I don't own Microsoft Office, so I'm the only guy in the crowd unable to view these files. Is there a way to see them without purchasing Office?

NEED A RAISE?

Before you storm into your boss's office, check out the "Automated Salary Review," a PowerPoint presentation. It'll teach you invaluable negotiating skills (*http://snipurl.com/salary2*).

The Fix: Sure is. All you need to know is the secret handshake—and the right link. Head for *http://snipurl.com/ PP_Viewer* and download Microsoft's free PowerPoint 2003 viewer. The program will let you view entire presentations created in PowerPoint 97 through 2003. By the way, Microsoft has finally released a utility that lets you view, print, and copy Word documents if you lack a copy of Word. This is the first new Word viewer since the age of Word 97. Get it at *http://snipurl.com/word_view.*

VIEW AND EDIT IN POWERPOINT

Using PowerPoint's Slide Show feature is a handy way to get a taste of what your audience will suffer through. Editing slides while viewing them isn't so handy. The trick is to use PowerPoint's pseudo picture-in-picture option. Press the Ctrl key while clicking the Slide Show icon in the lower-left corner of PowerPoint (it's the fifth icon from the left and cleverly looks like a screen).

You'll see a miniature slide show in the upper-left corner of your screen while PowerPoint—and its editing features—are in the foreground. A mouse click anywhere in PowerPoint lets you edit the presentation, and a click on the Resume Slide Show button shows you how your edit looks (see the image below).

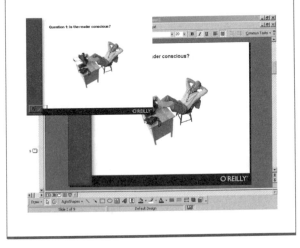

PRECISE IMAGE MOVEMENTS IN POWERPOINT

The Annoyance: I'm trying to fine-tune the location of an image in a presentation, but all I get are jerky little movements when I use my mouse. Is it my mouse, PowerPoint, or my not-so-steady hand?

The Fix: It's not you or your mouse. It's the way PowerPoint—in fact, all Office products—are designed to move images. As you move or resize an image, your mouse travels in small, incremental movements. Hold down the Alt key while moving the mouse and you'll be able to make infinitesimally precise adjustments. Cool, no? In fact, the trick's good on all Office products.

OUTLOOK AND OUTLOOK EXPRESS ANNOYANCES

MAKE OUTLOOK A WORD-FREE ZONE

The Annoyance: All of a sudden Outlook is opening Microsoft Word when I create a new email, and I can't seem to get things back to normal. How did that happen, and more importantly, how do I stop it?

The Fix: Yours is a very common grievance. It occurs when you fiddle with Outlook's settings, inadvertently click something, and forget that you've done it. (I do this all the time.) In Outlook, choose Tools → Options. In Version 97, select the E-mail tab if it's not already selected, uncheck the "Use Microsoft Word as the e-mail editor" box, and select OK. In Versions 2000 and XP (2002), select the Mail Format tab and uncheck "Use Microsoft Word to edit email messages."

OUTLOOK EXPRESS'S HIDDEN ONE-CLICK ENCRYPTION OPTION

The Annoyance: There are so many creeps on the Internet, and some of the email messages I send contain information they'd love to get their mitts on. To prevent that from happening, I got a digital certificate for signing and encrypting certain messages. But the Sign and Encrypt buttons don't appear in the Outlook Express toolbar, so I can't sign or encrypt a message with a single click.

The Fix: You can get these buttons on the message toolbar, just not on the toolbar of the main Outlook Express window.

The Sign and Encrypt buttons appear by default in the toolbar of a message-editing window (where you compose a new message or newsgroup post, forward a message, or reply to a message). If the buttons don't appear in the window, do the following:

- Be sure the toolbar hasn't been truncated because the window is too narrow to display all buttons. If a >> symbol appears at the right end of the toolbar, make the window wider or click >> to display the buttons that don't fit, as shown in Figure 4-37.

- If the buttons really aren't in the toolbar, right-click the toolbar and choose Customize. You should be able to add, remove, or rearrange the buttons to suit your needs.

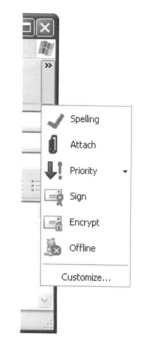

Figure 4-37. The Sign and Encrypt buttons—plus a few others you didn't know were lurking there—normally appear when you click the >> symbol.

REATTACH YOUR DETACHED ATTACHMENTS

The Annoyance: When I receive a message with an attached file, both Outlook and Outlook Express refuse to let me save or open the attachment.

The Fix: This is a security measure. The vast majority of viruses and Trojan horse programs are distributed through email attachments, and there are plenty of people who have unwittingly done untold damage to their computers and their friends' computers by opening attachments they shouldn't have. Microsoft shut this door, and rightly so. The problem is that it's hard to work with attachments that you know are safe.

The first solution is, unfortunately, a lifestyle change. Inform your correspondents that you no longer accept executable files or other unsafe file types. Ask them to zip all files before they send them to you, which has the added benefit of creating smaller attachments. Outlook and Outlook

Express happily accept *.zip* archives. (You're still responsible, however, for ensuring that the files within the zip file are virus-free before you open them. Be sure your antivirus program is up to date and properly configured to scan email attachments and other files as you open them.)

Of course, some of your friends are too stubborn to honor your request—or can't figure out how to zip files. Your options:

- In Outlook Express, open Tools → Options, click the Security tab, and uncheck "Do not allow attachments to be saved or opened that could potentially be a virus." Click OK and retrieve the attached file. Then return to the Options dialog box and check the box. Leave it set except for those rare times when you need to get a particular attachment. Trust me.

- Outlook doesn't offer such a simple workaround. You'll find lots of arcane workarounds (including various Registry hacks and even editing *.dll* files), utilities, and information about Outlook attachment blocking at the wonderful Slipstick Systems site at *http://snipurl.com/getexe*.

One goofy, but effective, workaround is to open Outlook Express (that's right, Express) and import the Outlook message into Outlook Express. (Choose File → Import → Messages.) Then disable attachment blocking in Outlook Express as described above.

If you need to receive attachments often, the best solution is Ken Slovak's Attachment Options, which you can download from *http://www.oreilly.com/pcannoyances*. Attachment Options adds a new tab to Outlook's Options dialog box that lets you control how Outlook accesses attachments.

TWO EMAIL CLIENTS, ONE CONTACT LIST

The Annoyance: Outlook Express 5 and Outlook 2000 can share a single Contacts folder so that I can manage all my contacts in one place. It's a fantastic feature, but it's disappeared from Outlook Express 6 and Outlook 2002.

The Fix: For those who still use Outlook Express 5 and Outlook 2000 (or Outlook 98), let me first explain how to set this up. First, open the Address Book by clicking the Addresses button in the Outlook Express Toolbar, and choose Help → About. If the dialog box doesn't show a path to a *.wab* file, you're already sharing your Contacts folder with Outlook. Congratulations. If sharing isn't set up, you can go through the Tools → Options dialog box in Outlook Express. There are some limitations:

- You must be using Outlook Express 5.0 or 5.5.

- You must be using Outlook 98 or Outlook 2000, and it must be configured in Internet Mail Only mode. To find out, choose Help → About. The line above the copyright notice indicates which mode—Corporate/Workgroup, Internet Mail Only, or No E-mail—Outlook is in.

- You can use only the Contacts folder in the default Personal Folders (*.pst*) file in the default profile.

- You can't use shared contacts with multiple identities in Outlook Express.

Although contact sharing is no longer supported in Outlook 2002 or Outlook Express 6 and has been removed from the Options dialog box, it's available with a Registry edit. Here's how:

1. In Registry Editor, navigate to the *HKEY_CURRENT_USER\Software\Microsoft\WAB\WAB4* key.

2. If a value named UseOutlook does not exist, choose Edit → New → DWORD Value. Name the new value UseOutlook. (For help using the Registry and Registry Editor, see "What's the Registry" in Chapter 2).

3. Double-click the UseOutlook value and change its value data to 1.

With the value data set to 1, Outlook Express no longer uses a *.wab* file with Windows Address Book; instead it uses the Contacts folder in Outlook. If you later want to disable contact sharing, delete the UseOutlook value or set it to 0.

EMAIL IS FOR EMAIL

The Annoyance: Outlook 2002 displays an address bar along with Go, Stop, and Refresh buttons in its main window, as you can see in Figure 4-38. This makes Outlook a crude web browser, and in fact, you can display web pages within Outlook's window. But I don't use it and it takes up valuable space. It's resizable, so I drag it over to one side to make it as small as possible. (Mini-annoyance: You can't get rid of the word "Address".) But the next time I start Outlook, the address bar returns to full size. How can I make it go away for good?

The Fix: It turns out that Outlook *does* remember the size of the address bar—to a point. If you drag the sizing handle (the small vertical bar to the left) so that the address bar occupies only half its original space, the address bar remains shrunk the next time you open Outlook. But if you drag the sizing handle all the way to the right (or double-click it) so that the address bar is at its absolute minimum size, it returns to its full ugliness with the next start.

Here's what's going on: Outlook stores the size of the address bar in the Registry when you close Outlook, and it reuses that size the next time you start the program. If you drag it all the way to the right, Outlook stores the size

as 0 (logically enough). When you restart Outlook, it misinterprets the 0 and assumes you want full width (187). You can fix Microsoft's stupidity in two ways:

- Resize the address bar *almost* to its minimum size—but don't drag all the way to the right.
- To get the smallest size that Outlook will reliably restore, open Registry Editor and navigate to the *HKEY_CURRENT_USER\Software\Microsoft\Office\ 10.0\Outlook\Options* key. Double-click the Address-BarWidth value and set it to 1.

A NIFTY OUTLOOK ORGANIZER

The Annoyance: I'm an email junkie—I easily receive over a hundred emails a day, and maintain an archive of over 10,000 messages. My beef: Outlook is lousy when it comes to searching and organizing all this stuff.

The Fix: I might suggest a 12-step program for your addiction, but no matter—scrounge $40 and pick up a copy of Caelo's Nelson Email Organizer. NEO organizes, catalogs, and indexes your email to the max, without touching the actual messages. As a result, you can do sophisticated (and fast) searches and save them; automatically redirect mail by sender, type, date, etc.; prioritize

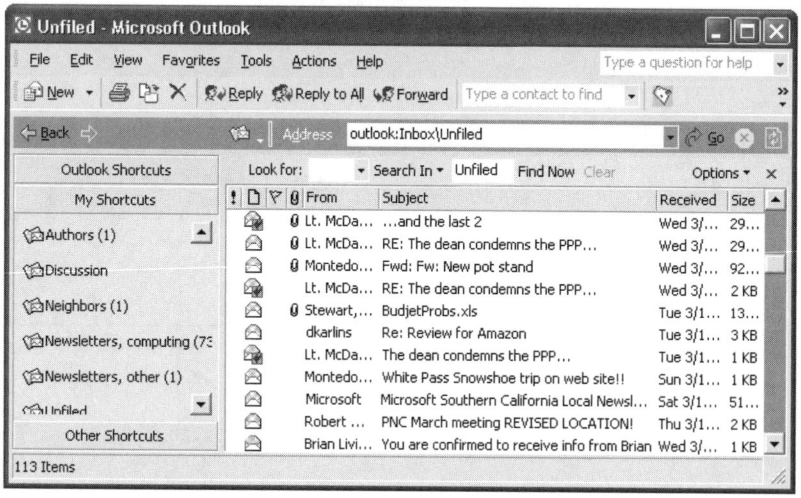

Figure 4-38. Sick of the useless Address bar? You can get rid of it—almost.

mail; and more. Integration with Outlook is seamless—you can hop between the two programs by clicking a button. Another plus: NEO works with Windows 9x and later and Outlook 97 and later. Alas, it doesn't support Outlook Express. I suspect many of NEO's features will find their way into Outlook. Until then, download the 30-day free trial from *http://www.oreilly.com/pcannoyances*.

OUTLOOK'S ADD-IN WON'T LEAVE

The Annoyance: I tried an add-in program for Microsoft Outlook XP and decided to uninstall it. But the damn thing won't go. Every time I run Outlook, I get an error message saying Outlook can't install or load the add-in! (See Figure 4-39.)

The Fix: Looks like you're stuck with an add-in that doesn't know when to quit. Here's how to give this annoyance its walking papers. Open Outlook and select Tools →

Options, click the Other tab and then the Advanced Options button. Click the Add-In Manager button; in the dialog box that appears, uncheck the add-in and click OK, and then OK twice more (see Figure 4-40). If the program isn't listed there, go back to the Advanced Options dialog and click the COM Add-Ins button, select the add-in, and click the Remove button.

A VIRTUAL TIME-WASTER

If you're anything like me, you love internet time-wasters. here's one that'll easily kill an hour. Click each of Bewitched's links. If you're restless, just go to "whirligig" and click your mouse a while (*http://snipurl.com/whirligig*).

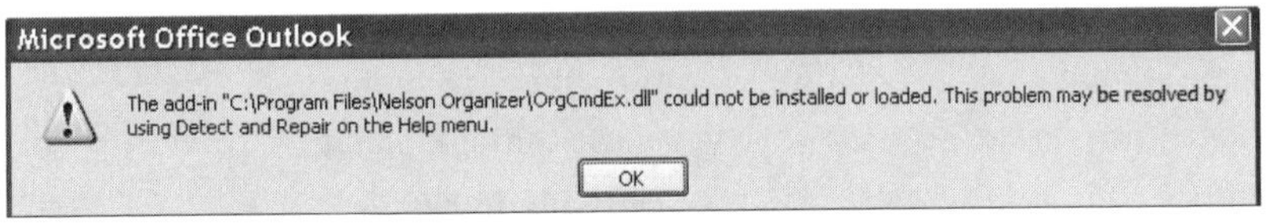

Figure 4-39. This is the pesky error I received every time I launched Outlook.

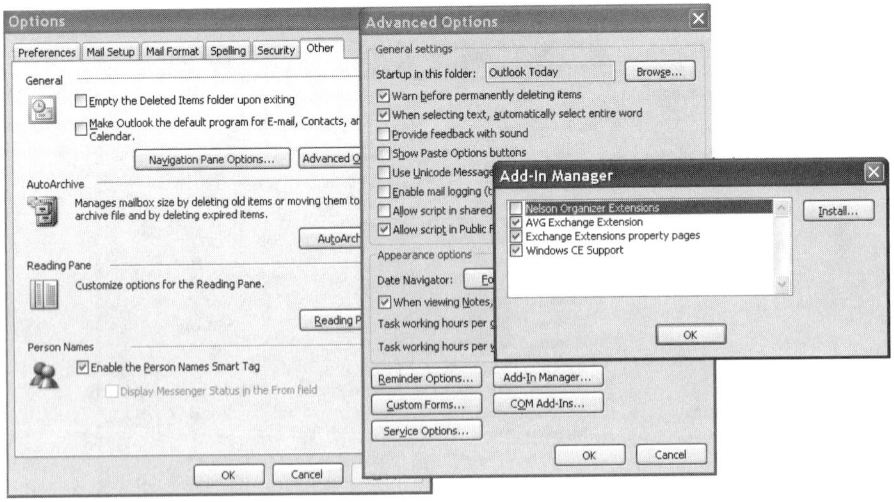

Figure 4-40. Outlook add-ins may hang around long after you've decided to stop using them—or after you've uninstalled them—giving you an annoying error message.

OUTLOOK AUTOCOMPLETE PUZZLER

The Annoyance: When I start to address an email in either the To or Cc field in Outlook, the first address in the drop-down list is an obsolete one. The address I want to use is the one right below it. Not only can't I skip past the first address, I can't get rid of it because it isn't in my Contact list! How did it get there and how do I get rid of it?

The Fix: This is a frustrating problem with an easy solution! You're a victim of Outlook's autocomplete feature: Outlook keeps track of everything you've ever typed in the To and Cc boxes, hoping you'll want to use them again some day, but they're not saved in any address book. When you type the first few letters in the address field and the old name appears, press the Up and Down arrow keys to highlight it, then press Delete.

LICKETY-SPLIT OUTLOOK SEARCHES

The Annoyance: I upgraded to Outlook 2003. I like the new features, but searching is still slow. And you still can't search in email attachments.

The Fix: Fret no more. You want the aptly named Lookout, an add-in that's one of the coolest Outlook productivity tools around. You can search inside practically any file on your drive, including spreadsheets, Word documents, Favorites, HTML files, and, yes, email attachments. You can search in a variety of ways using Boolean-type operators such as `Steve +Bass -guitar`. Try special keywords—"lastweek" and "yesterday", for example—to narrow your search to everything in the last week or just the other day, or search only email with attachments. (See Lookout in action in Figure 4-41.) Click a result and you'll launch the application associated with the file. Searches are really fast because Lookout uses an index to find files. Pawing through your hard drive and creating the initial index may take a few minutes or even a few hours, however, depending on the number of files on your PC and the speed of your system.

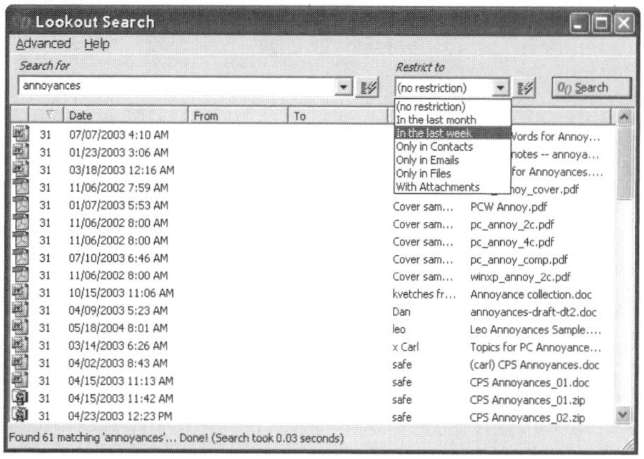

Figure 4-41. Lookout is a must-have add-in for Outlook users. It can do lickety-split searches half a dozen different ways, from email and contacts to Word documents and worksheets.

Here's the surprise: this used to be a commercial product costing $40. But now that Microsoft's acquired the company (they wanted to use it on their MSN site), it's a freebie.

Unfortunately, Lookout won't work without Outlook (Versions 2000, XP, or 2003), but if you spend most of your day with Outlook opened, you really must download this valuable tool. You can pick up a copy at *http://snipurl.com/lookoutsoft* or *http://snipurl.com/outlook_lookout.*

REMIND ME TO SET A REMINDER

The Annoyance: I don't know how I got along before I had a computer and Outlook to remind me of every appointment, deadline, and task I would rather miss. It pops up a friendly reminder just in time for me to think up an excuse not to go. But sometimes Outlook forgets to display reminders—or it displays them hours after they should have appeared!

The Fix: If reminders don't appear, they've probably been disabled. In Outlook, choose Tools → Options. In Outlook 97, click the Reminders tab and make sure "Display the reminder" is selected. In Outlook 2000 and later, click the Other tab, then the Advanced Options button and the Reminder Options button. Make sure the "Display the reminder" box is checked.

If reminders work sporadically, Outlook's database needs a reminder of who's in charge.

1. Close Outlook.
2. Click the Start button and choose Run.
3. In the Run dialog box, type `outlook /cleanreminders` and click OK.

Outlook purges all its reminders, and then scans your appointments, tasks, and follow-up flags to rebuild the reminder list in the database.

DATE-FORMAT ALTERNATIVES

Instead of typing a due date for a task in Outlook 2000 or 2002, enter a description, such as "last Friday of the month". Outlook will automatically convert that to numerical format. Try some: "first Monday in March", "30 days from now", "two months from last week", or "Cinco de Mayo".

SWEET PRINTS FROM OUTLOOK'S CONTACT LIST

Do you want to print envelopes or labels right from Outlook's contact list? Use Aladdins Envelopes & Labels, a nifty tool that allows you to do what Outlook ought to—select one or dozens of contacts, select either an envelope or the size label you want to use, and print. It's that simple. Aladdins Envelopes & Labels stores up to 20 label formats and 10 envelope styles, perfect for one envelope with your personal return address, another with your company's name, and another with, say, a logo. The one downside? At $39.95, Aladdin Envelopes & Labels isn't cheap, and it doesn't work with Outlook Express. There's a free trial version available at *http://www.oreilly.com/pcannoyances*.

I LIKE MY DATES BOLD

The Annoyance: I can tell by glancing at Outlook which days have appointments because those days are displayed in boldface—at least they're supposed to be. But sometimes Outlook doesn't correctly mark busy days in bold. What's the fix?

The Fix: Like the previous annoyance, this one requires you to clean house:

1. Close Outlook.
2. Click the Start button and choose Run.
3. In the Run dialog box, type `outlook /cleanfreebusy` and click OK.

Outlook rebuilds the list of busy days and displays them correctly in bold on the monthly calendar.

A BETTER HOME FOR YOUR DOCUMENTS

The Annoyance: Microsoft Office products have a love affair with the My Documents location. How can I make them store files where I want them stored?

The Fix: There are a few ways to sidestep Microsoft's obsession with tossing everything into My Documents.

1. Windows Me lets you rename the folder, and Windows 2000 and XP let you choose another location where documents are saved when you choose My Documents:

   a. Close Microsoft Office and any other editing programs.

   b. Right-click My Documents (on the Windows desktop, in a Windows Explorer or folder window, or on the Start menu) and choose Properties.

   c. In Windows Me, highlight the name in the text box at the top of the General tab and rename the folder. In 2000 and XP, in the Target field, change the existing location (likely *C:\Documents and Settings\username\My Documents*) to wherever you want things saved. For working on this book, for example, I chose *c:\annoyances\documents*.

   d. Click OK. If you ever change your mind, you can restore the default by renaming the folder (Windows Me) or following the steps above and clicking the Restore Default button (Windows 2000 and XP).

2. In Microsoft Office 2000 and XP applications, you can easily change the default folder for the Save and Open dialog boxes.

   • In Word, select Tools → Options, click on the File Locations tab, and adjust the locations as desired.

   • In Excel and Access, select Tools → Options, go to the General tab, and edit the "Default file location" field.

   • In PowerPoint, select Tools → Options, click on the Save tab, and edit the "Default file location" field.

3. If you use Office 2000, there's a Microsoft tool that lets you add custom places to Office dialog boxes, including Open and Save As. The tool lets you edit the five available locations in the left pane, and if you choose small icons, you can add up to 10 user-defined locations. The file you need is *places.exe*, and it's available at *http://www.oreilly.com/pcannoyances*. Note that when you download the file, you'll discover that Microsoft includes a dumb self-extraction tool. What's important is that you read the *readme.doc* carefully—it tells you exactly how to install the *places* utility.

WINDOWS MOVING COMPANY

Windows will ask whether you want to move all the files in My Documents to your new location. Don't rush this decision; for now, answer *no*. You can easily move the files later using Windows Explorer.

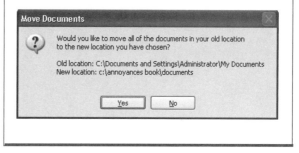

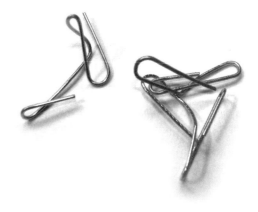

5

Windows Explorer
ANNOYANCES

If you've ever buried a file in the Tomb of the Unknown Folder and then gone on an hour-long treasure hunt to find it, you know what it's like to be annoyed with Windows Explorer. A huge 200 GB drive is terrific while you're happily saving files, but a nightmare when you have to find them again. It's like buying a 47-room castle: a dream come true, until you can't remember where you left your eyeglasses.

With over 100,000 files and folders on my system, I've developed lots of workarounds for many of Explorer's annoyances. I'll also tell you about a handful of free file management utilities and two terrific alternatives to using Windows Explorer at all.

SEARCH ANIMATIONS BEGONE

The Annoyance: I hated Clippy and you showed me how to dump it. [See "Give Clippy His Walking Papers (Really)" in Chapter 4.] How about eliminating the irritating animation in XP's Search feature?

The Fix: Animation begone! In Windows Explorer, press F3 and you'll take your last look at the dumb animation. Click the Change Preferences link at the bottom of the Search pane, click "Without an animated screen character," and say *adios* to the creature.

Here's an odd time-saver: if you press F3 from the Windows desktop, you jump right into the Search pane's "All files and folders" search. Why? Ask Bill.

A SHORTCUT TO MORE RECENT DOCUMENTS

The Annoyance: The Start menu's My Recent Documents is a handy way to quickly retrieve files I've been working on. But the list is limited to 15 documents.

The Fix: With a quick fix, you can have access to a heck of a lot more of your recently used files. The trick is to place a shortcut to the secret folder that tracks recently opened files on the desktop. Navigate to the *My Recent Documents* folder (its location varies depending on your version and setup of Windows; it's often at *C:\Documents and Settings\username\My Recent Documents* in XP and 2000 and at *C:\Windows\Recent* or *C:\Windows\Profiles\username\Recent* in 98 and Me). Once you find it, right-click and drag it to the desktop, release the button, and select "Create Shortcuts Here" from the menu to create a shortcut. Double-click this folder and you get a mondo list of recently opened documents going back months. Just double-click the desired file to open it.

Like any folder, you can customize it to your heart's content. I deleted dead links and files that I'm not likely to access again. You can also sort on name or date by clicking the respective headers.

ICON BEAUTIFICATION

Are you tired of staring at the same old bland, lifeless Windows folder icons? Give them some sizzle with Change Icon, a cool little freebie that'll let you do just that. The colorful icons make it much easier to find the folders by topic. For instance, I changed my Book Chapters folder icon to a set of keys, and my Photos folder now looks like a camera—handy for spotting folders when you're rummaging through a folder tree list. Grab a copy at *http://www.oreilly.com/pcannoyances*.

×	Name ▲
	Book Chapters
	Downloads
	Inbox
	Originals
	PC World Files
	Photos
	Program Files
	Trip to China
	ChangeIcon.exe

QUICK ACCESS TO MY COMPUTER

The Annoyance: Every time I load Windows Explorer, it takes me to *My Documents*. Call me a dinosaur, but I liked it better when Windows Explorer opened *My Computer* instead.

The Fix: If you want to open Windows Explorer with *My Computer* selected and the folders pane displayed on the left side, and if you have a Windows keyboard (that is, a keyboard with the Windows logo key), simply press WinKey-E.

ONE FOLDER, MANY PLACES

The Annoyance: Is there a quicker way to access a folder? Or to automatically open a specific folder in Windows Explorer?

The Fix: You bet. The possibilities:

- If you want to open a folder—any folder—from the Start menu, simply drag the folder's icon from Windows Explorer to the Start button. Without releasing the mouse button, wait until the menu pops up, and drag to the desired location on the menu. A heavy black bar indicates where the link will end up when you release the mouse button. You can drag the folder from just about any place you can view it, such as a Windows Explorer window, the Windows Explorer Address bar (drag the folder icon), an Open or Save dialog box, and so on.

- If you want to open a folder in Explorer by clicking a button on the Quick Launch toolbar, drag the folder to the Quick Launch toolbar.

- If you want to open a folder from a desktop shortcut, right-click the folder, and drag it to the desktop, drop it, and choose "Create Shortcuts Here."

Warning. . .
If you left-drag the folder as you do for creating Start menu and Quick Launch shortcuts, Windows moves the folder and its contents to the desktop instead of creating a shortcut.

WHEN ONE EXPLORER SHORTCUT IS NOT ENOUGH

The Annoyance: I work with the same six folders, and what I *really* want is a way to choose which folder to open before launching Windows Explorer.

Save Notepad Files Without the .txt Extension

Notepad insists on saving files with a *.txt* extension. This is mighty irritating if you use Notepad for creating the occasional HTML file.

The solution is a real no-brainer—once you know the secret. When you save the file, just put quotes around the filename in the "Save as" field, such as "duh.html".

The Fix: That's such a handy (and obvious) feature, no wonder Microsoft didn't include it! Until they do, you'll need to create a shortcut for each folder you want Windows Explorer to open.

First create a shortcut on the Start menu, Quick Launch toolbar, or desktop of the desired folder (as described earlier in "One Folder, Many Places"). Right-click the folder shortcut and choose Properties. On the Shortcut tab, edit the contents of the Target field by inserting `explorer /e,` (including the comma) before the folder name (see Figure 5-1). The `/e` switch forces Windows Explorer to open in "explore" view instead of "open" view. (You want the Folders tree pane to appear.)

For example, you might end up with a Target line that looks something like:

```
explorer /e, "C:\Documents and Settings\Steve\My Documents\Birding"
```

You can replace the path between the quotes with any folder location, as in:

```
explorer /e, "C:\incoming\downloads"
```

If you want Windows Explorer to point to a specific file when it opens, all you do is add `/select,` (don't forget the comma) after the `/e,` followed by the path and filename, like this:

```
explorer /e,/select, "C:\incoming\downloads\annoyance.jpg"
```

Figure 5-1. You can create a shortcut that opens a specific folder in Windows Explorer. Have more than one favorite folder? Create another shortcut.

DISCONNECT YOUR SAVED WEB PAGES

The Annoyance: When you save a web page in Internet Explorer, it saves the page's text and HTML code in a single file and stuffs supporting files, such as graphics, in a folder. For example, if you save a page named *Roni's Journal*, you also get a subfolder named *Roni's Journal_files*. Here's what bugs me: if I move or delete the supporting files' folder, Windows Explorer also moves or deletes the main HTML file and vice versa. The HTML file and the files folder seem to be inextricably connected.

The Fix: Keeping the HTML file with its supporting files is a good thing. But you can treat them separately. In Windows Explorer, choose Tools → Folder Options. Click the View tab, scroll down in the Advanced Settings list to the "Managing pairs of Web pages and folders" section, and check "Show both parts and manage them individually." To return to the default behavior, select "Show and manage the pair as a single file."

By the way, you can avoid this messy solution altogether. In Internet Explorer, choose Save As and in the "Save as type" menu, select "Web Archive, single file (*.mht)." Doing so saves everything—text, graphics, the whole shebang—in a single file. This way, the page's components can't get separated. Select "Web Page, HTML only (*.htm, *.html)" if you don't need all the graphics, animation, and other supporting files.

USING THE "READ-ONLY" CHECKBOX FOR FOLDERS

Right-click a folder, select Properties, and you get a wealth of information—how many files the folder contains, how much disk space they occupy, and so on. In the Attributes section of that dialog box, you might also notice a "Read-only" checkbox. You think, "Hurrah! I can finally make a folder read-only and keep people from mucking with my files!"

But you can click that checkbox until you're blue in the face, and every time you return to the Properties dialog, it will be grayed out (or on some systems, green), indicating an "indeterminate condition." What's going on? Inconsistent interface design and sloppy analysis, that's what.

Whenever you open a folder's Properties dialog box, Windows *always* waffles on the attributes because it doesn't check the read-only status of every file in the folder. But no matter—bottom line, you can't set a folder as read-only. When you check that "Read-only" box, you're setting all the files in the folder as read-only, but not the folder. This is still a handy feature, but Microsoft could have given us clearer cues about what's going on. Note: checking the "Read-only" box only makes the current files in the folder read-only; files that you subsequently add to the folder won't be affected.

DUMP WINDOWS EXPLORER: TWO SLICK ALTERNATIVES

I don't think Microsoft pays too much attention to Windows Explorer. The "new" features the company incorporates with every release of Windows are invariably "been there, done that" copies of existing shareware or freeware tools. I suggest you ignore Windows Explorer and choose either ExplorerPlus or Total Commander.

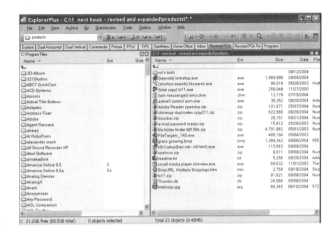

In my humble opinion, Novatix's ExplorerPlus is the best Windows Explorer replacement on the planet. Take a look at the top figure to see how cool it is to open two file-viewing panes and drag files between folders (see top figure). That alone is worth the price of admission. Other features include:

Multi-panes

You can open to side-to-side views, top/bottom panels, or, like Windows Explorer, no panels.

Layouts

I set up dual panes for seeing two folders I use often—the files for this book and for my "Home Office" column. Then I save the layout so I can instantly return to these two folders. I have different layouts for the user group folder, for my program files, and other situations. I can instantly switch among the layouts by clicking a tab just below the ExplorerPlus toolbar. This, folks, is very cool.

File Management Tools

You can quickly copy and move, rename multiple files, add notes to specific files, change the color of folder icons, and synchronize folders and files (see the middle figure).

Viewers

The built-in viewer lets you preview practically any file, document, multimedia file, or image (see the bottom figure).

DUMP WINDOWS EXPLORER: TWO SLICK ALTERNATIVES *(continued)*

FastFind

Lets you save searches, preview found files, and search within Zip files.

FTP

A built-in client for transferring files to your web server.

And if you're an old-time computer user, you'll appreciate ExplorerPlus' ability to emulate Norton Commander or Xtree Gold, two ancient DOS file managers. (Select Options → Preferences → Keyboard.)

By the way, unlike its predecessor, PowerDesk Pro, ExplorerPlus is bug-free. You can download a trial version of ExplorerPlus at *http://snipurl.com/explus_trial*. Once you play around with it, you may want to buy it for a mere $35 (for CD) or $30 (for download).

Total Commander is nipping at the heels of ExplorerPlus. Like ExplorerPlus, the $34 Total Commander is a dual-pane file manager (see the figure) that's highly configurable and has countless options, most of which are available via 60+ keyboard shortcuts.

I like the Directory Tree, a handy way to quickly navigate through an enormous hard drive (see bottom-right figure), and the Multi Rename feature is more powerful than any other I've used. The built-in file splitter (for copying a single file onto two or more disks) is great, as is the Combine File tool (which pulls the file back together). The program includes a download manager and a built-in FTP client that's fast and easy to use. Total Commander also emulates Norton Commander. A trial version is available at *http://www.oreilly.com/pcannoyances*.

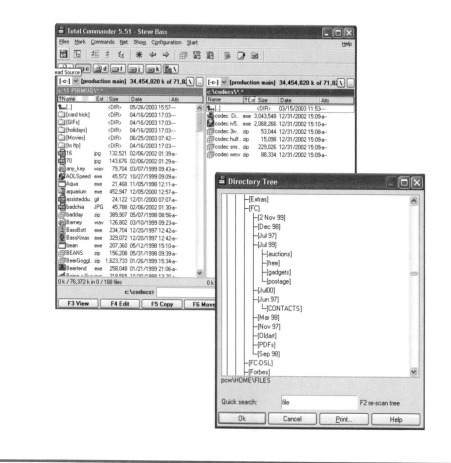

A BETTER WAY TO NAVIGATE

The Annoyance: Windows Explorer isn't much help when I'm submerged—and totally lost—in a subterranean folder on my hard drive. I feel like I could use a road map, something that Explorer doesn't supply.

The Fix: There are a few ways to better navigate with Windows Explorer.

The Title Bar view

Choose Tools → Folder options, click the View tab, and check the "Display the full path in the title bar" checkbox. In Figure 5-2 (top), you'll see it does just that.

The Address Bar view

If you don't already have the Address bar showing, select View → Toolbars → Address Bar. Now you'll see the current subfolder in the address bar. (See Figure 5-2, bottom).

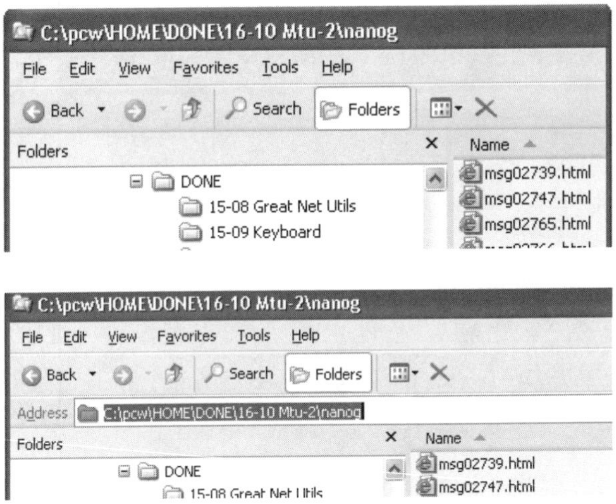

Figure 5-2. Top: If you're deep in the caverns of your hard drive, a quick glance at the menu bar will show you exactly where you are. Bottom: You might prefer using Explorer's Address bar both to see where you are and to navigate through your hard drive.

The third-party utility view

If you have lots of deeply buried folders, try Fast Directory Finder. This freebie indexes folders and lets you find them fast; it's also a super tool for finding folders across a network. It's available at *http://www.oreilly. com/pcannoyances*.

WHEN YOU CAN'T DELETE A FILE

The Annoyance: Windows Explorer won't let me delete certain files. I get an oh-so-unhelpful message about the file being "used by another person or program" (see Figure 5-3). There's no one else around, and no other programs are open. Any brilliant ideas?

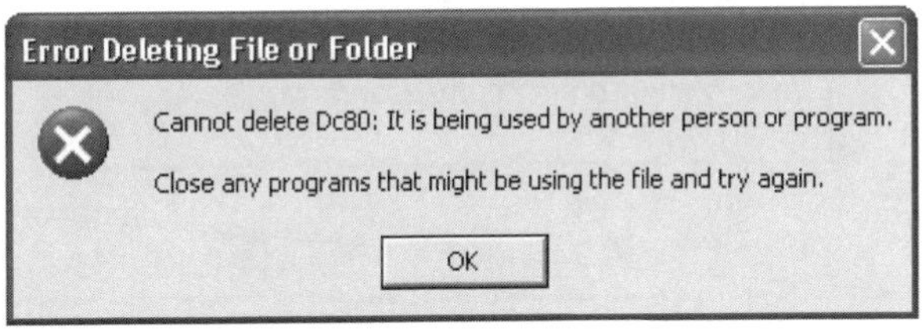

Figure 5-3. Do you get this message when you try to delete an *.avi* file? Me too.

The Fix: To prevent one program from accidentally clobbering a file that's in use by another program, many programs "lock" their open files so that they can't be deleted or changed by another program. I can live with that. But sometimes I *have* closed all other programs so that the only thing running is Windows Explorer, which I was planning to use to delete the file. (Note: some programs don't properly close document files when you're done with them. If the file you want to delete was open during the current session, close its application, not just the document.) But get this: it might be *Windows Explorer* that has the file open.

That's right: depending on how you've configured Windows Explorer, selecting a file can display a preview in the left pane. (This is especially common with *.avi* files.) Windows stupidly thinks the file is locked and prevents you from deleting it. The workaround:

- Close the preview pane. Display a different Explorer Bar (such as Search or Folders) or, more drastically, choose Tools → Folder Options and, on the General tab, select "Use Windows classic folders." Then select the file and delete it.

- Open a command prompt window, close Windows Explorer, and delete the file using the `del` command.

An easy way to open a command prompt window in the current folder is to use Microsoft's PowerToy, Open Command Window Here, which you can download from *http://www.oreilly.com/pcannoyances*.

Still can't nuke that file? Exit and restart Windows—that should release any file locks. Another trick to try: delete the folder that contains the file you want to delete. (Of course, move any files you want to keep to another folder—or, if possible, move the target file to a different folder before deleting it.)

If Windows still refuses to delete the file, boot your computer into a command-line interface instead of Windows. If you're using Windows Me or Windows 98, boot from a DOS system floppy disk, which you can create when you format the disk. A bootable DOS disk can also give you access to your Windows XP or Windows 2000 files, provided they're on a FAT-formatted volume.

But XP and 2000 PCs usually rely on NTFS, and in this case, a DOS boot floppy won't work. To access files on an NTFS-formatted volume, turn to the Recovery Console. Check Windows online help for information about using Recovery Console. In Windows Explorer, select Help → Help and

STOP THE YELLOW INFO FILE POP-UPS

From Explorer, select Tools → Folder Options → View, and scroll to "Show pop-up description for folder and desktop items." Uncheck the box, and those annoying yellow pop-ups will no longer bother you.

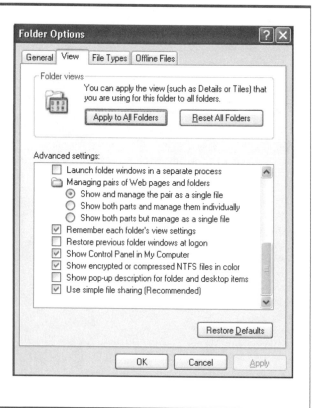

Support Center, and type "Recovery Console" in the search field. Note: by default, it's configured so that you do not have access to many of your files for security reasons.

MAKE EXPLORER CRASH-PROOF

The Annoyance: It's bad enough that my fancy programs crash and burn, but now Windows Explorer is suddenly crashing!

The Fix: You'd think Windows Explorer would be more stable, but I've seen it die on many occasions. One cause is a corrupt file in the folder you're trying to display. Switch to list view. Trying to render the corrupt file as a thumbnail can make Explorer go bonkers.

There's also a quirk that makes Explorer crash on some Windows 2000 setups. Install Service Pack 3 (or later) to squash this particular bug.

LOOK WHAT I FOUND! BUT DON'T TOUCH...

The Annoyance: The other day, I used the Search command (on XP's Start menu) to find some files. I selected multiple files so I could copy them en masse. But Windows refused to cooperate, instead displaying bogus messages like "Cannot copy file. Cannot read from source disk or file." Why can't I copy, move, or delete more than one file at a time in the Search Results window?

ANCIENT COMPUTER GAMES

You've probably had enough annoyances for now. So how about spending a few hours with some terrific timewasters such as Battle Tank, a nifty blast from the past (*http://snipurl.com/Tank*).

The Fix: Normally you can, but the rules change when the results include files from the Temporary Internet Files folder. The files there are not truly discrete files like you'd find in a normal folder; they're part of a single, indexed file.

Windows Explorer can decipher this index enough to display the files and work with them individually, but not in groups. You'll find similar limitations when you work with "compressed folders" (a.k.a. zip files). Windows Explorer displays the content just like normal folders, but when you try to manipulate these files, you'll discover that something's fishy.

COPYING FILE PATHS

The Annoyance: I often want to copy a folder's path and name so I can insert it into an email message or save a file to a specific spot. Why should that be so difficult?

The Fix: It's easier than you think. Open Windows Explorer, navigate to the folder, highlight the path in the Address bar above, and hit Ctrl-C. Voilà, it's in your clipboard. Can't see the Address bar? Select View → Toolbars → Address Bar.

BROADEN WINDOWS' SEARCH HORIZONS

The Annoyance: When your hard disk contains a gazillion files, it's just about impossible to remember where you put everything, or even what you named the file. That's why I search for specific text within files. Yet sometimes, Windows doesn't find my file!

The Fix: The problem is that Windows XP doesn't search all files, only certain types (based on file extension). The original version of Windows XP could only search inside Microsoft Office files, HTML pages, and a handful of other types. Installing Service Pack 1 for Windows XP adds "filter components" for dozens of additional file types, so that should be your first move if you're plagued by this annoyance.

If you want to search for a file type XP doesn't normally search, you must add a wacky Registry value. Microsoft Knowledge Base article 309173 at *http://snipurl.com/ ms_309173* explains the details.

A more comprehensive solution is to tell Windows to search *all* file types, regardless of extension (see Figure 5-4). This will slow down searches, but it does find files that wouldn't otherwise be found. Here's how:

1. Right-click *My Computer* (on the desktop, on the Start menu, or in a Windows Explorer window) and choose Manage.

2. In the console tree in the left pane, expand the "Services and Applications" item.

3. Right-click Indexing Service and choose Properties.

4. On the Generation tab, check the "Index files with unknown extensions" box and select OK, and then close the Computer Management window.

MYSTERIOUS FILE EXTENSIONS REVEALED

If you've got to figure out that obscure file extension, dig into The File Extension Source, an excellent reference site that lists almost a zillion extensions: *http://snipurl.com/file_ext*.

SEARCH FASTER BY EXCLUDING ZIPPED FILES

The Annoyance: On the other hand, Search can be a little too aggressive in its searches. I archive old documents in zip files. Search looks through all my zip files,

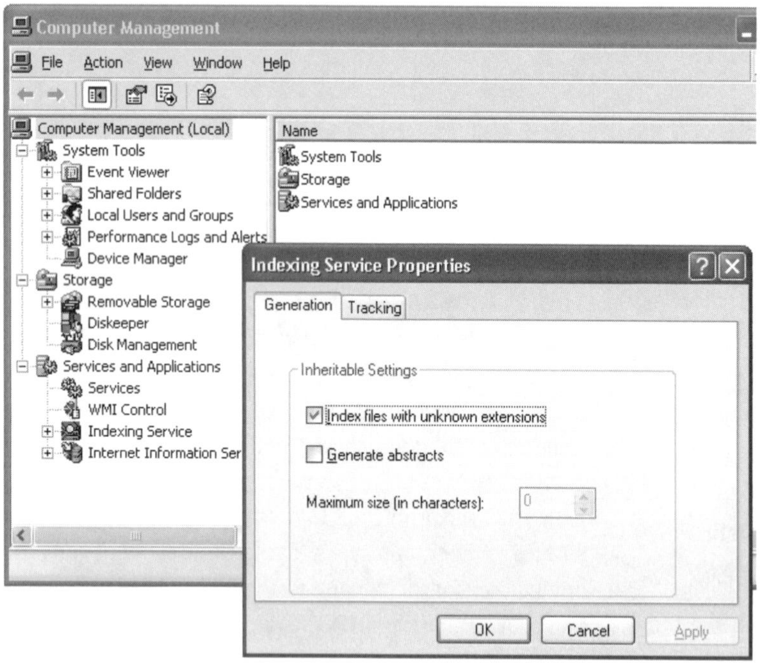

Figure 5-4. Here's how to force Windows to search all file types, regardless of extension.

dredging up lots of old, archived, and irrelevant stuff. I archive old files so they *won't* be included in searches. Is there a fix for this?

The Fix: Windows XP, as you've probably discovered, has co-opted the *.zip* file extension and calls such files "compressed folders." This is mostly a plus, since it acts just like a normal folder—you can add, remove, and use files. To further the illusion that zip files are compressed folders, Windows by default searches them. The only way to prevent that is to unhook zip files from Windows, which you do as follows:

1. Choose Start → Run and type:

       `regsvr32 /u %systemroot%\system32\zipfldr.dll`

2. Reboot your computer.

This will leave you without the built-in zip integration. You can reenable it by using the same command without the /u.

MANAGE ZIPPED FILES

The Annoyance: I'm using Windows 98 and rarely have to deal with zipped files, so I don't need to bother with third-party tools such as WinZip or FreeZip. But what do I do when the occasional zip file comes my way?

The Fix: You could upgrade to Windows XP—it has a built-in zip extraction tool. But if you insist on sticking with Windows 98, use ExplorerPlus (a replacement for Windows Explorer) for all your zipping and unzipping needs; even the free version does a terrific job. With ExplorerPlus, there are two ways to do it:

- If you want to extract the file (or files) into the same folder where the zip file resides, right-click the zip file and choose ExplorerPlus. (See Figure 5-5.)

- With ExplorerPlus showing two panes open side-by-side, just right-drag the zip file to the opposite panel, release the mouse button, and choose Extract Here. (See Figure 5-6.) Download a trial version of Explorer-Plus at *http://snipurl.com/explus_trial*.

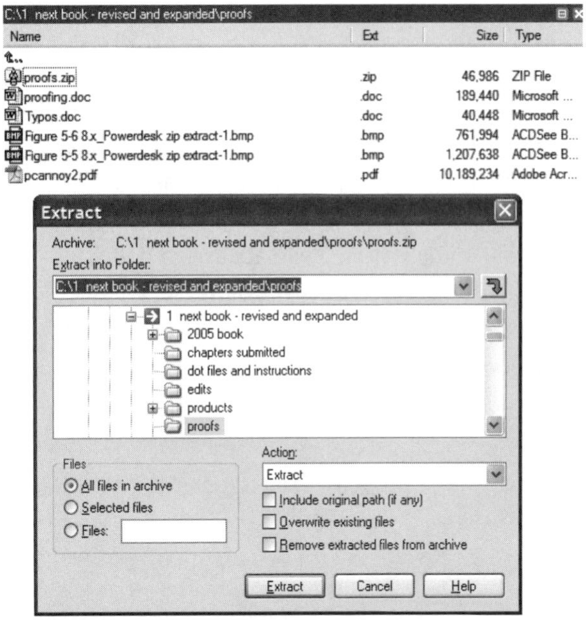

Figure 5-5. Using ExplorerPlus, you can extract zipped files into the same folder containing the zip file with a minimum of clicks.

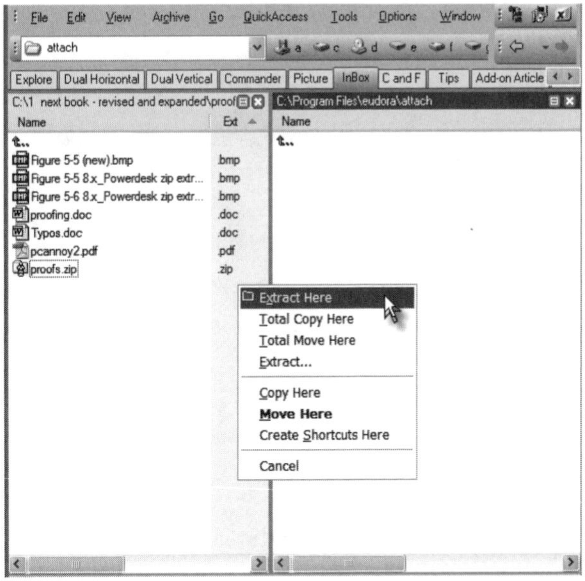

Figure 5-6. Using ExplorerPlus with two panes open makes it very easy to extract zipped files.

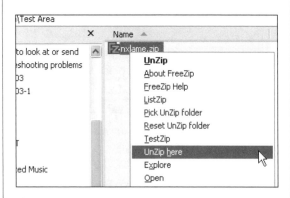
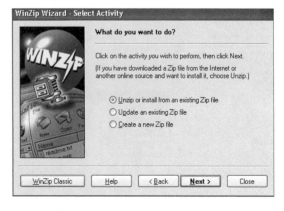
BEYOND WINZIP SELF-EXTRACTOR

The Annoyance: I downloaded a cool utility from Microsoft's site. When I double-clicked the file, a dialog box asked me to unzip the file into a folder. Once the file was successfully unzipped, there were no further instructions. What do I do next?

The Fix: Microsoft uses a really dumb unzipping program, the WinZip Self-Extractor (see Figure 5-7). Here's what to do: once the unzipping tool is finished, click the Close button. Then use Windows Explorer to go to the folder where you saved the file. In some cases, you'll need to run an installation program, often named Setup.exe; other times, you'll need to find a *readme.txt* or *readme.doc* file that supplies additional instructions.

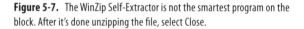

Create a folder you'll remember—mine is *downloads*—and unzip all your files to it so they'll be easier to find.

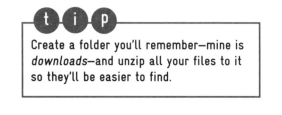

Figure 5-7. The WinZip Self-Extractor is not the smartest program on the block. After it's done unzipping the file, select Close.

RENAME MULTIPLE FILES

The Annoyance: I bought a digital camera, and every picture I take has a similar name, like *pic0001.jpg*, *pic0002.jpg*, and so on. Can Windows Explorer rename more than one file at a time? I'm using Windows 98.

The Fix: If you insist on sticking with Windows 98 rather than upgrading to XP, you'll be stuck with a dumb(er) version of Windows Explorer. Here are some alternatives:

- Upgrade to XP. Windows XP lets you rename a group of files just by selecting the files, right-clicking, selecting Rename, and renaming the first file. All the other files will have the same root name followed by a number in parentheses.

- RJHExtensions gives you an easy way to rename multiple files, plus shred and encrypt files. The freebie is available at *http://www.oreilly.com/pcannoyances*.

- If you're technically savvy, you'll love the Bulk Rename Utility (see Figure 5-8). You can download a free copy at *http://www.oreilly.com/pcannoyances*.

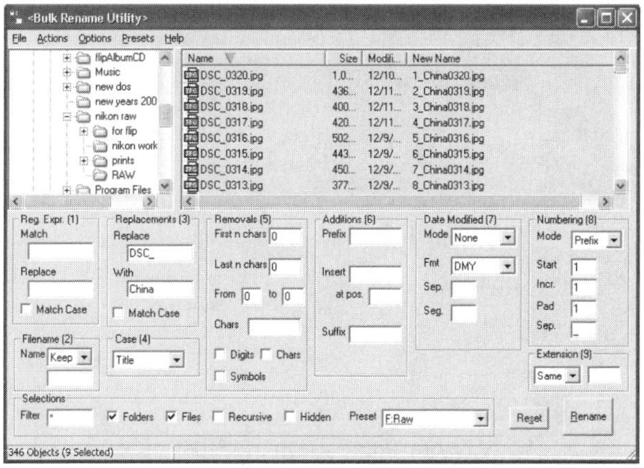

Figure 5-8. The Bulk Rename Utility has a dozen ways for you to rename both files and folders.

- FileTargets isn't great at file renaming, but it's superb at letting you quickly move or copy files, or copy the filename and path to the clipboard. Download a free copy from *http://www.oreilly.com/pcannoyances* (see Figure 5-9).

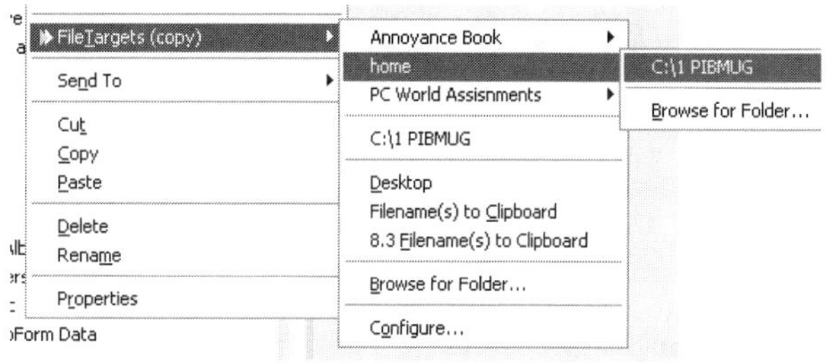

Figure 5-9. Use FileTargets to grab a bunch of files and copy them to folders you use often.

GIMME BACK MY FILE ASSOCIATIONS

The Annoyance: I installed a new MP3 player, and it's mysteriously taken over all my media files—video, WAVs, music—even photos. Talk about annoying!

The Fix: File associations—the program you want to open a particular type of file—are sometimes filched by other programs that see themselves as the center of the computing universe. Unless you pay careful attention during installation, programs such as RealOne Player can commandeer file association settings for dozens of formats. Here are two ways that may fix the annoyance:

- Open the application you don't want associated with the files, go to the Options or Preferences menu, and look for a setting to un-associate the files. Repeat the process with the program you want to associate with the files.

- Right-click the file, select Open With → Choose Program, and select the application from the list (or browse to the program). Make sure you check the "Always use the selected program to open this kind of file" box (see Figure 5-10).

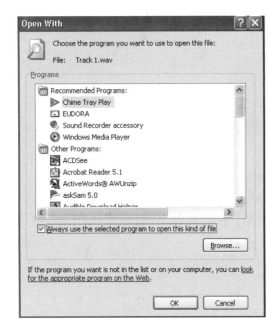

Figure 5-10. You can choose the program to open a type file with a simple right click

RIGHT-CLICK FOR QUICK PRINTS

The Annoyance: I've located a file with Explorer that I want to print. Isn't it dopey to have to double-click the file to open the application, and then find the Print command—just to print the file?

The Fix: You're right, there *is* a better way to do it, but the kids in Redmond don't make it obvious.

The quickest way to print a document, no matter *what* the application, is to let Windows Explorer do all the work. Right-click the file and select Print. Explorer will open the program that's associated with the file extension and issue the print command. Explorer's neat and tidy, too, closing the application when it's done.

FILE ASSOCIATION HELPERS

Windows 98 doesn't have nearly the degree of options that XP has. Until you upgrade, here are two programs to help you with file associations:

- **OpenExpert lets you choose which programs to use on the fly. That way, when you want to open an image file, you can choose a file viewer or a picture editor. Ditto for deciding between, say, Netscape and Internet Explorer to view an HTML page. The tool is easy to use—right-click a file, choose Open With → Add application, and select the program (see figure). OpenExpert is a freebie for home use (if you use it commercially, the fee is $20 per user, minus discounts starting at 20%) and is available at *http://www.oreilly.com/pcannoyances*.**

- **ChangeExt is another free Windows Explorer add-on that displays details about a file with a right-click. Besides handling file associations, it can copy the filename and path to the clipboard. You'll find it at *http://www.oreilly.com/pcannoyances*.**

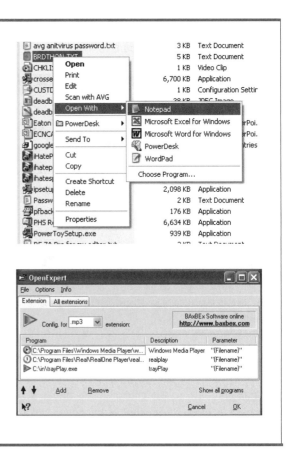

QUICK NOTES IN WINDOWS

The Annoyance: I need a quick, on-the-fly way to store notes with files—and I don't want to bother with a utility, free or not.

The Fix: Gotcha. Windows's file-annotation function is far from polished, but it's a quick and simple way to add notes to important files. In Windows Explorer, right-click the file and choose Properties (or just select the file and press Alt-Enter). Choose the Summary tab (Windows XP) or Custom tab (all other versions of Windows), and type your note in the Comments field (see Figure 5-11). Oddly enough, this option isn't available for some file types, including some video formats. (If you don't see any blank fields on the Summary tab, click the Simple button on the lower right.) Now when you send the file to someone, your notes travel with it. To read the notes, follow the same steps to display the Summary tab and Comments field.

![storm damage.txt Properties dialog box showing Summary tab with Title "storm damage.txt", Subject "Storm Damage Dcumentation", Author "Steve Bass", empty Category and Keywords fields, and Comments "This is the primary document detailing the damage we sustained during the major storms of December, 2004 throughout southern California. The cod was submitted to Yenta Insurance and their agent, John Schmendrick."]

Figure 5-11. Add notes to practically any file and they'll stay with the file no matter where it goes—or to whom you send it.

QUICK NOTES IN KEYNOTE

If you liked the idea of "Quick Notes in Windows," and you don't mind using a third-party program and you need something a bit more capable, turn to KeyNote. (Not to be confused with Apple's Keynote presentation software.) This puppy is an electronic Day-Timer on steroids: it has a tabbed notebook, outliner, and personal information manager. I use it as a scratchpad to quickly jot down notes and ideas instead of opening Word. You can download this freebie at *http://snipurl.com/keynote*.

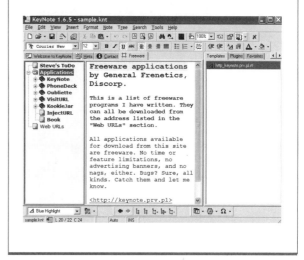

ENCRYPT FILES FOR SECURITY

The Annoyance: I was outraged to find a coworker poking around in a folder on my PC. Besides storing the files on a removable disk that I can lock in a drawer or booby-trapping my PC, is there any way to protect my files?

The Fix: Many people share their PC with somebody from time to time, whether a family member at home or a colleague at work, so it's worth encrypting all your sensitive files to keep Nosy Nellies at bay. There are a few ways to do it.

In Windows XP Pro and 2000 (with NTFS-formatted drives), open Windows Explorer and right-click the folder you want to encrypt. Choose Properties, select the General tab, click the Advanced button, and check the "Encrypt contents to secure data" box (see Figure 5-12). Click OK twice, and the folder's contents are locked up tight, accessible only to those who have your login information. Any files you subsequently move to the folder will also be encrypted; drag a file out of the folder, and it will be automatically unencrypted.

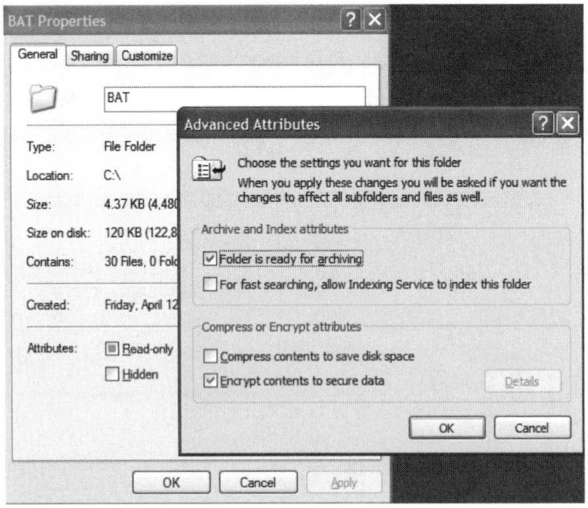

Figure 5-12. Explorer has a built-in way to encrypt files.

If you're using Windows Me or 98, visit *http://snipurl.com/ Cryptainer* and grab a copy of the free Cryptainer LE utility. This handy tool creates a hidden, encrypted virtual drive (see Figure 5-13).

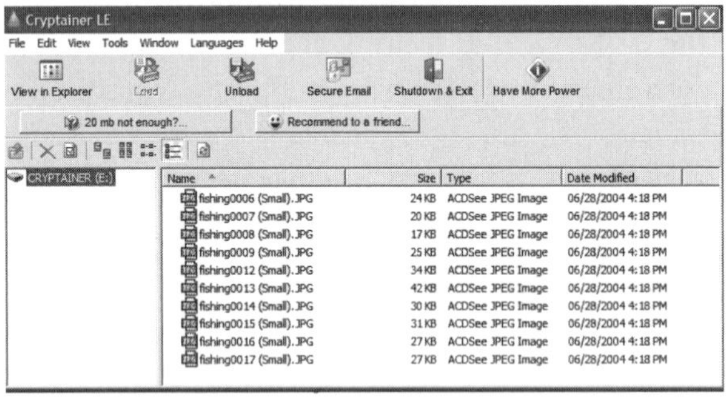

Figure 5-13. Want to keep your files and folders from prying eyes? The free Cryptainer LE can create a hidden drive available just to you.

A niftier way to keep your info from prying eyes is to start your computer by plugging in a special USB gizmo that acts like a car key. Often called a dongle (though never in mixed company), one notable offering in this category is Griffin Technologies' ControlKey. Once configured, only someone with a ControlKey can even boot your computer. Not only that, but you can make specific files and folders off-limits to some users, or limit your child's access to the Internet, instant messaging, or practically any application. The $60 device is small and looks very much like a USB flash memory stick (see Figure 5-14). Check it out at *http://www.controlkey.com.*

The ControlKey is flexible, and the software that comes with the gizmo lets you dictate what happens when you remove the key: it can lock your PC, put it in standby mode, or simply block Internet access. ControlKey also prevents hackers from booting your system into Safe Mode and then taking over your system.

> **t i p**
>
> ControlKey works only with Windows XP, and it can lock up files and folders only on NTFS-formatted drives.

Figure 5-14. The ControlKey can lock down your entire notebook or desktop—or only certain portions, such as online access or instant messaging.

SHARE BIG FILES THE EASY WAY

The Annoyance: I have a bunch of big video files I want to share with my buddies. I can't attach them to email—at 5 MB apiece, they're just too big. I wish there were an easy way to do it, especially for my friend the novice.

The Fix: Wish no more. I've got a cool program that lets you move files to a folder on your PC that your buddies can "see" on their PCs almost instantly. FolderShare is a free, secure peer-to-peer file-sharing program that's so convenient I use it almost daily (see Figure 5-15) .

Figure 5-15. Here's what FolderShare looks like on my PC—shared libraries for my O'Reilly editor, another for file sharing with PC World colleagues, and one for my illegal file-sharing buddies. You can see who has access to the Judy_Transfer library in the righthand panel.

Here's how it works: you invite someone to share a specific collection of files called a library, all housed in one ordinary folder. Your buddy will have to download a small application that lets him "connect" to the library. He then associates a folder on his computer with the library and downloads any of the library's files to his machine via drag and drop in Windows Explorer.

Depending on how you configure FolderShare, you can have a remote file in a pal's library appear automatically in your FolderShare folder. The alternative—and this is perfect if you're on dialup—is to just have a placeholder appear, reminding you to go to the site and download the file. Not to worry, only the files in the FolderShare folder are available to others; your other folders are safe from prying eyes. One more security issue you needn't worry about: all file transfers are authenticated via RSA key certificates and encrypted via AES (Advanced Encryption Standard) over SSL (Secure Sockets Layer). FolderShare is an ideal way to bypass email and FTP servers when sharing big files. The free version of FolderShare allows up to three files to be queued for download. You can work with as many as 100 libraries, each of which can have up to 3,000 files (the maximum size of any single file is 2 GB). For $4.50 per month, you get the ability to automatically sync files across multiple computers. Visit *http://snipurl.com/foldershare2* to download your copy.

If you'd rather not bother with Folder-Share and prefer splitting the files into manageable chunks for emailing, check "Split 'em and Join 'em" in Chapter 6.

A THUMBNAIL VIEW FOR FILE ATTACHMENTS

The Annoyance: I'm trying to attach an image—a JPG, actually—to an email. When I open the dialog, I'm faced with a lengthy list of obscure filenames. Sorting through the stack and trying to figure out what the image is by filename is nonsense. Why can't I see the image itself?

The Fix: This is so simple, you're going to laugh. (I did because it was something that had flummoxed me, too.) When you open the dialog, just switch the view from whatever it is currently—probably Details or Icons—to Thumbnails (see Figure 5-16).

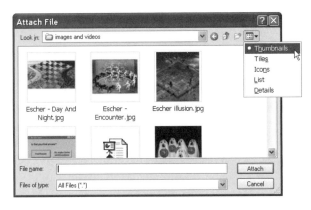

Figure 5-16. Want to view files before you attach them to an email? Just choose Explorer's Thumbnails option.

ALL THUMBS.DB

The Annoyance: Solve this mystery for me. What are those *Thumbs.db* files that have started materializing in many folders on my computer?

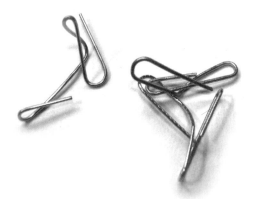

The Ultimate Escape

The best I could do on Escape (*http://snipurl.com/ dodgeit*), a tough and deeply annoying game, was 9 seconds. I could probably do better with my eyes closed. You'll find out right away that bumping the black frame ends the game. [*Note from Editor: It's highly addictive. I spent the afternoon playing this and got no editing done.*]

The Fix: They have an ominous look, I know, but they're benign files. Windows generates them every time you open a folder and use the thumbnail view. Delete them if they annoy you, though Windows will recreate them the next time you use the thumbnail view. If you're obsessed with keeping these little files off your PC, you can turn off the thumbnail cache; with a fast PC, Windows will hardly break a sweat reading the files during a thumbnail folder view.

From the Control Panel, select Folder Options and click the View tab. Scroll down, check "Do not cache thumbnails," and click OK. By the way, you may get an "Illegal document" error if you use Microsoft's FrontPage and a *Thumbs.db* file exists in a folder on a web site you're editing. The solution is to get rid of the *.db* file from the web site.

6

Music, Video, and CD
ANNOYANCES

Remember the good old days, when we watched videos on a television and listened to music on a radio? That was *so* 20th-century!

Today, almost any computer you buy can play sound and video files, and many come with the ability to burn your own CDs and DVDs. But with great power comes great irritability. There's a maze of file formats, a gaggle of players, and the many complications surrounding disc burning.

This chapter touches on some of the bigger annoyances related to multimedia on your PC. And hey, if you get really annoyed, how about dusting off your TV and CD player and using them instead?

MUSIC AND VIDEO ANNOYANCES

KEEP ALL YOUR MUSIC THE SAME VOLUME

The Annoyance: I have lots of MP3s I've ripped onto my hard drive from my CD music collection. The problem is, Copeland's "Fanfare" is so loud it blasts me out of my chair, and the next song, Dave Brubecks' "Take Five," is way too soft. Can I impose the same volume level on all my cuts?

The Fix: The trick is to adjust—or normalize—the sound level as you're ripping the MP3 to disk, and many ripping programs offer that feature. The problem is what to do after the fact:

- Microsoft's Windows Media Player fixes the problem by normalizing the volume as you play the music. Look under View → Enhancements → Crossfading Auto Volume Leveling.

- If you want to fix the problem permanently, you'll need MP3Gain, a free—and very cool—utility that analyzes and normalizes the sound levels of each of your MP3 files. There's a copy on *http://www.oreilly.com/pcannoyances*.

PLAY SOUND FILES QUICKLY AND EASILY

The Annoyance: I have a big collection of sound files that I use in my email program to announce incoming mail from different people. When I want to choose a sound file, I don't want to load that 800-pound gorilla—Windows Media Player—to preview a tiny file.

The Fix: For tiny sounds, use a tiny player—WavPlay. Just launch it and navigate to the folder with the sound files

(see Figure 6-1). WavPlay even lets you set up to five presets so you can quickly scan specific folders. There's a free copy of WavPlay at *http://www.oreilly.com/pcannoyances*.

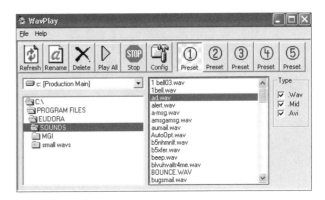

Figure 6-1. Instead of wasting time loading Windows Media Player, use WavPlay, a freebie dedicated to playing sound files.

iPOD ♥ THE PC

The Annoyance: I want an iPod, but I don't want to buy a Mac in order to use it. Talk about annoyances!

The Fix: A PC user contemplating an iPod? Oh, the horror! Well, the truth is, Apple's iPod may make many PC users contemplate a trip to the dark side. If that's the case, take a look at XPlay, a nifty $22 utility that lets you manage and download your MP3 files to an iPod by way of a FireWire or USB connection. Among other things, XPlay lets you use Explorer to drag and drop files to and fro the iPod, automatically synchronizes your PC's music collection with the iPod's, and more. XPlay works with Windows 98SE and later; a trial version is available at *http://snipurl.com/xplay2*.

TURN OFF REALONE'S MESSAGE CENTER AD

The Annoyance: I hate the Message Center on the RealOne media player. This ad window sits in the Windows System Tray, bogging down my PC and randomly appearing with irritating ads, alerts, and alleged news—even when RealOne isn't running. How do I get rid of this digital poltergeist?

The Fix: If you seek salvation at Real's site, you won't get very far. It says—with a straight face, yet—that the Message Center "cannot be turned off." However, it does tell you how to prevent it from popping up when RealOne isn't in use. In the RealOne Player, choose Tools → Preferences. In the Category window, expand the Automatic Services, and uncheck the "Periodically check for new messages" box, and click OK.

But if you value your sanity, rid yourself of the Message Center, even when RealOne is up and running. You won't find that tip at Real's site. So here it is: first, summon Windows' Task Manager. (In Windows XP, press Ctrl+Alt+Delete, then click the Processes tab.) Look for a process called *realsched.exe* or *evntsvc.exe*; highlight it and click the End Process button.

Next, delete the same file from Real's *Update_OB* folder. Go to *\Program Files\Common Files\Real\Update_OB* and once again locate a file called *realsche.exe* or *evntsvc.exe*. Delete this file, and you'll eradicate the Message Center—and make the famously pesky RealOne a little less pesky.

SMART MARKETING

The guy's (almost) a marketing genius. He's been covered all over the Internet. Too bad he doesn't have an area code on his truck, eh? *http://snurl.com/plumbtruck*.

GOOD RIDDANCE TO REALPLAYER

The Annoyance: The RealPlayer media player adds far too many icons to my desktop, and it constantly asks me if I wanted to change my media-file associations. RealPlayer also displays lots of ads and pop ups, and my firewall frequently alerts me that RealPlayer is trying to phone home. Can I dump it and still play music and video formatted for RealPlayer?

The Fix: It's easy to dump RealPlayer—and Apple's equally insistent QuickTime video player—and replace them with an app that is absolutely free and does just as good a job. Well, mostly.

But first, a disclaimer. The products I'm about to mention successfully handle a Real audio or video stream most of the time but, unfortunately, not 100% of the time, and definitely not with RealPlayer or QuickTime files streamed off every site you visit. If you're a real RealPlayer fan and *must* have it, skip to the next sidebar, "Welcome Back (to a Special) RealPlayer."

With this disclaimer under your belt, uninstall RealPlayer and QuickTime via Windows' Add or Remove Programs control panel. Then download Real Alternative, which plays RealAudio and RealMedia files and has plug-ins for Internet Explorer, Opera, Netscape, and Mozilla, so you can play music and videos right off the Web. It's available at *http://snipurl.com/alt_realplayer*. The QuickTime Alternative is at *http://snipurl.com/quickplayer*.

If you want something fancier for playing RealPlayer files (and MP3s), try the free JetAudio at *http://snipurl.com/jetaudio*.

By the way, if uninstalling and installing all these apps make your media-file associations go wacko—and they may, because you're uninstalling Real—read "Gimme Back My File Associations" in Chapter 5 for tips on re-associating your player programs with the appropriate file types.

REALONE'S ICONS ARE A REAL PAIN

The Annoyance: Near the top of my list of irritations is RealNetworks' RealOne Player. It's infuriating that RealOne salts my PC with desktop icons and browser links. The program also lights my fuse when it offers me confusing choices for audio and video file associations. Quick, get my blood pressure meds!

The Fix: If you're installing RealOne from scratch, pay close attention to each installation screen. Always choose a custom installation to see more options. On the "Program Location and Desktop Settings" screen, uncheck the

WELCOME BACK (TO A SPECIAL) REALPLAYER

There's a special version of RealPlayer 10 that hasn't a bit of spyware or adware, never nags you, and doesn't litter your system with icons. The version isn't stripped down, either; it's just missing all those annoyances.

It's found at a perfectly legit site, but few people know that the RealPlayer offered there is different. And I'd like to keep it that way because once word spreads, things may change. So consider it a perk of your purchasing *PC Annoyances* and keep it under your hat.

It's at the BBC Radio site at *http://snipurl.com/cool_realplayer*. The unofficial story, according to one source, is that the BBC's charter prevents it from "shower[ing] their viewers with craptastic ads for random American companies," so to get the BBC-to-Web broadcast in Real format, Real had to produce an ad-free player. True or not, you still get a version of RealPlayer, in all its glory, without the annoyances.

When you install RealPlayer, there's only one nag, but it's minor and easily resolved. RealPlayer still attempts to add an entry to your Registry because it wants to check for updates whenever you boot your system. If you'd prefer it doesn't, click Tools → Preferences, open the Automatic Services item on the left, and choose Auto Update. Uncheck the "Automatically download and install important updates" box and click OK. If you want to check for updates manually, just click Help → About RealOne Player, and press the "Check For Update" button.

As RealPlayer installs, you'll be faced with a few choices, all easy to handle. The first is an amazingly polite dialog that asks where you'd like to see RealPlayer icons (see top figure).

The other installation issue is the Default Media Player dialog. RealPlayer automatically assigns extensions best suited to itself, such as RealPlayer's *.RA* and *.RAM* files. That's fine. But it also tries to co-opt other audio and video files, such as MP3, CD, MPEG, and AVI (see bottom figure.)

My advice: keep your existing players assigned to these non-Real formats. Uncheck *every* box in order to ensure

that RealPlayer plays RealPlayer files only. To see what *is* assigned to these files—and see what RealPlayer tried to take over—click the dialog's Advanced button. If there are any files you'd prefer to assign to RealPlayer, you can modify the settings here.

When the next-to-last dialog appears asking you to register with RealPlayer, click Cancel and, in the next dialog, choose Exit. If anyone at RealPlayer approaches you, tell them Bass said it was okay not to register.

Unlike most RealPlayer installations, this special BBC version is extraordinarily polite and asks you nicely if and where you'd like its icons placed.

When you install this special version of RealPlayer, you'll find all the file association boxes checked. Don't get bamboozled—uncheck all the boxes and live happily ever after.

locations you think are nonessential. (I unchecked all of them; I knew that a RealOne icon would end up in my Start menu anyway.) At the "Default Media Player" screen, choose Customize, scroll through the choices, and carefully select which of the 14 audio and video file types you want to associate with RealOne.

Already have a RealOne (or RealPlayer) on your PC? Dump all of the program's icons except for the ones you use most often, such as the one from your desktop. Next, remove the RealOne shortcut from your System Tray. (You don't need it, since the player loads automatically whenever you open the associated file.)

STOP REALPLAYER FROM AUTO-STARTING

The Annoyance: Whenever I boot up Windows, a RealPlayer icon sticks itself in the Windows System Tray and refuses to leave. How can I give this unwanted guest the bum's rush?

The Fix: The problem goes beyond an icon in your System Tray. Even if you get rid of the software that launches that icon, RealPlayer will pop up, unannounced, with pesky messages.

There are several culprits here. One is a tiny program that constantly checks the Real site for updates. Another applet called the Message Center constantly checks the Real site for messages—often annoying marketing messages—and pops up those messages whether you like it or not.

To kill the Message Center annoyance, open RealPlayer and choose Tools → Preferences. Click Automatic Services in the panel to the left, then the Configure Message Center button on the right In the screen that appears (Figure 6-2), uncheck the "Check for new messages" box. Click OK and close the Message Center screen that appears for no good reason. Click OK again when the Preferences screen appears.

To tell RealPlayer to stop checking for automatic updates, follow the same steps as above. But this time, double-click Automatic Services and click the Auto Update item beneath it. Then, on the right, uncheck the "Automatically download and install important updates" box, and click OK.

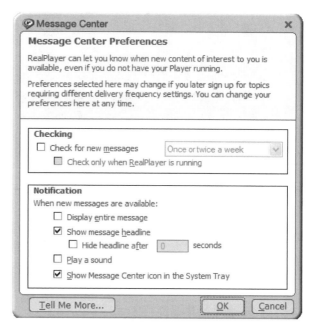

Figure 6-2. Kill RealPlayer's most annoying annoyance by telling it not to check for new messages in the Message Center.

TAKE YOUR MUSIC ANYWHERE

The Annoyance: I want to take my home collection of MP3s to work. I've burned a few CDs to take to the office, but with all this great technology, there's got to be a better way than schlepping all these CDs.

The Fix: There is. Load Chime Software's AjooBlast Server, a cool, free little remote access program that lets you listen to the music on your home PC (or your buddy's system) from any PC in the world. AjooBlast is a small program, and totally secure—access is only to the folders you allow, and downloading your files is not possible; it's for listening only. The only downside is that if you're behind a router, you'll need to open port 8080. You can download AjooBlast from *http://www.oreilly.com/pcannoyances*.

MAKE WINAMP JUMBO SIZE

The Annoyance: In a world full of bloated media players, Nullsoft's venerable Winamp remains a champ in part because it's so lean and mean. If you ask me, though, it's too lean—its default window is so tiny that it makes my aging eyeballs ache. Maybe they should have called it "Squintamp."

The Fix: Click Winamp's Control Menu (the little + sign in the upper-left corner), select Scale, and choose a size over 100%. If you value your eyesight, try 200%.

THE MISSING VOLUME ICON

The Annoyance: I don't know what I did, but the volume icon in my System Tray has vanished. How can I get it back?

The Fix: In XP, open the "Sounds and Audio Devices" control panel. On the Volume tab, check the "Place volume icon in the taskbar" box, click Apply, then click OK. For earlier versions of Windows, open the "Sounds and Multimedia" (Me and 2000) or "Multimedia" (98) control panel. On the Sounds tab (Me and 2000) or the Audio tab (98), check the "Show volume control on the taskbar" box and click OK. The speaker icon will reappear in the System Tray.

STUBBORN VOLUME CONTROL SETTING

Is the "Place volume icon in the Taskbar" box already checked? Uncheck the box, click Apply, check the box again, and hit OK.

TOO MUCH/NOT ENOUGH VOLUME

The Annoyance: My PC's speaker volume keeps jumping up and down, depending on what's playing. When the volume level is just right for music, Windows' system alerts blast me out of my chair. I spend way too much time fiddling with the speaker volume. It makes me want to go back to cranking up the old Victrola.

The Fix: Have you considered ear plugs? Seriously, it's difficult keeping all the sounds coming through your PCs at the right level. A couple of tips:

1. Open Windows' Play Control tool. Summon it by clicking the speaker icon in the System Tray. If you don't have a speaker icon, seek out the advice in "The Missing Volume Icon" for how to display it.

2. In the Play Control tool, you'll notice that sliders are dedicated to different sound types: WAV files, CD player, Line in (such as a microphone), and so on. Set the master Play Control (the slider on the far left) a few notches below the highest setting. Then adjust the Wave and CD Audio volume settings at about 50%. Don't worry about the other sliders—for most users, these are the only settings to worry about. The Play Control is the master volume and supersedes all the other controls. Wave handles practically every system sound, including music you play from your hard drive, streaming music, and Windows' annoying error dings. CD Audio handles sounds, usually music, from your CD and DVD players.

3. Next, you'll want to go to each application you'd normally use to play sounds—Windows Media Player for WAV files, Musicmatch for CDs, and so on—and adjust

the volume in each application. Note that the volume control in some players (Media Jukebox, for example) are linked to the Windows Volume Control, so this trick won't work quite as well as I'd like.

Not interested in all this fiddling? Try these alternatives:

- If you're ready to take your volume control to the next level—and you're willing to spend $15—try ToggleVOL-UME. This neat-o utility is a great alternative to anything Windows has to offer for controlling your PC's volume. You can fine-tune the volume dynamically by pressing the Ctrl key while moving the wheel on your mouse (see Figure 6-3). With it, I also configured my F11 key to instantly mute sound, and reprogrammed the numeric keypad for various preset volumes. Get a trial version of ToggleVOLUME at *http://snipurl.com/togglevolume*.

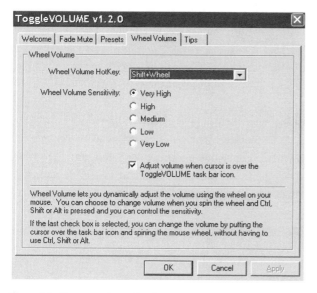

Figure 6-3. Fine-tuning the way ToggleVOLUME uses your mouse to control the volume is a snap.

- Want something similar to ToggleVolume that won't cost you a dime? Take a gander at Nir Sofer's Volumouse (see Figure 6-4). It's a powerful tool that lets you create rules for how your mouse wheel changes the sound volume of specific components, such as the microphone, headset, or line-in. It's available at *http://snipurl.com/volumouse*.

Figure 6-4. Volumouse takes volume control to another level by giving you the power to adjust the volume of your microphone, headset, and other audio components with just a flick of the wheel on your mouse.

Smart Keyboards Handle the Sound

If controlling sound via software on your PC is a pain, get a new keyboard with built-in volume controls. For example, Logitech's $29.95 Media Keyboard (*http://snipurl.com/MediaKeyboard*) launches audio and video players with the press of a button, lets you control volume with a touch, and more. If you prefer something from Microsoft, consider their $26 Digital Media Keyboard Pro (*http://snipurl.com/MS_keyboards*).

VOLUME CONTROL ON THE DESKTOP

Want to put the volume icon on the Windows desktop? You can't drag it from System Tray. Instead, open Windows Explorer, search for *sndvol32.exe* (it's probably in the *\Windows\system32* folder), and drag it to the desktop.

AUTOMATICALLY FIX MP3 TAGS

The Annoyance: I downloaded several hundred MP3 files in the last two days, but their MP3 tags are all screwed up. Most don't have track numbers, or the right artists or categories. I could spend weeks getting them tagged correctly. Isn't there an automated way of doing it?

The Fix: The tags you refer to are called ID3 tags, and they contain information about MP3 songs—title, artist, album, genre, and so on. This is the information you view when you're playing songs or assembling libraries in players such as Musicmatch Jukebox and Windows Media Player. When you rip music from a CD to MP3 format, your ripping software automatically creates those tags as well.

But music you download from the Internet has been ripped from CDs by many different people using many different programs. That means that the tagging for each song will be very different or incorrect or even missing. Most MP3 players, sound editors, and disc ripping/burning programs let you manually change these tags. For example, in Windows Media Player, right-click a file, choose Advanced Tag Editor, and you can edit the tags for the file (see Figure 6-5). But doing that by hand for hundreds of files would be nutty.

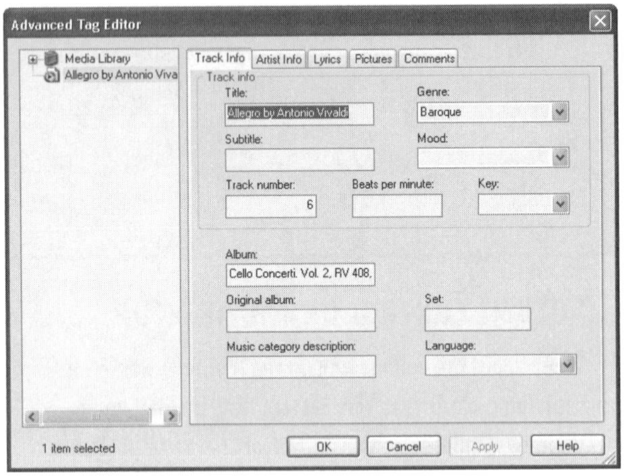

Figure 6-5. Editing tag information in Windows Media Player can be a laborious process.

Get a Standalone MP3 Tagger

What if you don't have (or want to use) Musicmatch Jukebox? The solution: the freeware MP3 Book Helper available from *http://snipurl.com/B_Helper*. As with the Musicmatch Jukebox's Super Tagging feature, this utility checks a database to find the correct ID3 tags for your files and lets you apply the tags to batches of files.

To automate the process, turn to Musicmatch Jukebox from *http://snipurl.com/MMatch*. Musicmatch Jukebox's Super Tagging feature can tag batches of files at a time. Not only that, but it will check an Internet music database, confirm what the tags should be, and then apply the corrected tags to your file automatically. To use the feature, open Musicmatch and highlight the files that you want to tag (see Figure 6-6). Then right-click them and choose Super Tagging → Lookup Tags. Musicmatch checks its Internet database, then pops up the correct tags for the tracks. Check the tracks for which you want to use the tags, click the Accept Selected Tags button, and you're done.

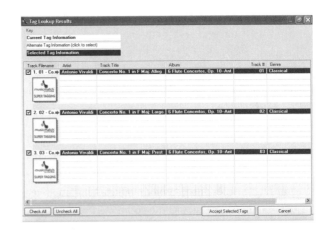

Figure 6-6. Super Tagging not only automates the process of tagging music files, but it makes sure the tags are accurate.

STREAM MP3s TO YOUR STEREO WIRELESSLY

The Annoyance: Whenever we go on long drives, I try to hook my Creative MP3 player to my car stereo's cassette player with an adapter. Too often the gizmo jams in the tape chute. It's so frustrating I stopped taking the MP3 player on trips.

The Fix: I used to have the same problem. Then I started using Aerielle's $40 AudioBUG. This small device—it looks like a tiny mouse—transmits data from your MP3 player (or any device with a standard 3.5mm audio-out connector) directly to your FM radio. It transmits on one of four FM frequencies: 88.1, 88.3, 88.5, and 88.7 MHz. You can use AudioBUG with any FM radio, including your home stereo system. See *http://snipurl.com/audiobug* for more information.

RECORD AUDIO FROM ANY SOURCE

The Annoyance: I listen to all sorts of great audio streams—music and radio shows—via Real's Player and Windows Media Player. But I can't figure out how to save any audio stream to disk.

STREAM SOUNDS TO YOUR MP3 PLAYER

If you don't want to go to the trouble of recording audio with Total Recorder, there's another option. For a fee, a company called Audible lets you listen to digital versions of books, radio shows, and newspapers (my wife loads her Audible-ready player with the "Fresh Air" and "This American Life" radio shows before leaving for her morning commute).

You can download content and listen to it on your PC or notebook, but most people are more inclined to listen on a player in the car or at the gym. You can use any one of a number of Audible-ready MP3 players, including Pocket PCs, iPods, Palm Handhelds, Rio players, and those sold by Audible (see *http://snipurl.com/audible*).

The Fix: You won't believe this, but they don't want you to save those files. But despite what they want, I'm going to tell you about Total Recorder, a dirt-cheap program that lets you grab anything you can hear over your PC's speakers and save it as a WAV, MP3, or half a dozen other audio formats. The program's not difficult to use, although you do need to temporarily modify your system's sound settings (the program guides you through the process). With Total Recorder, I can snatch radio interviews (National Public Radio's *Fresh Air*, for instance) for playback on my MP3 player (see Figure 6-7). The $12 standard version is ideal for most things you want to record off the Net. If you want to schedule everything—from opening NPR's site to starting and saving the recording automatically—you'll need the $36 Pro version. Try the program by downloading it from *http://www.oreilly.com/pcannoyances.*

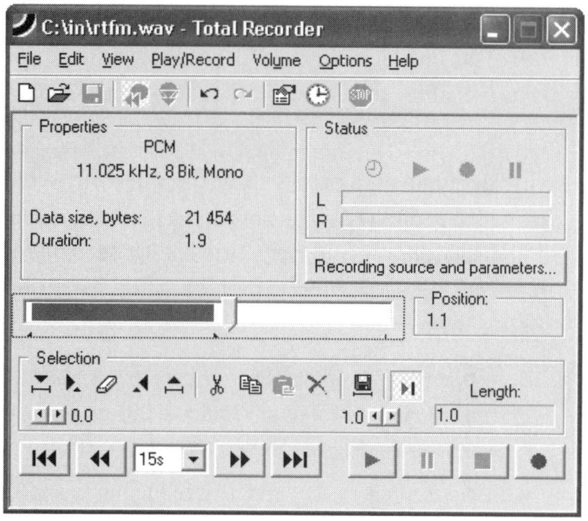

Figure 6-7. Snag that audio feed. With the $12 Total Recorder, you can save anything you hear over your PC's speakers.

Another tool worth considering is Admiresoft's Super Mp3 Recorder (*http://snipurl.com/spr_mp3*), which captures streaming audio and saves it in MP3 and WAV formats. It's shareware and free to try, but if you like it, you'll eventually have to pony up $19.95 for the Standard version, or $29.95 for the Professional version, which lets you do sound editing and can automatically start recording at preset times. RipCast Streaming Audio Ripper (*http://snipurl.com/ripcast)* is a similar program, but it's designed to work with SHOUTcast servers that deliver streaming MP3 files, so it won't work for all streaming audio formats. It's shareware and free to try, but if you continue to use it, you're expected to pay $17.95.

CAPTURE AND SAVE VIDEO STREAMS

The Annoyance: Total Recorder sounds cool. But what about saving video streams and Shockwave animations so I can play them again while I'm not online? Windows Media Player doesn't have this option, nor does RealOne.

The Fix: Most videos and Shockwave (a.k.a. Flash) files are automatically—if temporarily—saved on your hard drive as they're playing in your media player. Which means you can find, rename, and save the files for later playback. Here's how:

1. First determine the extension of the video file. While the video or Flash is being played, the filename is usually displayed in the player's title bar. Or search your hard drive for all files with that video extension. Here's how:

   a. To open the Windows Search bar, select Start → Find → Files or Folders (Windows 98) or Start → Search → For Files or Folders (Me, 2000, XP).

   b. In the search field, enter the following string of video filename extensions:

      `*.avi, *.mpg, *.mpeg, *.asf, *.mov, *.rm, *.wmv`

      Add `*.swf` if you want to search for Shockwave/Flash animations as well.

   c. The trick is to find the video and Shockwave animation files right after you've played them. (In other words, don't close the player.) So search by date, looking for only current files.

What's a Codec? (And Why Should I Know?)

When a video is recorded and saved to disk, the raw footage creates an enormous file. For the video to be manageable—downloadable in a reasonable amount of time or storable in a minimum of space—it must be reduced in size, or compressed. At the other end—before you watch the video on your PC—it must be uncompressed. Videos are compressed with a program called a codec (which stands for compressor/decompressor). Two popular codecs are MPEG and QuickTime. (See the sidebar "Decipher That 'Missing Codec' Error.")

FIND STREAMED FILES HIDING ON YOUR PC

Sometimes when you stream music or video files to your PC, Windows will automatically save the files in your Internet cache, which is typically found in *C:\Documents and Settings\<yourname>\Local Settings\Temporary Internet Files*, where *<yourname>* is your account name in XP. Open Windows Explorer, browse through the folder, and look for files in MP3, MPG, MOV, AVI, SWF, and other media formats. Keep in mind that what you'll find here is hit or miss. You typically won't find RealPlayer files, but you'll almost always find Flash movie (SWF) files, and often MP3s and MPGs. However, before you go poking around, save your work—grabbing files out of this cache can sometimes crash Explorer.

2. When you find the file (it will probably be in the browser's cache folder, typically *\Documents and Settings\<yourname>\Local Settings\Temporary Internet Files*), save it with a new name in a new location. Once saved, open the file by double-clicking it.

SPLIT 'EM AND JOIN 'EM

The Annoyance: People who post videos on the Internet often split them into dozens of individual files. That makes it easier to upload and download them, but it also means watching each file separately. Is there some *easy* way to bring them together?

The Fix: Fear not, *auteurs*, there's a way to view the video all at once. Boilsoft's $20 AVI/MPEG/RM/WMV Joiner and $25 AVI/MPEG/ASF/WMV Splitter can splice segments together to create a single, unified file. Both utilities take a modest amount of skill to operate—even a video newbie can get it right the first time. Simply add the files you want to merge and click one button. Conversely, to split a large file, just locate it, decide on a file size (or choose selected portions of the video), and click a button. Simple, no? Go to *http://snipurl.com/boilsoft* to download trial versions of the programs.

CAPTURE AND SAVE VIDEO STREAMS, PART II

The Annoyance: I checked the *Temporary Internet Files* folder like you suggested, but I can't find some of the videos I watched on the Internet. There's gotta be a way to capture streaming video, right?

The Fix: Get VideoCap's Easy Video Capture from *http:// snipurl.com/vidcap*. (There's a free working demo; the full package costs $29.95.) Not only does it record streaming video, but it can capture anything that occurs on your screen—a great way to create training videos. The program saves video in AVI format, so if you want captured video in another format, get a copy of AVI MPEG Video Converter at *http://snipurl.com/vidconv*.

iTUNES ANNOYANCES

iTUNES BANKRUPTCY

The Annoyance: I've installed iTunes (*http://snipurl. com/tunes*) and set up an account with my credit card so my music-mad daughter can download music legally. Although she's not breaking any intellectual property laws, she's certainly breaking my bank account. Is there any way I can control how much music she buys, without her having to beg me every time she wants to download a song?

The Fix: The best solution is to set up a monthly music allowance. Here's how:

1. In iTunes, click on Music Store, and in the upper-right-hand portion of the screen, click your account.

2. Log into your account if you haven't already.

3. From the screen that appears, click Setup Allowance; in the next screen, select the amount of the allowance and fill in the Apple Account name of the person you're setting up the allowance for (see Figure 6-8). If none exists, select "Create an Apple Account for Recipient," and create a new account.

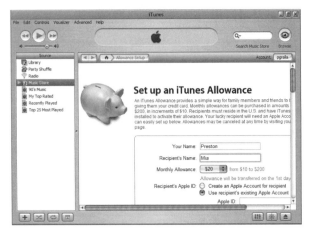

Figure 6-8. Make sure your kids don't break the piggy bank by setting up a monthly iTunes allowance.

4. From now on, when your daughter uses her account, she'll be able to buy up to the amount you've set for her. She'll also see how much money she has left in the account. If she doesn't spend all of her money in a given month (fat chance!), the remainder will be added to her next month's allowance.

Kids sometimes make snap decisions when they buy music and later regret it. You can minimize impulse purchases by turning off the "1-Click" setting. When 1-Click is on, clicking the Buy button in the iTunes store immediately pays for the tune and automatically downloads it, and there's no turning back. Change a few settings, however, and selected songs are first put in a shopping cart. That way, your kids can later look in their shopping carts and decide if they really want to buy those tunes. To turn off iTunes' 1-Click and use the shopping cart, choose Edit → Preferences → Store, select "Buy Using a Shopping Cart," and click OK.

MOVE iTUNES COLLECTION TO A NEW PC

The Annoyance: I have several gigabytes of music files in iTunes, and I just bought a new PC. For the life of me, I can't figure out how to get them from my old PC to my new one.

The Fix: Don't fret; it's easy to do:

1. Copy the files to several CDs or a single DVD. Make sure that you *copy* them, and don't burn them as audio CD tracks. You'll find your iTunes files in your *My Music* folder.

2. Start iTunes on your new PC. Choose Edit → Preferences, click the Advanced tab, and check the "Copy files to iTunes Music folder when adding to library" box if it's not already checked (see Figure 6-9).

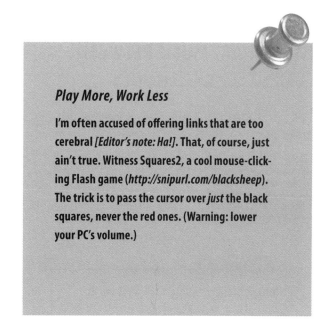

Figure 6-9. When importing music from another PC into iTunes, make sure you check the "Copy files to iTunes Music folder" box.

3. Put the CD or DVD in the disk drive of your new PC. Drag the song folders from the CD or DVD to the Library icon in the iTunes window. The folders and all the songs in them will be copied into iTunes. (From iTunes, you can also choose File → "Add to Library" to copy them.)

> If you're selling, scrapping, or giving away a computer that has iTunes installed on it, make sure you "deauthorize" it. If you don't, it will still count as one of the up to five computers you can play iTunes files on. To deauthorize your computer, in iTunes select Advanced → Deauthorize Computer, select Deauthorize Computer for Apple Account, and enter your Apple ID and password.

BACK UP YOUR iTUNES!

The Annoyance: My system crashed and took all the music I purchased at the iTunes Music Store. Will Apple replace my tunes?

Play More, Work Less

I'm often accused of offering links that are too cerebral *[Editor's note: Ha!]*. That, of course, just ain't true. Witness Squares2, a cool mouse-clicking Flash game (*http://snipurl.com/blacksheep*). The trick is to pass the cursor over *just* the black squares, never the red ones. (Warning: lower your PC's volume.)

The Fix: Alas, the news isn't good. According to an iTunes expert, Apple's policy is that users should always back up their purchases. Once they're lost, they're lost. It's not unlike buying CDs at a local store and asking for a replacement if they were stolen from your home.

You can back up your iTunes to a hard drive, CD or DVD, or other media. The details are at *http://snipurl.com/iTunes_backup*.

STOP iTUNES FROM POPPING AND CLICKING

The Annoyance: I just imported over a dozen music files into iTunes from an audio CD, and now every track has pops and clicks. Is this iTunes' way of forcing me to buy music online?

The Fix: Nope. iTunes just does a very poor job of copying music from audio CDs. Delete all the music files you've imported, because you won't be able to fix them. Select iTunes → Preferences → Importing and check the "Use error correction when reading Audio CDs" box. The problem should go away, although you'll find that it now takes longer to import music from CD.

CAN'T SHARE MUSIC BETWEEN COMPUTERS WITH iTUNES

The Annoyance: I have two computers, both with iTunes installed. But whenever I try to share music between them, I get the error message "The shared music library is not compatible with this version of iTunes." What's up?

The Fix: Your computers have different versions of iTunes. Upgrade both to the latest version and you'll be set.

You can share music with another PC only if it's on your network and if iTunes is running on both computers.

SCRAMBLED iTUNES SONG TITLES

The Annoyance: I use several different programs for ripping music. When I imported the music into iTunes, all the titles are scrambled. Now my music collection looks as if it's in Swahili, but my music isn't Swahili music.

The Fix: The problem is that your ripping programs store ID3 tags in a different way than iTunes does. To fix the problem, open your iTunes music library and select all the songs with scrambled titles. Then choose Advanced → Convert ID3 Tags. In the dialog box that appears, check the Reverse Unicode box and click OK (see Figure 6-10). The song titles should now be fixed.

Figure 6-10. Don't want your song titles to read like Swahili? Use this dialog box to fix them.

WINDOWS MEDIA PLAYER ANNOYANCES

WINDOWS MEDIA PLAYER WON'T COPY MUSIC TO MP3 PLAYER

The Annoyance: I've ripped music from a CD using Windows Media Player, and now I can't copy it to my portable MP3 player. What gives?

The Fix: By default, Windows Media Player takes a rather draconian approach to stopping copyright violations. It automatically copy protects your files, and will only let you copy them to other devices or to a CD if you pay for them, even if you've ripped the music from your own CDs. There's a simple solution: turn off copy protection. Select Tools → Options, click the Copy Music tab, and uncheck the "Copy protect music" box.

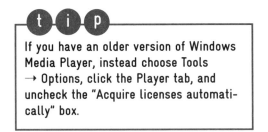

If you have an older version of Windows Media Player, instead choose Tools → Options, click the Player tab, and uncheck the "Acquire licenses automatically" box.

WINDOWS MEDIA PLAYER'S VANISHING TOOLBARS

The Annoyance: I'm almost too embarrassed to ask, but where in the world is the Windows Media Player's menu bar?

The Fix: In what may be one of the worst design choices of all time (second to Microsoft Bob, that is), the Windows Media Player menu bar is normally hidden from view. To make it appear, move your mouse to the top of the player window and voila—it appears. Move your mouse away and it disappears. If you find this behavior disconcerting, you can force the menu bar to appear at all times. Click the small double-headed arrow button in the upper-left corner of the player window, and the menu bar will appear and stay put. Click the button again to hide it.

WHY DOESN'T MY VIDEO PLAY?

The Annoyance: I get so annoyed when someone sends me a funny video and I can't play the thing. Why doesn't Windows Media Player know what to do with these videos?

The Fix: When you've got the right file format running in the right media player at the right speed, it's a technological marvel. But too often the video player says, "Hey, that's an Apple movie, pal! Take a flying leap," or words to that effect.

There are two fixes. The first is easy: just forget it. The video was probably boring, or something you wouldn't want your spouse to see anyway. But if you must see the video, take a deep breath:

1. Open Windows Media Player. Look at Tools → Options and click the Player tab, and make sure the "Download codecs automatically" box is checked. Then try playing the video again. There are many different digital video formats, and a different playback codec is required for each one. You may be missing the one you need.

2. Still no luck? The next best bet is making sure you have the latest version of Windows Media Player—Version 10. You can download the one you need from *http://snipurl.com/mswmp*.

3. You can also try an alternate media player, such as Real's RealOne Player, which you can download from *http://snipurl.com/free_real*.

4. If you're using Windows 98, Me, or 2000, and Windows Media Player 7.1 can't handle your mystery video, try the brute-force approach. The low-level drivers that underlie Windows Media Player Version 8 are part of a subsystem called DirectX, which may be

able to recognize your video. You can install DirectX 8.1b on Windows 98, Me, or 2000; if you're still stuck on Windows 95, you need DirectX 8.0 Runtime. Both are available at *http://snipurl.com/directx*.

LET ZONEALARM DO ITS JOB

Every time Windows Media Player tries to access the Internet, ZoneAlarm alerts you with an annoying box. You may be tempted to tell ZoneAlarm to leave WMP alone by checking the "Remember this answer next time I use this program " box on ZoneAlarm's alert. But I don't recommend it.

ZoneAlarm's doing the job you asked it to do—watching for any suspicious incoming or outgoing communications. Windows Media Player is a particularly meddlesome program; it wants to supply album covers for the MP3s you're playing (good), but also uses unique ID numbers to exchange information about you with other web sites (not so good). So it's going to be a pain, but if you want to maintain your privacy, I recommend you make the decision whether to let Windows Media Player access the Internet on a case-by-case basis. If WMP is heading off to retrieve a video you requested, fine, let it go to work. But if it just casually pops up on its own, I recommend that you have ZoneAlarm block it.

If you don't have ZoneAlarm, download Zone Labs' free version from *http://www.oreilly.com/pcannoyances*.

PLAY VIDEOS WITHOUT THE WEB BROWSER

The Annoyance: When I'm playing a video file, such as a movie clip or music video, in Window Media Player it's fairly common for my browser to pop open and take me to a site I had no intention of visiting. How can I kill this "feature"?

The Fix: You're the victim of a dreaded HTML script that's often embedded in Windows Media files. There's a convoluted Registry fix to turn the scripting off, and it's detailed in a Microsoft Knowledge Base article. But the fix is more overwhelming than the annoyance. (See for yourself: *http://snipurl.com/wmp_scriptfix*.) A quicker, easier way is to use Brett Bartholomew's WMPopKill, a small utility that operates like an on/off switch with Media Player. To use the tool, you may need to patch Media Player; WMPopKill automatically attempts to get the patch. You can get WMPopKill at *http://www.oreilly.com/pcannoyances*.

ADD RIPPING TO WINDOWS MEDIA PLAYER

The Annoyance: MP3 is the most popular digital music format on the planet, but Windows Media Player 9 can't rip songs in MP3 format.

The Fix: Of course, you could switch to another media player like...oh, virtually any other one in existence. But if you're a Windows Media Player aficionado and can spare ten bucks, you can add MP3 ripping to Microsoft's player. Choose Tools → Plug-ins → Download Plug-ins. In the resulting browser window, click MP3 Creation Plug-ins. You can then buy and download Cyberlink's MP3 PowerEncoder (from *http://snipurl.com/powerencoder*), InterVideo's MP3 XPack (from *http://snipurl.com/xpack*), or Sonic Solutions' CinePlayer MP3 Creation Pack (from *http://snipurl.com/cineplayer*). Each of these plug-ins is $10, and each gives WMP the ability to rip MP3 files.

START YOUR PLAYER WHERE YOU LEFT OFF

The Annoyance: When I launch Windows Media Player, I want to get to my own media. But the program automatically loads the Media Guide (a.k.a. WindowsMedia.com), a Microsoft web site that loads slowly even over a broadband connection and seems to think I'm a Cher fan.

The Fix: There's a simple solution. Go to Tools → Options. On the Player tab under "Player settings," uncheck the "Start Player in Media Guide" box and click OK. From now on, the player will start up in Now Playing mode, which conveniently picks up where you left off in your last session.

BRING YOUR PLAYER'S MENU OUT IN THE OPEN

The Annoyance: Windows Media Player usually does what I need. But all of a sudden, its menu bar vanishes, except when I hover the pointer over where it used to be. It's enough to make me drag my Victrola out of the closet.

The Fix: See that tiny, round button with the up and down arrows in the upper-left corner of the player? You probably clicked it unwittingly; click it again and the menu bar will reappear. You could also hover the pointer to make the menu bar appear, then click View → Full Mode Options → Show Menu Bar. If you're a keyboard jockey, use Ctrl-M and Ctrl-Shift-M to display and hide the menu bar.

AN OLD LOOK FOR A NEW PLAYER

The Annoyance: I'm using a recent version of Windows Media Player, but I don't really need its ornate fripperies, like the ability to "skin" it with different visual motifs. Actually, come to think of it, I'll take mundane but functional any day.

The Fix: Oddly enough, you can use Windows Media Player's skin customization feature to make the program mimic its old, pre-skinnable look and feel. In Full Mode, click Skin Chooser in the Media Player taskbar to the left. (If the taskbar is hidden, select View → Full Mode Options → Show Menu Bar.) In the scrolling list of skins in the left pane, select Classic, and then click the Apply Skin button. Presto—WMP looks like its old self again.

QUICKTIME ANNOYANCES

KILL THE QUICKTIME ICON

The Annoyance: Every time I start my PC, a small QuickTime icon appears in the Windows System Tray. No matter what I do, I can't get rid of the thing!

The Fix: Right-click the icon and select QuickTime Preferences → Browser Plug-In. Uncheck the "QuickTime system tray icon" box, and then close the dialog. The icon won't appear anymore.

WINDOWS MEDIA PLAYER SUPERCOOKIES POSE A PRIVACY THREAT

I was really bummed when I discovered that Windows Media Player uses a unique ID to exchange info about me with web sites. The information is probably benign—like my age, salary, pension plan, and sexual proclivities (just kidding, I hope)—but I'd prefer the program didn't share anything with anybody.

While you're at the appropriate tab, uncheck the "I want to help make Microsoft..." box in the Customer Experience Improvement Program area. If you don't, information about your Windows Media Player use is sent to Microsoft. Microsoft naturally claims that the information is only used in the aggregate, but if you're a privacy buff, uncheck the box.

There's a quick, easy way to turn off SuperCookie tracking. Open Windows Media Player; then, depending upon your player version, choose Tools → Options or View → Options, select the the Privacy tab or the Player tab, uncheck the "Allow Internet sites to uniquely identify your player" or "Send unique Player ID to content providers" boxes and click OK (see figure). If you're intrigued and want to learn more about SuperCookies, check out Richard M. Smith's privacy site at *http://snipurl.com/supercookie_details*. More fun,

though, is watching a SuperCookie in action, at *http://snipurl.com/supercookie_demo*.

Stop SuperCookies dead in their tracks by unchecking "Send unique Player ID to content providers."

However, even though the icon no longer appears, Quick-Time still stealthily loads a small applet called *qttask.exe* every time you reboot. To banish this pest, open the System Configuration Utility. Select Start → Run, and type **msconfig** in the Open box. Choose the Startup tab, uncheck the box next to *qttask*, click OK, and then click either the Restart or Exit Without Restart button, as your mood dictates. In theory, this should stop the persistent sucker from loading on startup. And it does. But the next time you run QuickTime, the program stealthily undoes your change and *qttask.exe* loads on startup. Don't bother deleting the relevant Registry key—when QuickTime runs again, it re-creates that key.

The permanent solution? Rename or delete the file *qttask. exe*. QuickTime works perfectly well without it. Find it in the *C:\Program Files\quicktime* directory, unless you've installed QuickTime somewhere else.

NONSTOP QUICKTIME ERROR MESSAGE

The Annoyance: Whenever I open QuickTime, I get the error message "No Disk, Please Insert Disk In Drive D" no matter what I do. Make it go away!

The Fix: You probably recently viewed a QuickTime movie on a CD or DVD, and QuickTime is looking for the disc when it starts. To get rid of the error message, launch QuickTime, choose File → Open Recent → Clear Menu, and confirm your choice.

QUICKTIME WON'T PLAY NICE WITH BROWSER

The Annoyance: I've installed QuickTime, but whenever I visit a web page with a QuickTime movie, instead of seeing the movie in my browser, I see a broken QuickTime logo. Why won't this software play movies?

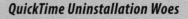

QuickTime Uninstallation Woes

When you uninstall QuickTime, you may get an error message saying that a QuickTime file is in use, and so the program can't be removed. The problem? You left a Control Panels window open. Close the Control Panels window, then uninstall QuickTime. This time, it should go off without a hitch.

The Fix: You've installed QuickTime but not the ActiveX control required to play movies from directly inside your browser. To fix this, go to *http://snipurl.com/qtime*. A dialog box will appear, asking if you want to install the QuickTime ActiveX control. Accept it and the control will be installed on your PC. From now on, you'll be able to view QuickTime movies right inside your browser.

QUICKTIME, STOP NAGGING!

The Annoyance: Every time I run QuickTime, it asks me whether I want to upgrade to QuickTime Pro. No, no, a thousand times no! Can you hear me now? How can I turn this off?

The Fix: The latest version of QuickTime seems to have done away with this annoyance, so my best advice is to download and install the latest version of the free (non-Pro) player. One trick for those stuck with an older version: set your system clock several years into the future, run QuickTime, and when the upgrade notice appears, tell it that you want to be notified at some later date. Then quit QuickTime and reset your system clock to the correct time. Users report that this disables the upgrade notice.

MUSIC SOUNDS LIKE AN OLD 78

The Annoyance: When I play music with the Quick-Time player, it sounds like a scratchy old 78. Is this a feature or a bug?

The Fix: Neither—it's wonky settings. Open the Quick-Time player and choose Edit → Preferences → QuickTime Settings. From the dialog box, select Sound Out from the top drop-down menu; in the "Choose a device for play-back" drop-down, select "waveOut: Windows' preferred device". In the Rate drop-down menu, use 44.100 kHz, and then select the "16 bit" and Stereo radio buttons below that menu. (See Figure 6-11.)

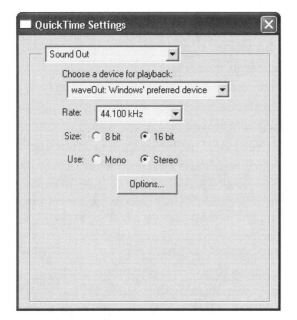

Figure 6-11. If QuickTime audio sounds like a scratchy old record, these settings should solve the problem.

PLAY QUICKTIME MOVIES WITHOUT QUICKTIME

The Annoyance: I've finally had it with QuickTime. Non-stop error messages, applets that load in the background without telling me...I don't need all this *tsouris*. Isn't there a way I can view QuickTime movies without actually using QuickTime?

The Fix: Yes, with a free plug-in for Internet Explorer, Opera, Netscape, and Mozilla. Uninstall QuickTime using the "Add or Remove Programs" control panel. Then get QuickTime Alternative from *http://snipurl.com/qt_alt*. One big plus: the plug-in also lets your browser play QuickTime files embedded in web pages.

CD AND DVD ANNOYANCES

REMOVE CDS WHEN THE POWER'S OFF

The Annoyance: My CD-RW drive refuses to eject a disc. Must I resort to the paper clip trick?

The Fix: Not necessarily. Restart Windows. As it's booting up, press the eject button and the drive should pop open. If not, shut down your PC and turn it on again, tap the CD-ROM drive's eject button, grab the disc out of the tray (even as the tray is still extending), and nudge the tray back in. As soon as it's fully retracted, press the PC's power button to turn it off.

USE 74-MINUTE CDS WHEN SHARING DISCS

The Annoyance: I've been happily using 74-minute/650 MB blank CD-Rs for years. But the newer 80-minute/700 MB discs are just as cheap, so I tried some. Only problem is, some of my buddies complain that their CD drives can't read the discs.

The Fix: It's not your fault: it's your cheapskate buddies and their old CD drives. CD-Rs store data in a spiral tract that starts at the inner part of the disc and works its way toward the outer edge of the CD. The drive's laser must follow the spiral to read or write data. An 80-minute disc's data spiral is wound more tightly than a 74-minute disc's, and older CD drives can't adjust their laser heads to read it.

There's no easy way to know if your buddies' CD drives can read 80-minute media—until they try and can't. Best bet? If you're going to share CDs with friends, stick with 74-minute blanks. Or tell your buddies to cough up for a new CD drive. Or get new buddies.

TO NUDGE OR NOT TO NUDGE...

Do you remember your first CD player? I do, and I'll never forget the sales guy saying that it's not a good idea to nudge the CD-ROM drive's tray in order to close it—that I should always use the button.

Yet I've often nudged the tray closed on my computer with no apparent ill effects. But I wanted the skinny. So I asked tech guys at two CD drive companies.

Plextor's guy said that the trays on all Plextor's drives can be closed with a light nudge, but that the company doesn't recommend this practice. The reason is that force is a relative term. Pushing the tray lightly will close the tray, while pushing the tray too hard can jam the gears, disabling the drive.

On the other hand, Sony's guy said that you can nudge the tray or use the button. "Nudging has no long-term effect on reliability of our drives since they are designed to be used either way."

Me? I'm nudging.

OFFICE-SUPPLY WORKAROUND

If your CD drive's eject button conks out, power down the PC and find a paper clip. Straighten it out and gently stick this technologically sophisticated implement into the small hole on the front panel of the drive. That'll manually force the tray to pop open.

BURN CDS, BUT HOLD THE LABELS

The Annoyance: My six-year-old daughter delights in playing music CDs. That's cool, but she also takes pleasure in dropping them, scratching them, and flinging the $15 discs at the dog. So I've made duplicates and hidden her original CDs, and I let her maim the copies. The question is, should I stick labels on those dupes?

The Fix: In a word: no.

There are lots of gadgets available that make cool-looking labels, but a label can harm a CD-R and even trash your drive. Over time, the label can shrink (or your kid could rip it off), pulling off the disc's protective layers and distorting the reflective layer that holds your data and music (see Figure 6-12). If the label (and yes, you've gotta use the circular

Figure 6-12. CD labels can damage—even rip off—the critical reflective layer of a disc. Don't use 'em.

ones) isn't precisely centered, the disc will wobble as it spins, making the disc unreadable. Worse, if the label comes off while the disc is spinning, your drive could be trashed.

My advice: label the disc on its clear, inner ring with a felt-tip marker. That way you don't have to worry about the ink possibly eating away at the disc's protective layer.

PERMANENT LABELS FOR CDS AND DVDS

If you have the bucks, you can directly—and safely—label your CDs and DVDs with a printer that has a special feature designed for the job. Epson's $200 Stylus Photo 900 and $349 Stylus Photo 960 both print text and pictures directly onto CDs and DVDs. Both models hold the disc in a small tray that slides into the printer. The Epson 900 feeds from the back, a really annoying design, while the 960 lets you slide the disc in from the front.

Both printers are top-notch performers (read *PC World*'s review at *http://snipurl.com/epson900_review*), but there's one downside: you must buy specially coated CDs and DVDs with an "Ink Jet Printable Surface." The special CDs run half a buck more than regular ones; coated DVDs range from $3 to $7 more, depending on brand.

CD BURNER RUNS HOT AND COLD

The Annoyance: How's this for irritating? Some days my external USB CD burner—which is connected to my PC via an add-in USB/FireWire card—works perfectly, but other times my computer doesn't recognize the darn thing. And here I thought the disc was supposed to be burning, not me.

The Fix: Hose down, baby—help is here. Whenever any external device is seen and then not seen, check all the usual connections. Make sure the drive is securely plugged into its AC adapter, and the adapter into a wall plug. (*Don't* try to power the drive off the USB line.) Make sure you're using the vendor's supplied and/or recommended USB data cable, that it doesn't have any kinks or cuts, and that it's snugly attached on both ends (to the right plug on the drive, and to the right plug and card in your PC). Still acting wonky? Plug the drive into a different USB port on the card. (While you're at it, test all the USB ports with some other USB device. If they work fine, chances are your drive may be down for the count.) No improvement? Borrow another USB cable and try it out. Still on the fritz? Pop open the PC and make sure the USB/FireWire card is firmly seated in its slot. If it is, move it to another slot (but not next to the AGP video adapter, since that could cause motherboard woes). Reconnect everything, restart your system, and see how it goes. Still unstable? Borrow another USB/Firewire card and see if that works.

One of the above steps should nip the problem in the bud. If not—and assuming your USB/FireWire card and CD burner are mechanically and electrically sound—you may have a software or firmware mismatch. Take the following steps in turn and see if the drive works reliably. First, check your documentation (and if need be, contact the vendor), and make sure your drive, burning software, USB/FireWire card, and version of Windows are all mutually compatible. Download and install any new drivers for the CD burner and card. Still got grief? Install relevant firmware updates for the card and drive. If these steps don't solve your annoyance, seek out a qualified repair facility.

CD CONTENT WITHOUT THE CD

The Annoyance: I hate schlepping all my software CDs when I travel with my notebook. Particularly irksome are the games that yell bloody murder if they're not loaded from CD.

The Fix: Farstone's Game Drive is a $30 utility that saves compressed CD images to your hard drive. You can then run many games—and most other content from a CD—without the physical disc. You can load as many as 22 CDs (limited by available hard drive space). Bonus: hard drives are faster than CD drives, so your games run a lot quicker. Grab a free trial version at *http://snipurl.com/gamedrive*.

CHECK THAT DISC BEFORE YOU BURN

The Annoyance: I've burned a bunch of critical files on a CD, and I want to make doubly—maybe triply—sure they were copied correctly. But my CD-burning program doesn't check for file corruption or other problems.

The Fix: I have just the insurance policy you need. It's CDCheck, and it's a keeper. Use it to do readability verifications, binary comparisons, and CRC file creation checks. It's great for every file you burn on CD, and especially valuable for backup CDs. (See Figure 6-13.) The tool compares the files on the CD with the originals on the hard drive and can even recover damaged files in some cases. The utility is free (and for all it does, that's quite amazing). Grab a copy at *http://www.oreilly.com/pcannoyances*.

A VIRTUAL STAPLER

Multimedia was made for this. Choose a classic model or something a little newer and sleeker. Once you get tired of clicking, check the gallery and watch a fascinating movie about the no-staple stapler (*http://snipurl.com/staple*).

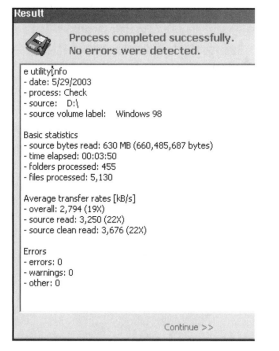

Figure 6-13. Top: CDCheck scrutinizing a disc. Bottom: The CD got a clean bill of health. If an error had occurred, CDCheck's Help file details what's wrong with the disc and what you can do.

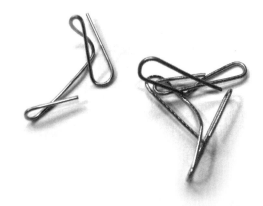

READ AND WRITE READ-ONLY FILES

The Annoyance: I copied a bunch of photo files to a CD-R for long-term storage, but when I copied a few of them back to my hard drive for editing, my photo program nixed the idea, saying I wasn't allowed to modify them. What gives?

The Fix: CD-R is a write-once medium—files burned to disc can't be modified, so the burning software naturally sets each file's attributes to "read-only." Copy a file from CD to hard disk, and that attribute is still set. To unlock the file, try these two solutions:

- In Windows Explorer, locate the file on your hard drive, right-click it, choose Properties, and uncheck the "Read-only" box. If you have lots of files to change, hold down the Ctrl key while you click as many individual files as you want, right-click, choose Properties, and uncheck "Read-only" (see Figure 6-14).

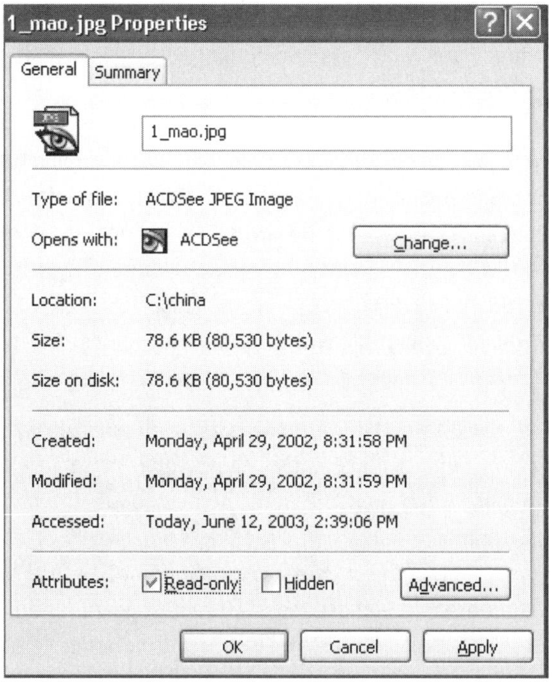

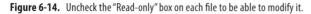

Figure 6-14. Uncheck the "Read-only" box on each file to be able to modify it.

- A quicker, more elegant way is with David Crowell's CROA, a freebie. Right-click on a folder and choose "Clear Read-Only Attributes (CROA)" (see Figure 6-15). Grab a copy from *http://www.oreilly.com/pcannoyances*.

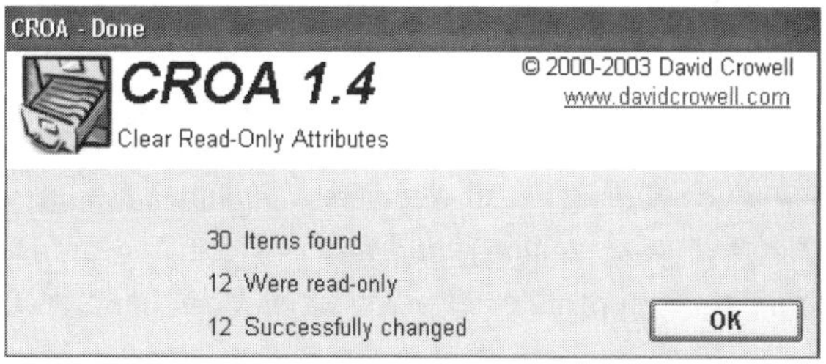

Figure 6-15. Let CROA do the dirty work for you and change the read-only attributes of all the files in a folder automatically.

KEEP THE CD DRIVE CLOSED AFTER WRITING

Windows XP has a mind of its own. After writing a CD, it insists on ejecting the disc. You can eliminate this annoyance and save wear and tear on your CD drive. Open My Computer, right-click your CD-RW drive, and then click Properties. Select the Recording tab and uncheck the "Automatically eject the CD after writing" box (see figure).

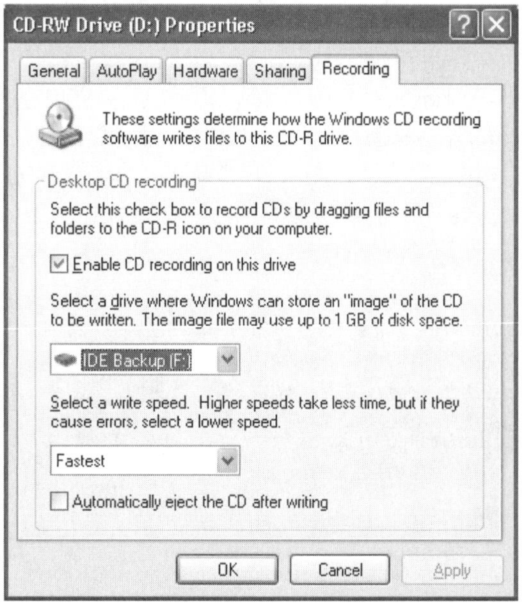

QUICK AUDIO FILE CONVERSIONS

The Annoyance: Opening a fat app like Roxio's Easy CD Creator to convert a single MP3 or WAV file is overkill. Got a quicker way?

The Fix: A quicker, cooler way is to use dBpowerAMP Music Converter (dMC), a handy freebie that does WAV-to-MP3 conversions (and vice versa). Right-click a music file in Windows Explorer, and a small icon appears (see Figure 6-16, top). Click either Mp3 or Wave, and dMC's

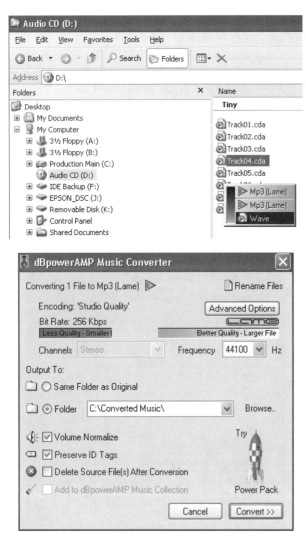

menu allows you to change the output folder and rename the converted file (see Figure 6-16, bottom). The program is available at *http://www.oreilly.com/pcannoyances*.

CREATE QUICK MP3 LISTS

The Annoyance: I want to list a bunch of MP3s and email the list to a friend as a text message, but I can't figure out how to do it.

The Fix: It's easy if you use PrintFolder 1.2, a free utility whose sole purpose is to quickly save or print a list of files from any folder. Check it out at *http://www.oreilly.com/pcannoyances*.

PRESERVE LONG FILENAMES

The Annoyance: Ever since Windows 95 came out, I've been freed from the old limitation on filenames. Instead of cryptic filenames like *ITIN1094.DOC*, I can use names like *Itinerary For October 1994 Trip To South America.doc*. But when I burn these files to CD, my clever filenames are turned into something even more cryptic—like *ITINER~1.DOC*.

The Fix: You get truncated filenames whenever you burn a CD using the ISO 9660 format. ISO 9660 is a standard CD format that can be read by virtually any computer with a CD-ROM drive—regardless of what operating system it uses. But ISO 9660 doesn't support long filenames, which would be incompatible with DOS and other older operating systems. You can get around this in several ways:

- Use a different CD format, such as Romeo or Joliet. (No, I didn't make those names up.) These formats support long filenames, but the CDs you create might be readable only on PCs running Windows 95 or later and on Macs. For most folks, that's not such a bad limitation. (If you use the CD-burning capabilities built into Windows XP, you're already getting Joliet CDs.)

Figure 6-16. Top: Choose the file from the music CD you want to convert. Bottom: Start dBPower Music Converter and watch it do the conversion.

- If compatibility is paramount, use WinZip, "compressed folders" in Windows XP, or a similar tool to compress your files into a .ZIP archive file. Give the .ZIP an 8.3 filename and burn it to a standard ISO 9660 CD. The files within the .ZIP archive retain their full, original names and folder structures.

POPULAR CD-WRITING PROGRAMS

BlindWrite. Free trial; $34.99 to keep.
http://www.blindwrite.com

FireBurner. Free trial; $32.95 to keep.
http://www.fireburner.com

Ahead Nero Burning ROM. Free trial; $69.99 to keep.
http://www.ahead.de

Easy Media Creator 7. $79.95.
http://www.roxio.com

CDRWin. Free trial; $34.95 to keep.
http://www.goldenhawk.com

These files are also at *http://www.oreilly.com/ pcannoyances*.

BURN USABLE CDS FROM ISO FILES

The Annoyance: I downloaded a movie trailer in ISO format and copied it to a CD-R. But I can't make it play.

The Fix: You can't just copy an ISO file to a disc and expect the contents to magically transform themselves into a playable CD. You must restore the image to CD, which is very different from copying files to the CD.

First, you need a program that can burn ISO images to CD. The two best for the job are Nero Burning ROM and Roxio's Easy CD Creator. Here's a step-by-step guide for using Nero Burning ROM (these directions also work for .CUE and .BIN files):

1. Load Nero, select File → Burn Image, select the ISO image, and click the Open button (Figure 6-17).

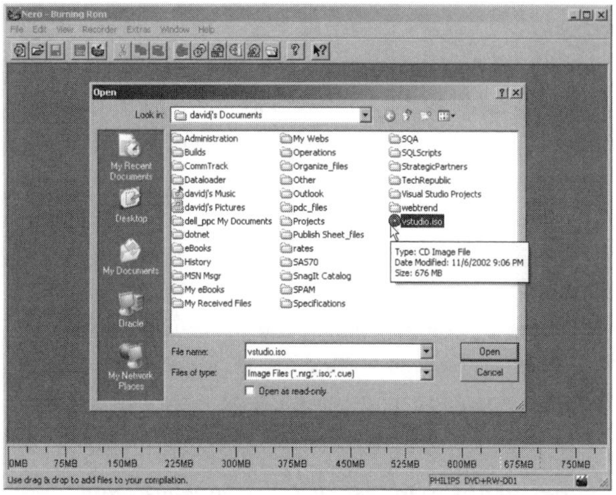

Figure 6-17. The Open dialog box allows you to select your ISO image file.

2. The Write CD dialog box appears (Figure 6-18). Now, pay attention to the next step or you'll just add another coaster to your collection. If you're burning a data ISO or a Windows installation CD, it doesn't matter what write speed you select. You should, however, select the Disc-At-Once or Disc-At-Once/96 write method.

If you're burning an ISO video CD, choose the slowest write speed you can; the write method should be Disc-At-Once. (The reason is that DAO burns the entire disc, from beginning to end, in one fell swoop, ensuring you can work around the ISO image's LipCrypt encryption.)

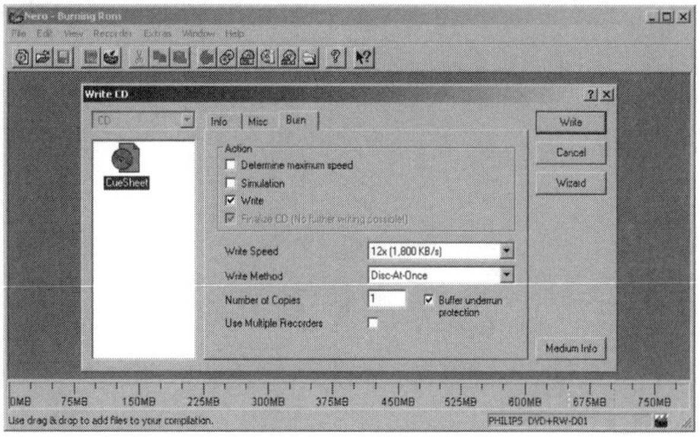

Fsigure 6-18. The Write CD dialog box with the fastest write speed marked and Disc-At-Once option marked.

PEEK INSIDE ISO FILES

The Annoyance: I have an ISO image that contains a few files I need. Why can't I extract the ones I want? And what about adding new files after I've created an ISO file?

The Fix: ISO files are compressed, much like zipped files, which makes them tricky to work with. The good news is that there are some tools that can view the contents of an ISO file or let you add to the ISO (see Figure 6-19). Four of the most popular applications are:

WinISO

Free trial; $30 to keep. *http://www.winiso.com*

WinImage

Free trial; $30 to keep. *http://www.winimage.com*

IsoBuster

Free; $25.95 to register. *http://www.smart-projects.net/ isobuster*

Undisker

Free trial; $40.44 to keep. *http://www.undisker.com*

WinISO and IsoBuster also let you view the contents of other image files, such as Nero .NRG files, CloneCD .IMG files, and .CUE/.BIN files. These files are also at *http:// www.oreilly.com/pcannoyances*.

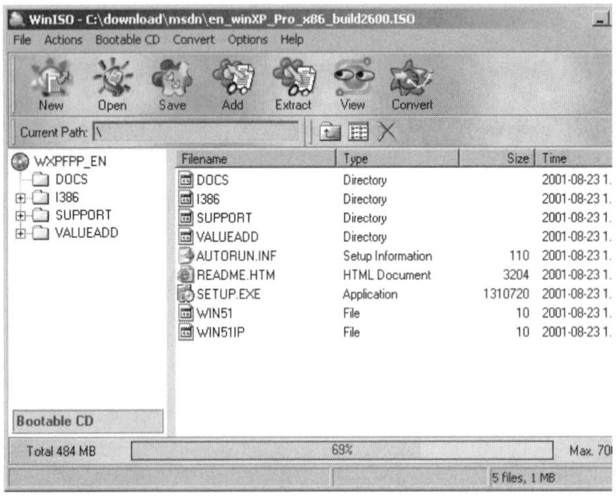

Figure 6-19. WinISO shows ISO files as if you were viewing a CD with Windows Explorer. With this sort of a utility, you can add, update, or delete content within an ISO file.

FIND INVISIBLE .BIN FILES

The Annoyance: I have .BIN and .CUE files in the same folder, but my CD-burning software can't see the .BIN file. Why not?

The Fix: Chances are you moved these files at some point. The .CUE file is probably still pointing to where the .BIN file used to reside.

For example, if your .CUE file contains:

```
FILE "f:\video\LukeAndLaura\image-name.BIN" BINARY
TRACK 1 MODE2/2352
INDEX 1 00:00:00
```

it tells your CD-burning software that the .BIN file is on the F: drive, in the *\video\LukeAndLaura* folder. (To view the contents of a .CUE file, open it in Notepad or any text editor.)

You can either change the path in the .CUE file or, even easier, just remove the path info from the .CUE file (leaving `FILE "image-name.BIN" BINARY` in this example).

.CUE, .BIN, AND .ISO FORMATS

CD-burning programs use various formats, notably .ISO and, to a lesser extent, .CUE and .BIN. (.CUE and .BIN were made popular years ago by one program—CDRWin. You need both the .BIN and .CUE files to burn an image to disc.)

The .CUE file, also known as the CueSheet, contains the track layout information for Video CDs, Super Video CDs, or other data track layout information. The .BIN file holds the actual data to be written to the disc. Many programs—including Nero, BlindWrite, CloneCD, and FireBurner—have full or partial support for these two formats.

Unlike the .BIN/.CUE format, an .ISO file contains the entire CD image—the data layout information and the data.

AUTOPLAY, GO AWAY (OR COME BACK)

The Annoyance: The other day I popped a music CD into my CD-ROM drive, and in the Audio CD Properties dialog that appeared, I clicked "Open folder to view file using Windows Explorer". But then I foolishly clicked "Always does the selected action." Now whenever I stick in a CD, this dumb dialog shows up. How can I undo this?

The Fix: To reset Windows' AutoPlay, open My Computer, right-click your CD drive, select Properties, click the AutoPlay tab, and click the Restore Defaults button (see Figure 6-20). If the AutoPlay tab is missing in XP or 2000, close the Properties dialog box, click Start → Run, type `services.msc` in the Open box, and press Enter. Scroll to and double-click the Shell Hardware Detection item, and in the "Startup type" drop-down, select Automatic. Click either the Start or Resume button, click OK, then exit the Services window. The CD drive's Properties dialog box also has AutoPlay options for pictures, video files, and other CD content; this is your chance to reset them to their default values as well (see Figure 6-21).

Figure 6-21. While you're poking around in AutoPlay's settings, make sure to check the default values for Pictures, Video and Music files, and the other items.

NO, I DON'T WANT TO BURN THE CD RIGHT NOW...

The Annoyance: When I first started burning CDs, I'd open Windows Explorer, select a bunch of files in the file pane, and drop them onto my CD-RW drive icon. Then I'd click that little pop-up that says "You have files waiting to be written to the CD," and on the window that appeared I'd click the "Write these files to CD" link on the CD Writing Tasks pane. But what if I don't want to burn the CD immediately because I'd like to add more files later and then burn them all at once?

The Fix: Go ahead and drag the first set of files and ignore that pop-up message (it'll go away). Drag more files over at your convenience. When you're ready to burn, open My Computer or Windows Explorer, right-click your CD drive icon and choose "Write these files to CD" (see

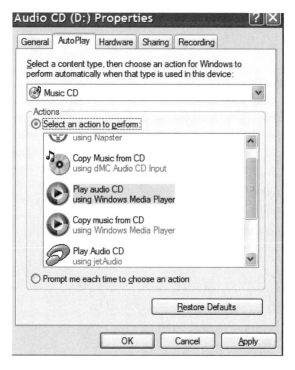

Figure 6-20. Click the Restore Default button to get your AutoPlay settings back to normal.

Figure 6-22). Or to see the CD Writing Tasks pane, right-click the CD drive icon and choose Open. If you want to delete any files, choose "Delete temporary files".

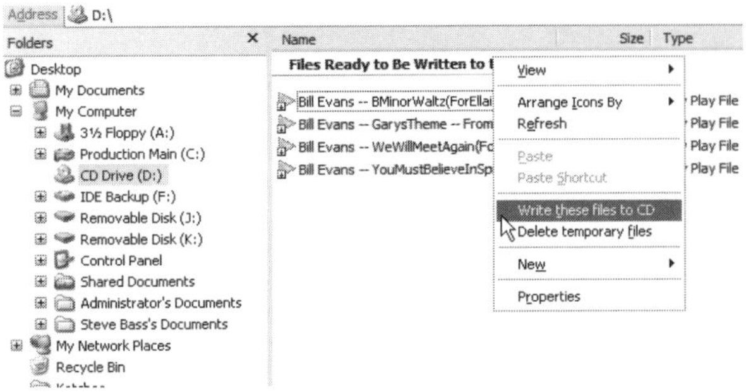

Figure 6-22. Windows doesn't make it easy to burn files to a CD after you've closed the CD Writing Wizard. Do it by using Windows Explorer.

By the way, don't worry about deleting these files after burning them to CD. You're deleting copies of the files—not the originals—that are in XP's temporary storage area. In fact, swing by the *C:\Documents and Settings\ username\Local Settings\Application Data\Microsoft\CD Burning* folder to see if any old files are loitering about, taking up hard disk space.

DVD+R VERSUS DVD-R?

The Annoyance: I just bought a DVD±R/±RW drive to burn DVD movies. Should I buy DVD+R or DVD-R media? The price for a 10-pack is about the same.

The Fix: It depends on which type is more compatible with your playback hardware. See what the manual says or check the drive manufacturer's web site. The alternative is to buy one disc of each type, burn the same video to both discs, and play them on the DVD players and DVD-ROM drives. The disc that plays in the most devices is the one to use. If there's no difference, buy the cheaper ones.

ORGANIZING DVDS AND MUSIC CDS

The Annoyance: My collection of music CDs and movie DVDs has grown exponentially, and Windows Media Player isn't very good at cataloging them. I want to organize these discs and be able to search them, so I can pick the right tune or the right movie to match my mood.

The Fix: There are a couple of great cataloging programs that are either free or dirt cheap. For DVD movies, grab a copy of DVD Profiler. Enter the UPC of a movie DVD into the program—or just stick the disc into your PC—and the program pulls down nearly two dozen details on the film from the company's 150,000-title database, from genre to cast listing to playing time. The program is so automatic, you can catalog your DVD collection way fast and search your catalog on a number of factors. Other pluses: downloadable reports from other users, the ability to track who's borrowed which movie, a charting function to watch your viewing trends, and more. There are two flavors of the program—free but with ads or $25 for a version unencumbered by ads. Browse to *http://snipurl.com/DVD_Profiler* to download the free version.

Want to do something with your collection of music CDs and MP3s? Turn to CD Trustee, which creates a database of song titles automatically. CD Trustee built a nifty database for me in a flash: I just popped in each CD in turn, and the program automatically looked it up in an online database and pulled down all sorts of info on the album, artist, tracks, and more. The entire process takes about 10 seconds. Once your catalog is up and running, you can search by song, artist, composer, or CD title (see Figure 6-23). The program can also print CD labels, jewel case covers, and inserts. CD Trustee costs $39.95, and there's a limited-use trial version available: *http://snipurl.com/cd_trustee*.

A similar, but not as comprehensive, utility is CDmax. The product's free, but if you like it, donate $15 to the creator. Check it out at *http://snipurl.com/CDmax*.

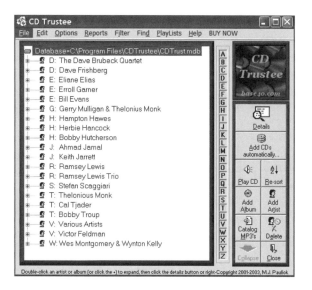

Figure 6-23. CD Trustee does a phenomenal job of cataloging music CDs and giving you quick access to just the one you want to play.

IS PC FRIENDLY NECESSARY?

The Annoyance: I rented a DVD movie to watch on my PC. But when I tried to watch it, up popped the installation for InterActual PC Friendly. Do I really need InterActual? And if not, what can I do to stop it from loading?

The Fix: You can just say no when InterActual's opening screen appears, and play the DVD. But you're going to miss out on all the nifty DVD-ROM content—the extra features the studio put on, such as web connectivity, additional games, and extra commentary. If you do install PC Friendly and don't want to clutter up your hard drive, just remove it after you've watched the DVD; use Windows Control Panel's Add or Remove Programs.

FASTEN YOUR SEAT BELT

Here's the video of a flight I took (wink, wink) from Anchorage to Nome: *http://snipurl.com/hownottoland*. (The link downloads a Zipped Windows Media video file.)

TAKE A RECURSIVE BREAK

Need a break and just want to space out? Try watching "Recursive" at *http://snipurl.com/swirl*. Wonder how it's done? The creator was kind enough to provide background at *http://snipurl.com/swirl_howto*.

INTERACTUAL DVD ANNOYANCE

If you use InterActual's PC Friendly DVD player with Windows XP, you may find that the photo gallery or other features don't work. Microsoft has a patch that'll fix you up lickity-split; see *http://www.oreilly.com/pcannoyances*.

Hardware
ANNOYANCES

Is your monitor flickering, your cable modem sputtering, or your printer putt-putting? I'll bet you've been annoyed by your keyboard and even your cell phone. I have dozens of ways for you to eliminate these irritations, plus a hefty handful of extra tips that deal with annoyances you didn't even know you had.

THE WONDERS OF A MODEM RESET

The Annoyance: I spent a couple of frustrating hours trying to figure out why my DSL connection can't access the Internet. I checked my connection with utility programs, reconfigured my pop-up and ad blocker, fiddled with Windows' TCP/IP settings, and called tech support—still no connection.

The Fix: A simple, two-minute reboot of your DSL or cable modem may be all it takes to get you back online. The mystery is why there isn't a diagnostic tool that can tell you it's time to reset your Internet access device. Until that magical tool arrives, here are a few steps you can take:

- If you're using DSL and can't get online, wait a bit—the modem should attempt to resync. If that fails, close the DSL dialer application, then reopen it and see if a connection is made. Still offline? Exit the dialer application, turn off the modem, wait several minutes, and then fire them back up. If that doesn't work, call your ISP.

- If you're having problems with your cable Internet connection, first make sure there isn't a line outage. If your cable-connected TV is showing static, now you know why your cable Internet access is down.

- Next, make sure all the components, from modem to cables to power, are properly connected. Still DOA? Turn off (or unplug) the modem for a few minutes, then turn it back on. Note which lights come on and stay on, and which ones don't—tech support may want to know. If everything lights up, you should be able to step online. If not, you may (depending on the system) have to turn off the modem and disconnect it from the coaxial cable for a few minutes, and then reconnect everything. If that fails, call your cable company.

HELP FOR SLOW DIALUP CONNECTIONS

- There's a good chance you can give your dialup modem connection a boost by trying a different dial-in or access phone number.

- If your ISP is a small outfit, it may have separate phone numbers for 56 Kbps modems. Make sure you're calling the right number.

- A phone cable that's longer than ten feet from your modem to the wall jack will affect performance: the longer the cable, the weaker the signal.

- For more tips, check *http://www.56K.com*.

ONLINE HELP FOR DSL AND CABLE MODEMS

Check these sites for the skinny on all things DSL and cable modem:

BroadbandReports
A wide-ranging resource site with dozens of links to other DSL and cable sites, reviews of providers, and valuable tips for using both (*http://www.broadbandreports.com*).

Everything DSL
Curious which is better, DSL or cable modem? Worried about hackers breaking into your PC? This site answers these and other burning questions (*http://www.everythingdsl.com*).

Cable Modem Help
The name says it all—it's an excellent resource with a comprehensive listing of cable providers, help for connecting your AOL account to cable, and even troubleshooting tips (*http://www.cablemodemhelp.com*).

Cable Modem Info
This is a good resource if you're looking for a cable Internet provider in your area, or if you already have cable modem and want help sharing it, check out this site (*http://www.cablemodeminfo.com*).

WIFI MIRACLE SPRAY

Increase Web throughput 100 percent—get WiFi Speed Spray today!!! If you're using any wireless product, you'll want to try out WiFi Speed Spray. This remarkable product speeds up everything wireless. Buy now while supplies last (*http://snipurl.com/wifi_spray*).

BRING THE ZING BACK TO DSL

The Annoyance: I have DSL access in my home office, and up until a few weeks ago, it was really fast. Now it's sluggish—web sites appear slowly, and files take forever to download. I've tried every speedup trick I know, even rebooting my DSL modem and router, to no avail.

The Fix: The same thing happened to me—my DSL line lost its zip. It was nothing I (or you) did wrong. It was my dumb Internet Service Provider. My router is set up to use specific domain name server (DNS) addresses supplied by my ISP (see Figure 7-1). The problem was that my ISP changed the DNS addresses but failed to inform its customers. The old DNS addresses worked, but the new ones worked better. Call your ISP, ask tech support if they've changed the DNS addresses, and ask for help in making the changes.

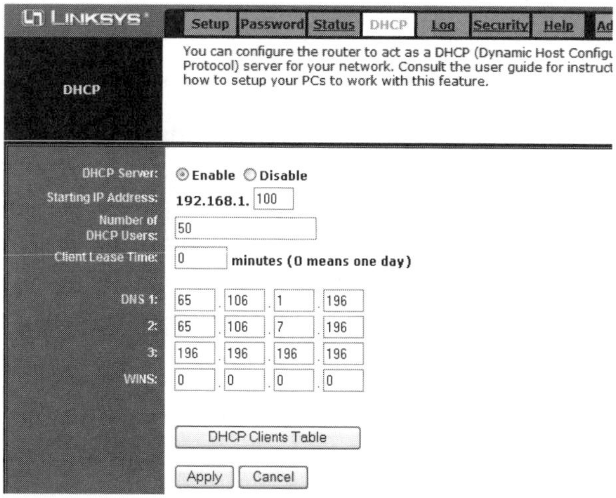

Figure 7-1. Change the DNS settings on a Linksys router from the DHCP setup page. Most routers have similar pages where you can change your DNS settings.

UNINTERRUPTIBLE POWER TO THE PC

The Annoyance: Every summer I know I have to deal with rolling blackouts. I don't mind shutting down my PC when the power's about to go down, but they only give us an approximate time—sometimes in a four-hour block.

KEEP YOUR BROADBAND CONNECTION IN HIGH GEAR

Use the ferrite chokes. **DSL, cable, and even dialup connections may be slow because of radio frequency interference. Those little cubes that snap around the modem's data cable and power line reduce RF interference. If you threw them out because you didn't know what they were, you can pick up a set at most electronic supply stores for under $5.**

Get a microfilter. **DSL users might experience static, humming, or noise on their phone line. If your DSL modem and phone uses a line splitter, call your ISP and get a microfilter, which reduces the interference between your phone and the DSL modem. Pinpoint devices in your office that can emit RF, slowing your DSL line. Isolate your modem from halogen lamps, 900 MHz to 2.4 GHz portable phones, security alarms, and similar devices. If you already have a filter installed but still have noise, ask your ISP for a new filter.**

Replace the copper. **If your home or office is in an old building, the copper wire may be old, frayed, and brittle. That will have an effect on the DSL line and, to a lesser extent, on dialup connections. Ask your phone company to replace your internal wiring—but be prepared to pay through the nose. The same advice goes for existing coaxial wire for your cable modem.**

The Fix: Invest in an uninterruptible power supply, a gadget that's cheap insurance when the AC goes MIA. A UPS is just a big battery that keeps your PC running long enough after the electricity goes out for you to turn the PC off properly. A small UPS costs roughly $40 and keeps your system up for about 5 minutes; my $100 APCC Back-UPS ES 725 keeps my PC alive for 10 minutes. Most UPSes also "condition" the line (evening out sags and spikes) and act as surge protectors. You can figure out the size UPS you need at APCC's site, *http://snipurl.com/apcc_sizer*.

PULL THE PLUG

What you absolutely do not want to happen when you bring your notebook in for a repair: *http://snipurl.com/pulltheplug*. **[Warning: this is a video clip.]**

MANAGE MULTIPLE BULKY AC ADAPTERS

The Annoyance: The engineers who design AC adapters for notebooks and handhelds should be sentenced to 20 whacks with a geometry textbook. Some transformers almost weigh more than the device they're powering!

The Fix: This is one of my A-list annoyances. I bought APC's $45 Professional SurgeArrest surge protector (see *http://snipurl.com/apc_surge*); it has eight outlets, three of which are spaced far enough apart to accept most AC adapters. Belkin's ten-outlet SurgeMaster (see *http://snipurl.com/belkin_surge*) has four outlets capable of accommodating hefty adapters. Since I have more than four large adapters, I bought a vertical rack-mount power strip designed for a workbench. It has eight outlets over its four-foot length, each about six inches apart.

You can take advantage of *all* the outlets on either the SurgeArrest or SurgeMaster using Cables Unlimited's clever extension cords. The first is a short, one-foot extension cord. The other is a short extension cord with a "Y"

connector, so you can plug two bricks into a single outlet (see Figure 7-2). Both products are under $9 and available at *http://snipurl.com/short_ext*.

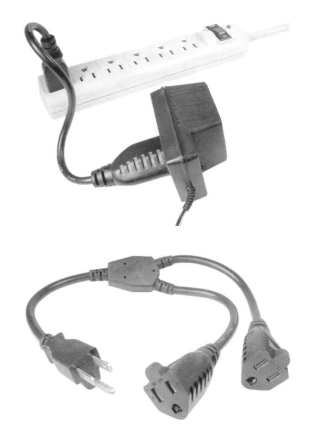

Figure 7-2. Top: Make full use of your power strip by using the Power Strip Liberator, a short extension cord from Cables Unlimited. Botttom: You can beat the system by plugging in two big AC adapters and using only one outlet on a power strip with the Power Strip Liberator II.

POWER STRIP CAUTION

Make sure you plug the short extension cords into the surge protector, not directly into the wall outlet, and use them only for AC adapters, not for more power strips or extension cords.

LIGHTEN YOUR POWER LOAD

The Annoyance: It never fails: I fall in love with some cute little gadget for my PC, only to find that it requires an AC adapter that could double as an anchor for an oil tanker. I have enough bricks under my desk to rebuild Hadrian's Wall. How can I clear out the brick-a-brac?

The Fix: A smart, though not cheap, fix for this AC traffic jam is the DC Hub from GoldX (*http://snipurl.com/goldx_hub*). This $30 hub can power up to five electronic devices that would ordinarily need their own AC adapters. You can run one 12-volt, one 9-volt, and three 5-volt devices simultaneously. It's ideal for providing a constant stream of power to different devices, such as a label printer, cordless mouse, cable modem, router, USB hub, and other typical items found connected to a PC. The downside? You also need the company's $30 PowerCore Base unit with surge protector to power the hub.

LIGHTEN YOUR LOAD WITH A UNIVERSAL POWER ADAPTER

If you don't like lugging around that brick-size, six-pound transformer to power your paper-thin notebook, try the $119 Targus Universal AC Adapter. This pricey (but well worth it) gizmo is two inches thick and weighs 4.5 ounces. Linked with the right connector (and many of them are included), it can power most notebooks and recharge many cell phones and PDAs. Check the site for specs (see *http://snipurl.com/targus*) and look for discounts at PriceGrabber (see *http://snipurl.com/Targus_discount*).

A 1989 COMPUTING BARGAIN

It's astonishing how inexpensive today's computers are. Consider this ad from 1989: *http://snipurl.com/old_pc*. (And note that the monitor's not included.)

CLEAR AND SHARP LCD FONTS

The Annoyance: Here's something that made me mad: I upgraded my system to Windows XP, bought a cool LCD monitor, and looked forward to seeing crisp, sharp fonts. But no, XP just ignored my hardware and forced me to dig around to find my LCD's type-display settings on my own.

The Fix: If XP won't do it for us, I guess we'll have to do it ourselves. There are three methods to turn on ClearType, Microsoft's font-rendering technology that makes characters easier to read on LCDs. Choose the method that's easiest for your situation:

The quickest

Right-click anywhere on the desktop, choose Properties, select the Appearance tab, and click the Effects button. Check the "Use the following method to smooth edges of screen fonts" box, and choose ClearType from the drop-down menu. Unfortunately, Windows uses the ClearType default and doesn't let you fiddle with the settings.

The best for fine-tuning

Go to Microsoft's ClearType site (*http://snipurl.com/set_cleartype*), check the "Turn ClearType on" box at the bottom of the page, then click the "Step 2" link and follow the prompts. Spend a few minutes adjusting and setting the options to your viewing preference.

ClearType on and off

If you'd like to fiddle more with your ClearType settings, or if you need to turn it on and off often, grab a free copy of ClearTweak Pro (see Figure 7-3) from *http://www.oreilly.com/pcannoyances.*

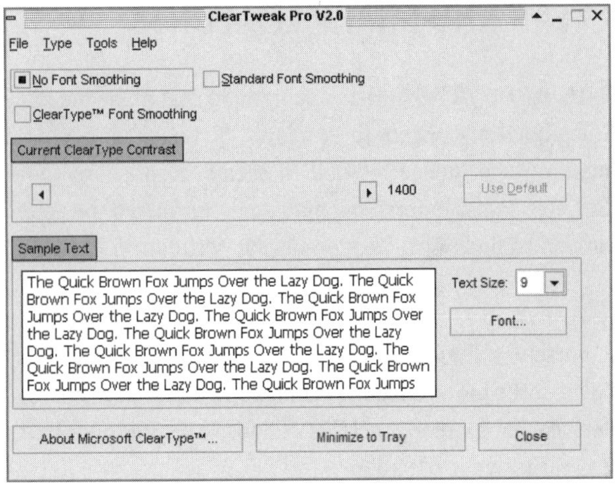

Figure 7-3. ClearTweak Pro is a nifty free utility for adjusting your notebook and desktop PC's LCD screen. It's also ideal if you need to turn ClearType on and off a lot.

PRIO GLASSES BRING MONITORS INTO FOCUS

In 1994, my monitor started looking fuzzy, and I realized it wasn't the monitor—it was me. That's when I discovered PRIO prescription computer eyeglasses. I went for a special eye exam, took off my old spectacles, and stuck on a pair of special PRIO glasses. I'm still wearing my PRIOs. I can't imagine sitting in front of a computer without them. It's easier to focus on the screen than with my regular glasses, images are sharp, and my eyes don't get tired. Even if you don't wear glasses or if you wear contacts, PRIOs can make a world of difference. Get more details on PRIO's site at *http://www.prio.com*.

CLEARTYPE BASICS

ClearType is a fascinating technology, especially if you wear a pocket protector and once enjoyed fiddling with a slide rule. Microsoft's ClearType site offers a good explanation of how the process works. Check it out at *http://snipurl.com/learn_cleartype*.

TUNE UP YOUR MONITOR

The Annoyance: The colors on my new monitor are not quite right, and unless it's my eyes, the monitor doesn't look as sharp as it should. I've used the monitor's built-in controls to no avail. Why aren't monitors easier to adjust?

The Fix: You spend lots of time staring at your monitor, so it makes sense to finely tune its settings. Unfortunately, monitor manufacturers don't provide much help. Turn to DisplayMate—in my opinion, the best product available for adjusting CRT and LCD monitors. DisplayMate gives me instant gratification because I can adjust my ViewSonic LCD's sharpness, color, and contrast and fine-tune dozens of other settings (see Figure 7-4).

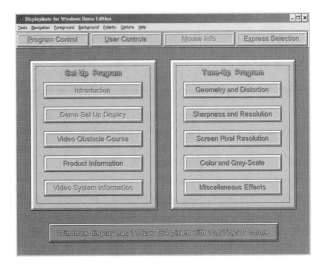

Figure 7-4. The DisplayMate free demo program is more than adequate for most people wanting to set their monitors' brightness and contrast, properly size and center screen images, check sharpness and resolution, and adjust the color.

The free version of DisplayMate is adequate for most people (get a copy at *http://www.oreilly.com/pcannoyances*). But once you start tinkering, you'll probably want the $70 standard version. Heck, just the chart comparing relative strengths and weaknesses of CRTs and LCDs is worth the visit to *http://snipurl.com/display_chart*.

The SMART Way to Check Your Hard Drive

Wonder when your hard drive's going to fail? Oh, it will, guaranteed, but there's a way to find out before it happens. PanteraSoft's HDD Health 2 disk utility uses Self Monitoring, Analysis, and Reporting Technology (SMART) to report on your drive's performance to your PC's BIOS. If your drive is about to become a doorstop, you'll get a bunch of pop-up and email alerts. The program even keeps a log of the drive's problems. Grab a copy from *http://www.oreilly.com/pcannoyances*.

HUSH...HUSH, SWEET MONITOR

The Annoyance: My six-year-old 17-inch monitor, which I affectionately call "Gramps," started making a high-pitched, drive-me-up-the-wall whine. I thought I'd landed in a low-budget sci-fi thriller.

The Fix: The whine is probably caused by a vibrating flyback transformer (don't ask; it's a voltage thing). You can muzzle the monitor by changing its refresh rate. To do so in Windows XP and 2000, right-click the desktop and choose Properties, click the Settings tab, then the Advanced button, then the Monitor tab (see Figure 7-5). Change the setting in the "Screen refresh rate" or "Refresh Frequency" drop-down, respectively, to 72 Hertz or higher. (The higher the refresh rate, the less eyestrain you'll suffer from, too.) In Windows 98 and Me, click the Adapter tab (not the Monitor tab) and change the setting in the Refresh drop-down menu.

An alternate fix is to perform "percussive maintenance": Give the monitor a good whack on the side. Really. This might stop the vibration, albeit temporarily. Keep in mind that repairing your monitor will likely cost more in the long run than replacing it. This may be your best excuse yet to buy that new LCD panel you've had your eye on.

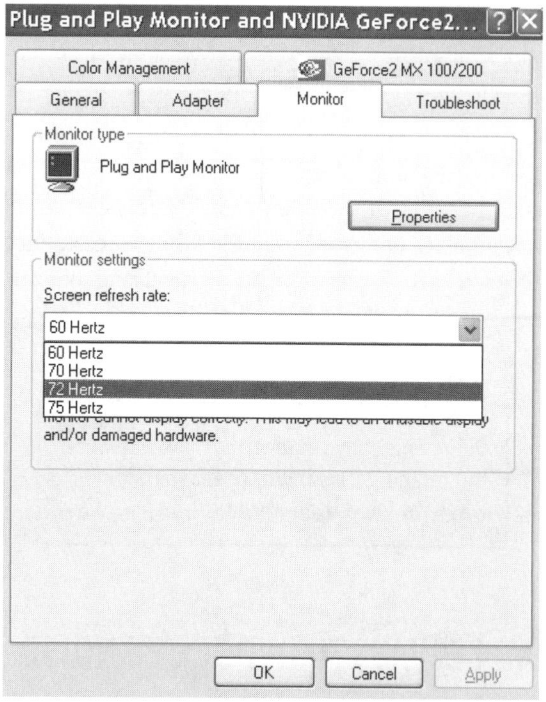

Figure 7-5. Change your monitor's refresh rate in the Display control panel to stifle an ear-piercing whine.

STRAIGHTEN UP AND DISPLAY RIGHT

The Annoyance: My mother called recently with yet another gripe about her PC (kvetching must run in the family). This time she was upset because she couldn't figure out why all of the images on her screen were tilted at a slight angle.

The Fix: It's a worthy kvetch, unless you like tilting your head when you type. The problem is with the monitor's controls. Your mother's monitor may have a button called "Image Tilt" or "Rotate". Simply turn the knob and you'll see the picture straighten out. If the monitor uses onscreen controls, look for a "Geometry" control—something that involves fiddling with trapezoids and parallelograms. Select the geometric shape from the onscreen menu that most closely resembles the monitor's current problem, and start pushing the + and - keys (or whatever the CRT uses for changing the value of the setting).

While you're digging through the settings on your mother's CRT, you might as well help her get more bang for her display buck. Most monitors come factory-set with an annoying black border; enlarge the display area to fill the entire screen by expanding the vertical and horizontal image areas until the black borders disappear.

> **t i p**
>
> Doing this may require that you adjust the image up or down, or maybe sideways, to keep it centered.

SIMPLE WAYS TO REDUCE PC NOISE

The Annoyance: I work in a small home office, and the noise from my PC is driving me bonkers.

The Fix: PCs are way too loud. Their hard disks grind, their fans whine, and their cases clatter. Bothersome? Yes. Insurmountable? Well, maybe, depending on the source of the noise. You can reduce some noise with a few simple tweaks.

First, turn your PC off, remove the case cover, turn the system back on, and use a car mechanic's stethoscope—or just a paper-towel tube—to isolate the noise source. Hold it near the cages that hold the hard drive, CD-ROM drives, and other internal peripherals.

Here are a handful of tricks to try once you've isolated the source of the noise:

- If your hard drive chatters, make sure the screws attaching it to the PC case are tight, and examine the bracket holding the drive to confirm that it's tightly connected to the PC.
- Power supplies can be noisy, and if yours is, replace it with PC Power & Cooling's Silencer. The least expensive model costs $55. (See *http://snipurl.com/pcpower.*)

- Check the gap around the case cover for vibrations; if you detect any, wedge in a piece of cardboard or use sealing foam. If the case's cover itself is rattling, try a couple of beads of silicon gel or caulking, which you can buy at a building supply store. You could also try Dynamat's Xtreme Computer Kit, a $30 adhesive-backed, heat-bondable vibration damper you place inside your PC (see *http://snipurl.com/dynamat*).
- If the fans are noisy, see if anything's touching the blades—make sure a wire or cable isn't being hit by the fan. You could replace the existing fan with a quieter one or one that automatically adjusts its speed based on heat within your PC. For a tremendous array of fans and other cooling devices, check CrazyPC at *http://snipurl.com/pc_cooling.*

For additional details on making your PC quiet, check out The Silent PC site at *http://snipurl.com/silentpc.*

> **GET THE RIGHT SCREWDRIVER**
>
> Compaq and other PC manufacturers seem to delight in using obscure Torx screws that have six shallow flanges, rather than traditional Phillips screws. If you need to open the case, you may need to buy a Torx T-9 screwdriver, which is available at most hardware stores.

LOST SCREW, BIG PROBLEMS

The Annoyance: I upgraded my PC's sound card recently and dropped the little screw that holds the add-in card in place. The screw's somewhere in the case and for the life of me, I can't find it.

The Fix: Find it, bub, because if you don't—and it dislodges from wherever it's sitting and lands on your system board—your computer's toast. A stray screw can short out your system board faster than a teenager can clean out an all-you-can-eat buffet. Turn off your PC, remove all the cables and the side covers, and gently tip and shake the system. If that doesn't free the screw, grab a flashlight and start looking for it. When you find it, place a tiny dab of wax or glue stick on the tip of a screwdriver and grab the errant screw that way. Still can't find the screw? You may need to pop the PC's lid, remove all the cards, and, if need be, the motherboard itself.

DO AS I SAY, NOT AS I DO

Want embarrassing? After almost 20 years of computing, I still find myself making remarkable mistakes. This one's a beauty: I always tell people to turn off the PC when they crack the case and work on the insides, but it's something I never do myself. My unsolicited advice? Do it. All the time, every time.

Here's why: I added a sound card to my wife's PC recently. Easy enough, right? Then, while the system was up and running, I replaced the cover. I've done it this way since I started tinkering with PCs in 1983, but this time it bit me in the butt. The metal case cover touched the sound card and the system board fried to a crisp...and never booted again.

P.S. My wife ended up with a brand new PC; to date, all I'm allowed to do is look at it—from a distance.

EXTRA POWER FOR DIGITAL CAMERAS

The Annoyance: My digital camera is great, except for the dozens of AA batteries I have to schlep with me to keep it powered.

The Fix: One of the pleasures of owning a digital camera is that I can shoot as many pics as I want without worrying about the cost of film or developing. And now I'm not even concerned about carrying extra batteries. DigiCom's very cool $30 Digital Camera Auxiliary Power Pack is a rechargeable lithium ion battery that links to the camera via a cable. It's about the size of a small cell phone, and in unscientific tests using my digital camera, I took 212 pictures before it ran out of juice.

There are versions for 3-, 5-, and 7-volt cameras (it's imperative to choose the correct one, so check your camera's manual). The Power Pack's not easy to find. You can find it for sale at *http://snipurl.com/digicom* or by doing a Google search.

WINDOWS SETTING BLOCKS DVD UPGRADE

The Annoyance: I want to update the firmware for my Sony DRX510UL DVD burner, and the site said to disable the DMA setting in Windows XP before doing so. But it neglects to tell you *how*.

The Fix: The Sony drive is terrific—it burns a DVD+R and DVD-R, and supports DVD-RW and DVD+RW. But ask Sony for support, and it responds with a virtual raspberry—its online instructions are complex and often impossible to understand. Luckily, fiddling with DMA isn't difficult. Here's how to turn it off:

Windows XP/2000

> Open the System control panel, choose the Hardware tab, and click the Device Manager button. Double-click "IDE ATA/ATAPI controllers" and double-click "Secondary IDE Channel" (your DVD drive is most likely located on the secondary channel; if not, choose "Primary IDE Channel"). Click the Advanced Settings tab, and under Device 0 (master) or Device 1 (slave) (depending on how your drive is set up), select PIO Only from the Transfer Mode drop-down menu. Click OK.

Windows 98/Me

> Open the System control panel and choose the Device Manager tab. Double-click CD-ROM, then double-click your drive. Select the Settings tab, uncheck the DMA option, and click OK.

Remember to reverse the previous steps once your DVD drive's firmware is installed.

CHECK FOR LOOSE CABLES

The Annoyance: My monitor works fine most of the
time but occasionally flickers on and off. If I reboot the
system, it works fine again, then flickers after a few hours.
It's driving me nutty.

The Fix: Check the cables. Repeat. Don't think it's something this simple? I once spent half a day diagnosing my
faulty dialup connection only to discover the telephone
line was plugged into the wrong jack on the modem.
Another fiasco was forgetting to reconnect the network
cable after moving my PC. By the way, this intermittent
problem can occur with a modem, scanner, or practically
any device that's connected to your PC with a cable.

HEY SANTA—DUCK!

Didn't get that terrific headset you wanted for Christ-
mas? Here's why: *http://snipurl.com/santa_duck*.

5 CABLES IN 1

The Annoyance: I have a bunch of USB devices—MP3
player, digital camera, PDA, and more—and they all have
different USB cables with different connectors, so when I
want to move tunes to my player and then download pix
from my camera, I have to keep switching cables! And
when I buy more gadgets, I'll have to buy (and fuss with)
still more USB cables.

The Fix: End the cable madness with the $30 QuickCon-
nect 5-in-1 USB Cable from GoldX (*http://snipurl.com/goldx*).
The cable has five interchangeable tips that attach to
either end, so instead of plugging in a different cable every
time you switch gadgets, you just change the cable's tip.
The cable can also connect a PDA directly to a USB printer.
You can buy the cable in lengths from 1.5 to 15 feet.

SAFELY REMOVE A USB FLASH DRIVE

The Annoyance: I often use a USB Flash drive (essentially, a key fob that holds gobs of data and plugs into a
USB port) to move files between computers. When I'm
ready to pull the drive out of the USB port, I dutifully

double-click the Safely Remove Hardware icon in Windows' System Tray. But then the inquisition begins: I have to select the device I want to remove, click Stop, then review another list of devices, click OK, and then click Close. This rigmarole makes me want to not-so-safely remove Windows.

The Fix: Fortunately, the fix is so easy you won't believe it. Don't double-click the Safely Remove Hardware icon. Don't right-click the icon. Just click it once with the left button, and the icon sprouts a menu of attached removable devices. Click the one you want to remove, and in a few moments a balloon tip lets you know it's safe to do so.

By the way, this same routine applies to other removable devices, including hard drives, CD drives, cameras, and MP3 players. Resist the temptation to ignore the Safely Remove Hardware icon and yank the device—it could lead to data corruption or loss in some cases.

LOCK DOWN YOUR USB FLASH DRIVE

The Annoyance: Those little USB Flash drives are really convenient. I can copy over hundreds of megabytes of data in a few seconds and carry it off in a package no bigger than a key fob. The problem is, so can unsavory data thieves. If I left my PC for just a few minutes, someone could easily make off with my personal files, completely undetected.

The Fix: Some corporations have banned USB drives as well as devices with similar capabilities, such as MP3 players. Of course, short of strip-searching everyone who leaves the building, such a ban is toothless. A few have chosen the more drastic solution of removing USB connectors or—gasp!—plugging them with epoxy. If you have Windows XP with Service Pack 2 installed, there's a less permanent, more effective solution, which involves editing the Registry.

Open the Registry editor (Start → Run, type **regedit**, and press Enter). Navigate to *HKEY_LOCAL_MACHINE\SYSTEM*

CurrentControlSet\Control. If there isn't a subkey named StorageDevicePolicies, create one. (Right-click the Control key, choose New → Key, and type **StorageDevicePolicies**.) In the StorageDevicePolicies key, create a DWORD value named WriteProtect if it doesn't already exist. (Right-click the StorageDevicePolicies key, select New → DWORD Value, and name it WriteProtect.) Double-click WriteProtect item and change "Value data" to 1. Click OK, exit the Registry editor, and restart Windows.

Now when Flash drives are plugged into your PC's USB port, they're treated as read-only devices; no one can save data from your PC to the Flash drive. To restore normal read and write operation, change "Value data" of the WriteProtect item to 0.

USB-TO-PS/2 MOUSE ADAPTER

The Annoyance: I have a hand-me-down HP notebook from my son. On a whim, I bought a USB mouse at a garage sale and only later realized I have just one measly USB port on the notebook (right, it's *that* old). And that's already taken by my USB printer.

The Fix: Instead of bothering with a USB hub, try a PS/2-to-USB adapter. You can probably find one at another garage sale, or buy one for under $5 at Provantage (*http://snipurl.com/provantage*).

GIVE YOUR LASER PRINTER A MEMORY BOOST

The Annoyance: I often have to print long, complex documents filled with images. My laser printer balks, and either the document won't print at all or it prints images on some pages and gibberish on others.

IF YOU USE A MAC

Here are some handy instructions that say a lot about Mac users: *http://snipurl.com/Mac_howto*. (And you'd better bookmark this one, in case you forget.)

The Fix: A quick-and-dirty workaround is to try printing one page at a time. If it's a Word document, and you don't need to see the images, print it in Draft mode. From Tools → Option, choose the Print tab, and under Printing options, check the "Draft output" box.

If you're willing to spend a few bucks, you can resolve the problem by increasing your laser printer's RAM. Increasing RAM not only sends documents flying out of your printer, but it also lets you add more complex images to files without the printer rebelling.

All laser printers come with memory—generally SIMMs, the same type of RAM many PCs use. (Inkjet printers don't use RAM; the document is held on the PC and spooled to the printer.) Unfortunately, manufacturers are stingy and include only 1 MB or maybe 2 MB of RAM in their laser printers, just enough to print an average document. But you can supplement this with more RAM; check your printer's manual for the type and size of RAM you can use.

SAVE BIG WITH LOW-RESOLUTION PRINTS

The Annoyance: My inkjet printer was cheap—I bought it for a mere $60. But I have to spend a fortune on inkjet refill cartridges that seem to last less than a month.

The Fix: It's pretty simple to extend the life of any print cartridge by setting the default quality of the printer to "draft" mode. Open the Printers and Faxes control panel, right-click the printer, and select Properties. Choose the Device Options tab and click Print Quality; select the lowest quality and exit the menus. Printout won't be nearly as sharp as you'd like, but for draft copies, it's more than adequate. And you *will* save money.

Another trick is to turn off the color. Yep, it's that simple. Unless color is crucial to your document, you're wasting ink and slowing down the printer. Head back to the Printers and Faxes control panel, go to Properties, and find the tab that lets you print in grayscale. Then print the page again. When you do need color, simply reverse the settings.

If you often need to output high-quality or color printouts, use the Printers and Faxes control panel's Add Printer function to install a second copy of the printer driver, but set the print quality to high. Name it "High Quality" or "Money Waster." Install another, but this time set it to color output and name it appropriately. When you need to change to the higher print quality or color for a print job, choose File → Print and select that printer from the drop-down menu.

INKJET LICENSE PLATES

Ever wonder what it feels like to make license plates in prison? Here's your opportunity to find out. You'll have hours of fun and waste scads of color ink when you print these beauties on you inkjet printer (*http://snipurl.com/license*).

PAPER-SAVING PRINT UTILITY

The Annoyance: It just galls me that half the time I print a web page, I end up with an extra page with one or two lines on it.

The Fix: Internet Explorer and other browsers do have a print preview function. In IE, select File → Print Preview and click through the pages. Don't need the last page? Press Esc, select File → Print, enter a page range, and click OK. Want complete control over what you print, how it looks, and (more importantly) what *doesn't* print? Pick up FinePrint, a clever $50 utility. Just preview what you want to print and delete the extra page. Better yet, you can print four miniature pages on one page, scale large pages to print on smaller pages, or send dozens of separate jobs to the printer, saving some for later printing or deleting others (see Figure 7-6). And if you're curious about what

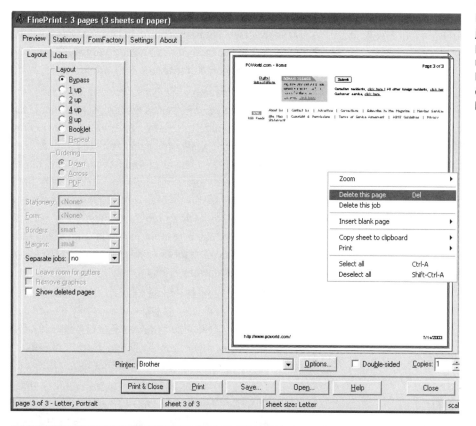

Figure 7-6. Top: A lot of web pages are just a bit longer than what fits on a single printed page. You can reduce waste by not printing the unneeded extra page. Bottom: If you have a long print job, you can cut down on the time it take to print by choosing FinePrint's 2-up setting.

happens when your printer misbehaves, take a look at Figure 7-7. You can download a trial copy of FinePrint at *http://www.oreilly.com/pcannoyances*.

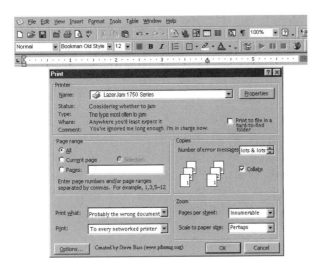

Figure 7-7. When good printers go bad....

KEEP THE PAPER FLOWING

The Annoyance: My year-old inkjet is driving me nuts with paper jams. No matter which kind of paper I use—plain or photographic—it chews it up.

The Fix: To avoid printer paper jams, make sure that all the paper in the tray is the same type and weight. (The most common paper weight is 20 pounds; it's usually listed on the package.) Don't mix photo paper, heavy card stock, and plain paper, for example. And always store your paper flat. If your printer uses a vertical feed tray and you don't print often, flip the paper around to prevent it from curling in the tray. Better yet, store it flat until you actually print something.

When it comes to cleaning the printer, various philosophies abound. We asked hardware maven Jim Aspinwall (author of the recently released *PC Hacks* from O'Reilly) for his take. His recommendations:

- Use the right paper. A high-grade 18- to 22-pound bond letter, 90 brightness or better (less rag), is best for most consumer printers. Feed it 60-pound stock or parchment and you're asking for trouble.

- Paper separation is a typical source of feed failure, and it's caused by paper that is too dry (static cling), too humid, or unable to separate because of tray friction. In dry environs, where the pages stick together as they come out of the ream or printer, take the paper out of the paper tray (or ream), hold one end of the stack firmly, and fan the pages. This can often break the static bond, as well as any "stickiness" that may be due to badly cut or coated paper. In humid environments, keep your paper in a dry, cool, flat environment until you're ready to print.

- Using those compressed air cans to blow out dust and debris can help, but beware where you blow. With laser printers, blowing around toner can muck things up. It's better to vacuum away paper chaff and toner.

- To clean the rollers, use only a slightly water-damp high-grade cloth (micro-fiber wipes are common these days) to remove the dust from as many surfaces and rollers as you can get to. Avoid using any chemical (alcohol, oil, silicone, solvents, Teflon, etc.) on rollers unless it's been approved by your printer manufacturer. So far, I've only been able to find "roller renewer" for the hard rubber rollers used in old typewriters. Definitely *not* the thing you want to apply to today's synthetics.

- Replace the rollers. Rollers should be evenly "spongy," not shiny or hard. Hard, shiny rollers can slip, causing paper jams.

FIX YOUR OWN PRINTER

You'll find dozens of additional tricks for laser printers at *http://fixyourownprinter.com*. (A buddy found a fix there for a paper feed problem he had with his HP LaserJet 5P printer, which is still chugging along after nine years.) Another great laser-advice site is *http://www.printertechs.com*.

MOVE YOUR SOUND CONNECTORS TO THE FRONT

The Annoyance: When I work late at night, I like to listen to music on my PC, but I don't want to wake up everyone in the house. Crawling under the desk to disconnect my PC's speaker cables from the sound card and connect my headset isn't what I consider fun.

The Fix: Many new computers have sound-card input and output ports on the front panel. But until you upgrade, here are two tips:

- Plantronics PC Headset Speaker Switch is a mouse-sized gizmo that connects your speakers *and* headset to the sound card. With a flick of a button, you can swap the sound from your speakers to your headset.

The gizmo costs $20 (see *http://snipurl.com/audiopc*), but I've seen it discounted for about $15 (see *http://snipurl.com/audiopc2* and *http://snipurl.com/audiopc3*).

- If you hate searching for ports and fussing with cables, get IC Intracom's Multimedia Control Panel. It brings two USB ports, as well as FireWire, joystick, microphone, and speaker ports to the front of your PC. The panel fits into any free, externally accessible (that is, having a removable front plate) 5.25-inch bay in your PC, and its connectors snake through the PC into the corresponding ports on the back of the PC. I've seen it on the Web for about $30 (see *http://snipurl.com/ctrl_panel*). If you just want the USB port or only the speaker connection, you might want to try a similar gizmo from FrontX that lets you choose the ports you want (see *http://www.frontx.com*).

DOCK YOUR NOTEBOOK

The Annoyance: I use my notebook for traveling, and when I get home, I use it as a desktop PC. It's a pain reconnecting all my peripherals at home, and then unhooking all the cables when I hit the road.

The Fix: This is an easy fix: use Belkin's Hi-Speed USB 2.0 DockStation. The $95 gadget has one parallel, one serial, and two 2.0 USB ports, as well as input for VGA and Ethernet. First connect your monitor, printer, keyboard, and other peripherals to the DockStation. Then connect two cables from the DockStation to your notebook, and you're in business. When you need to take off, just disconnect the two cables from your notebook. (See *http://snipurl.com/dockstation*).

USE YOUR NOTEBOOK AT HOME

The Annoyance: I use a notebook as a substitute for a desktop PC. But it's a real pain in the neck (literally). I have to put it on a stack of phone books so the screen is at the right height, but then the keyboard is too high!

The Fix: The solution could be the Oyster, a smart way to dock your notebook (*http://snipurl.com/oysterdock*). Open your notebook so it's flat, slide the keyboard end into the $150 Oyster, and voila—the LCD is facing you at eye level. Now connect a USB mouse and keyboard to the Oyster's USB ports (the gizmo includes a four-port USB 2.0 hub with a spot to hide the cables) and you're good to go (see Figure 7-8).

Figure 7-8. Sherpaq Mobile Products' Oyster lets you bring your notebook's screen up to eye level.

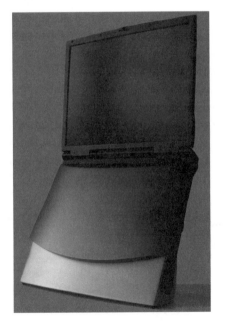

CONNECT YOUR FLASH MEMORY DRIVE WITH A USB CABLE

The Annoyance: I bought one of those cute little portable flash memory drives. It only holds 16 MB, but it was dirt cheap and a handy alternative to a floppy. What's not handy is crawling under the desk to stick it into the USB port on the back of my PC.

The Fix: I'm guessing your keychain-size flash memory drive was inexpensive; many of the larger-capacity drives come with a USB cable. You can pick up a six-foot male-to-female extension cable for under $5 at a local computer store or online.

NO-FUSS NETWORK BACKUPS

The Annoyance: Although I love my home-office network, lugging my external USB hard drive to each computer to back them up is a real bother. But no, no, no—I don't want to set up a file server.

The Fix: Instead of installing a server, share the drive with all the PCs in your network by attaching it to Linksys's Network Storage Link for USB 2.0 Disk Drives (NSLU2). This $99 device connects to a wired or wireless router (see *http://snipurl.com/Linksys_storage*) and lets everyone in your network access any attached USB 1.x or 2.0 drive for quick and easy backups. You can even share a USB Flash drive with the Linksys unit.

> **Warning...**
> During installation the Storage Link must format your USB drive, so make sure you've backed up everything on the drive first.

BIG HARD DRIVE CORRUPTION

The Annoyance: Ever since I upgraded my PC with a 160 GB hard drive, system hibernation stopped working correctly. Sometimes, instead of resuming from hibernation, the PC restarts! I've run ScanDisk and defragged the drive, but the problem persists. What gives?

The Fix: Somebody once said you can never have too much RAM or too big a hard drive. Somebody was wrong. Well, you're in deep doo-doo if you've got a big drive on a system using an early version of Windows XP—even with Service Pack 1 (SP1) installed. Older versions of XP can't perform certain system level functions (addressing and flushing caches, for example) with big drives, and that can lead to corrupted data. Solution #1: upgrade to Service Pack 2. (Just run Windows Update to snag this monster.) Solution #2: grab the dedicated fix from Microsoft at

http://snipurl.com/atapi1. If you want to learn more, check out Microsoft's Microsoft Knowledge Base Article 331958 at *http://snipurl.com/atapi2*.

UNWIRE YOUR PRINTER

The Annoyance: I'm a big wireless fan, but I have one device that remains tethered to my PC: my printer. I'd like to connect to it wirelessly and share it with my wife who has a computer down the hall. Can I cut the cord?

The Fix: Start snippin'. All it takes is a wireless print server. The Linksys Instant Wireless Print Server (WPS11) supports the 802.11b standard and can connect to one parallel printer. The company's Wireless-G Print Server (WPS54GU2) works on 802.11g networks (see Figure 7-9) and can connect to two printers (one parallel and one USB). Installation is pretty painless: basically, connect the Print Server to your wireless router or hub, and then connect the printer to the Print Server. Now everyone on your wireless network can access the printer. Both models cost about $130 (*http://www.linksys.com*).

Figure 7-9. The Wireless-G Print Server lets you wirelessly connect both a USB and parallel port printer, either in your office or down the hall.

GO WIRELESS WITH A WALL SOCKET

The Annoyance: Wireless is appealing. I'd like to use my notebook in the living room and have access to my desktop down the hall—and use its connection to the Internet. But the thought of spending tons of money and time on routers and cards and WiFi is unappealing. Isn't there an easier way?

The Fix: In less than 20 minutes, you can make the connection via—are you ready for this?—an ordinary wall socket. All you need is Belkin's PowerLine USB Adapter (about $100; *http://www.belkin.com*). Connect the notebook to the PowerLine adapter with a USB cable, and then plug the adapter into any electrical wall socket. Down the hall, connect the Belkin PowerLine Ethernet Adapter ($100) to your desktop computer and plug the adapter into a wall socket, too (See Figure 7-10). Once the drivers are installed, you'll be able to share the files and peripherals of each computer, including Internet access. PowerLine networking even works with versions of Windows as far back as 98SE. The company claims transfer speeds up to 14Mbps, and the gizmo uses 56-bit DES data encryption, so you needn't worry about a neighbor with a long extension cord viewing your files.

Figure 7-10. Don't want to run networking cable down the hallway? Not interested in messing with wireless? Get Belkin's PowerLine adapters and use your home's power grid.

STIFLE AMBITIOUS WIFI POP-UPS

The Annoyance: I finally got on the WiFi bandwagon, and my ambitious notebook keeps telling me there's more than one wireless network available for me to use. This pop-up pops up every time I try connecting to the Internet and it's driving me crazy.

The Fix: Your highly motivated wireless card needs to scale itself back and look just for your primary network.

1. In the Device Manager, open the "Network adapters" item and right-click your wireless LAN card.

2. Choose Properties, select the Resources tab, and uncheck the "Use automatic settings" box.

3. Select Basic configuration 0000 in the "Settings based on" line, and click OK.

EMERGENCY POWER FOR PALMS

The Annoyance: I love my Palm PDA, but I'm lucky if I get a day's worth of battery life out of it. That's not a problem at the office—I can snap it into its cradle and recharge it. But schlepping the cradle with me on a business trip is a pain. There must be a better way.

The Fix: When I'm on the road, I leave the cradle at home and bring Tech Center Labs' tiny $15 Power Adapter for Universal Connector Palms (*http://www.talestuff.com*). Plug one end into the cradle connector on your PDA, plug the other into the wall adapter normally attached to the cradle, and you're charging away. Another option: run your Palm with the company's $15 AA Emergency Charger for Universal Connector Palms, which uses rechargeable or regular AA batteries. And in dire emergencies, the company's $20 Universal 9 volt Emergency Charger will give your Tungsten Palm (and other PDAs, such as the Garmin) enough juice so you can finish that hand of solitaire.

POCKET PC FILE AND BATTERY WOES

The Annoyance: What about us Pocket PC folks out here? I have two gripes. Microsoft hides the battery-life indicator in the Settings → System → Power folder, requiring an annoying three clicks each time I want to see how much battery life is left. And like Windows, the Pocket PC is stuck with a dreadful file manager—in this case, the File Explorer.

The Fix: First, grab a trial copy of Omega One's Battery Pack Pro at *http://snipurl.com/batterypack*, a $20 utility that not only displays a desktop bar indicating your Pocket PC's battery life, but also calculates expected life based on your usage. Next, replace File Explorer with Resco's $25 Explorer 2003 (*http://snipurl.com/resco)*, a great productivity tool that lets you far more easily move, copy, delete, and create files and folders; can zip and encrypt files; and includes a nifty file viewer.

BOOST YOUR CELL'S BATTERY

The Annoyance: I hate it when I'm away from home and realize I forgot the charger for my dying cell phone. Can you hear me now? Hello? Helloooo?

The Fix: Among the handful of emergency gizmos I take with me when I travel is Cellboost, a small, 1.2-ounce disposable cell-phone recharger that's roughly the size of a cigarette lighter (see *http://snipurl.com/cellboost*). It takes about three minutes for Cellboost to give my phone's dead battery enough of a charge to make an hour-long phone call. The device costs between $4 and $6, depending on your phone model.

THIS CHAIR'S FOR YOU

As a cost-cutting measure, all cubicles will be retrofitted with these new, dual-purpose, ergonomic chairs: *http://snipurl.com/ergo_chair.*

RED SKIES AND BLUE ROSES

The Annoyance: I printed a photo on my inkjet printer, and the output was streaked and the colors didn't match what I saw onscreen. The sky was red, and the roses were blue! What went wrong?

The Fix: If you don't use your inkjet printer regularly—at least once a month—the ink cartridges get funky and print quality can plummet. My advice? Run the head cleaning utility and print a couple of color-intensive pages. If the fidelity of your output doesn't improve, buy a new cartridge. And from now on, print a color page at least once a week.

FRAMED DIGITAL PHOTOS

The Annoyance: I love showing off my digital-camera handiwork, but boy is it a hassle to bring everyone around my PC to view the images.

The Fix: I have just the thing: Pacific Digital's MemoryFrame, an appealing gadget that looks like a traditional picture frame, but stores and displays multiple digital images on a 5.6-inch LCD screen. Just connect the MemoryFrame via USB to your PC, camera, or memory card reader, and then load up to 55 images (in JPEG, TIF, PNG, GIF, or BMP format) into the frame's 16 MB of RAM and 8 MB of flash memory. Hang the MemoryFrame on your wall or place it on a tabletop to view a slideshow of your pictures (see Figure 7-11).

A BETTER MOUSETRAP?

If a friend, co-worker, or employee suffers from stupidity, these new buttonless mice can help (*http://snipurl.com/b_mouse*).

Figure 7-11. If you want it display your digital photos in the living room—or any room in the house—use the MemoryFrame. Just keep your checkbook handy—this puppy costs $270.

You can use the bundled Digital Pix Master software to create a slideshow on your PC before you load the images into the MemoryFrame. If you don't want to bother with a PC, the frame will create the show for you. Its built-in controls let you delete images, change timing and transitions, and make other alterations. A few quibbles: the Memory-Frame uses slow USB 1.1 connections, and the wire that connects to the AC adapter is an eyesore. (One plus: the 8 × 10" wireless edition has a built-in WiFi adapter, so you can transmit slideshows from your PC to the MemoryFrame wirelessly.) The biggest show-stopper: at $250 list, the MemoryFrame isn't cheap (the 8-by-10-inch model lists for $500). I have to say, though, that this puppy wows everyone who steps into my living room. Get it from *http://www.pacificdigital.com*.

A cheaper, if less snazzy, approach—burn your images onto a CD or DVD in JPEG format, and pop the disc into your DVD player connected to your TV. Most contemporary DVD players (even the $90 cheapies) can read these discs. Select the folder holding the pictures, and many players will display the images in slideshow fashion. Neat. And cheap.

CURLING PICTURES

The Annoyance: I just started scanning my 30-year-old collection of photos and many have a little curl. When I place one on the scanner and close the cover, it's hard to keep the photo from moving. Short of taking off the scanner cover and holding down the picture by hand, I'm not sure what to do.

The Fix: Use the glass from a picture frame to hold down those curling prints, then gently close the scanner cover. By the way, when I want to scan my wife's sticky, oil-splattered recipes, I sandwich the pages between two sheets of glass to keep my scanner's platen dainty and clean.

REMOVE SHADOWS FROM THE OTHER SIDE

The Annoyance: When I scan magazine articles, the print on the other side of the page shows through, leaving telltale spots.

The Fix: An old trick: slip a sheet of black paper behind the page. On a sheet-fed scanner, put the original in the plastic sleeve that came with the scanner to prevent it from jamming.

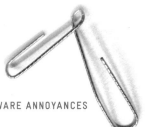

GRINDING, NOT SCANNING

The Annoyance: My scanner makes a grinding noise and then nothing happens. It was working fine yesterday, I swear.

The Fix: That was yesterday; today you have a solution. My hunch is that you (or someone in your office) inadvertently flipped the scanner's locking mechanism, which keeps the scanner's light bar in place for shipping. It's usually located on the back of the scanner, near the on/off switch; if not, check the scanner's manual.

SKEWED SCANS

The Annoyance: I have a horrible time scanning images that are crooked in the original material. The scanner software tries to straighten them automatically but rarely does a decent job, and I still end up with skewed results.

The Fix: Try this technique: on the back of the original, take a pencil and ruler and draw a straight line that matches the baseline of the image. Then use that mark to align the original on the scanner.

MAKE SCANNERS READ BETTER

The Annoyance: I bought a flatbed scanner to optically "read" newspaper and magazine articles. The optical character recognition (OCR) program recognizes the printed text and converts it to digital form, but there are still lots of errors. How can I improve my results?

The Fix: The mantra of OCR scanning is: the better the original, the better the scan. Here are five tricks that can help:

- Fiddle with the scanner's brightness and contrast settings. For instance, if the characters on the page you're scanning are dark or smudged, increase the scanner's brightness to make the image lighter. Conversely, thin or light characters need less brightness and greater contrast in order to make the letters stand out.

- Experiment with grayscale or black-and-white scanning modes.

- Avoid color paper. Before scanning, copy the original onto white paper.

- If the characters on the page are small—say, 9 points or less—scan at 600 dpi. For larger fonts, use 300 dpi.

- Remove creases from the page. Press a clipping between the pages of a thick book before scanning, or consider—don't laugh—ironing the clipping using low heat.

TRANSFER PHONE NUMBERS TO YOUR DIGITAL PHONE

The Annoyance: I find it distressing that with all the technology packed into my cell phone, I still have to enter phone numbers one at a time. It's boring and tedious, and I could use a workaround.

TURN YOUR SCANNER INTO A COPY MACHINE

Not every home office has a photocopier—but if you have a scanner and a printer, you basically do. I use ICarbon, a free tool that lets me fire a scanned document to my printer in seconds. ICarbon loads fast, and its black & white, grayscale, and color presets make the process a breeze. Download a copy from IDev at *http://snipurl.com/icarbon*.

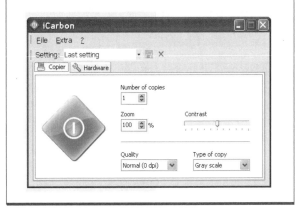

The Fix: One workaround coming up: the DataPilot Cell Phone Data Transfer Suite is a clever application that works by connecting your phone to a PC using a serial or USB cable that's included in the package. I used mine to connect an ancient Nokia 5160 digital phone to transfer phone numbers from Microsoft Outlook; the program also interfaces with Outlook Express, Act, Pocket PC, and Palm software (see Figure 7-12). If you don't use any of these contact managers, you can stick with DataPilot's phone book manager. Get more detail at *http://www.datapilot.com*.

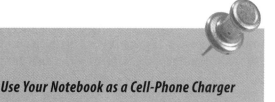

Figure 7-12. Let your computer do the job of creating, editing, sharing, and keeping current the data on your digital phone. Even better, you can use the DataPilot to turn your digital phone into a wireless modem.

LAPTOP SUPPORT EXTRAORDINAIRE

Think you have trouble with your notebook? Take a look at this: *http://snipurl.com/laptopsupport*.

Use Your Notebook as a Cell-Phone Charger

When I travel, I hate schlepping my cell-phone charger—it's just another thing to lug along. But if I'm also taking my notebook, I can use a device that lets me charge my phone right from my notebook's USB port. Even better, American Power Conversion's USB Mobile Phone Charger models run between $8 and $14. You can find the model you need for your cell phone at *http://snipurl.com/apc_charge*.

A THREE-TONE SOLUTION TO TELEMARKETERS

Telemarketers drive me crazy with their constant phone calls. Here's a way to cut down on telemarketing.

Remember the last time you called a number that was no longer in service: you heard three short tones like "doo... dah...dee." When the telemarketer's autodialer hears those frequencies (geeks only: 985.2 Hz, 1370.6 Hz, and 1776.7 Hz), it brilliantly deduces that your phone number's been disconnected or is not in service. The rationale is that as more telemarketers discover your phone number's been disconnected, you'll get fewer calls.

You can download these three tones as sound files and record them to your answering machine at the beginning of the greeting. Download the tones at *http://snipurl.com/telemrkt2*.

If you are willing to spend some money, try the TeleZapper, a $40 electronic gadget from Privacy Technologies. Just plug the device into an available telephone jack, and when you pick up the phone to answer a call, the TeleZapper lets loose with the three tones that tell automated dialers that your number's disconnected. Tests at Bass International Labs indicate that the TeleZapper works really, really well. Check it out at *http://snipurl.com/zapper*.

Index

Colophon

Our look is the result of reader comments, our own experimentation, and feedback from distribution channels. Distinctive covers complement our distinctive approach to technical topics, breathing personality and life into potentially dry subjects.

Genevieve d'Entremont was the production editor and copyeditor for *PC Annoyances*, Second Edition. Ann Schirmer was the proofreader. Peter Ryan and Genevieve d'Entremont did the typesetting and page makeup. Matt Hutchinson, Mary Brady, and Claire Cloutier provided quality control. Julie Hawks wrote the index.

Ellie Volckhausen designed the cover of this book using Adobe Illustrator and produced the cover layout with Adobe InDesign CS using Gravur Condensed, Glypha, and Adobe Sabon fonts. The cover is based on a series design by Volume Design, Inc.

Patti Capaldi designed the interior layout using Adobe InDesign CS. The text and heading fonts are Rotis Sans Serif, Lineto Gravur Condensed, and Myriad Pro; the code font is TheSans Mono Condensed. Julie Hawks converted the text to Adobe InDesign CS. The screenshots and technical illustrations that appear in the book were produced by Robert Romano, Jessamyn Read, and Lesley Borash using Macromedia FreeHand MX and Adobe Photoshop 7. The cartoon illustrations used on the cover and in the interior of this book are copyright © 2004 and 2005 Hal Mayforth.

Keep in touch with O'Reilly

1. Download examples from our books

To find example files for a book, go to:

www.oreilly.com/catalog

select the book, and follow the "Examples" link.

2. Register your O'Reilly books

Register your book at *register.oreilly.com*

Why register your books?
Once you've registered your O'Reilly books you can:

- Win O'Reilly books, T-shirts or discount coupons in our monthly drawing.
- Get special offers available only to registered O'Reilly customers.
- Get catalogs announcing new books (US and UK only).
- Get email notification of new editions of the O'Reilly books you own.

3. Join our email lists

Sign up to get topic-specific email announcements of new books and conferences, special offers, and O'Reilly Network technology newsletters at:

elists.oreilly.com

It's easy to customize your free elists subscription so you'll get exactly the O'Reilly news you want.

4. Get the latest news, tips, and tools

www.oreilly.com

- "Top 100 Sites on the Web"—PC Magazine
- CIO Magazine's Web Business 50 Awards

Our web site contains a library of comprehensive product information (including book excerpts and tables of contents), downloadable software, background articles, interviews with technology leaders, links to relevant sites, book cover art, and more.

5. Work for O'Reilly

Check out our web site for current employment opportunities:

jobs.oreilly.com

6. Contact us

O'Reilly & Associates
1005 Gravenstein Hwy North
Sebastopol, CA 95472 USA

TEL: 707-827-7000 or 800-998-9938
      (6am to 5pm PST)

FAX: 707-829-0104

order@oreilly.com
For answers to problems regarding your order or our products. To place a book order online, visit:

www.oreilly.com/order_new

catalog@oreilly.com
To request a copy of our latest catalog.

booktech@oreilly.com
For book content technical questions or corrections.

corporate@oreilly.com
For educational, library, government, and corporate sales.

proposals@oreilly.com
To submit new book proposals to our editors and product managers.

international@oreilly.com
For information about our international distributors or translation queries. For a list of our distributors outside of North America check out:

international.oreilly.com/distributors.html

adoption@oreilly.com
For information about academic use of O'Reilly books, visit:

academic.oreilly.com

Related Titles Available from O'Reilly

Annoyances

Access Annoyances

Computer Privacy Annoyances

Excel Annoyances

Home Networking Annoyances

Internet Annoyances

Mac Annoyances

PC Annoyances, *2nd Edition*

PC Hardware Annoyances

Windows XP Annoyances for Geeks

Word Annoyances

O'REILLY®

Our books are available at most retail and online bookstores.
To order direct: 1-800-998-9938 • *order@oreilly.com* • *www.oreilly.com*
Online editions of most O'Reilly titles are available by subscription at *safari.oreilly.com*